ON WORK, RACE, AND THE
SOCIOLOGICAL IMAGINATION

THE HERITAGE OF SOCIOLOGY

A Series Edited by Donald N. Levine

Morris Janowitz, *Founding Editor*

EVERETT C. HUGHES

ON WORK, RACE, AND THE SOCIOLOGICAL IMAGINATION

Edited and with an Introduction by
LEWIS A. COSER

THE UNIVERSITY OF CHICAGO PRESS
Chicago and London

EVERETT C. HUGHES (1897–1983) was a founding member of the "second generation" of American sociologists. He was closely connected with the Chicago School of Sociology, and had a profound influence on postwar sociologists, including Erving Goffman and Howard Becker. He edited the *American Journal of Sociology* from 1952 to 1960, and from 1952 to 1956 he was chairman of the Department of Sociology at the University of Chicago, where he taught for many years.

LEWIS A. COSER is Distinguished Professor of Sociology Emeritus at the State University of New York, and Adjunct Professor of Sociology at Boston College.

The University of Chicago Press, Chicago 60637
The University of Chicago Press, Ltd., London
© 1994 by The University of Chicago
All rights reserved. Published 1994
Printed in the United States of America
03 02 01 00 99 98 97 96 95 94   1 2 3 4 5

ISBN: (cloth): 0-226-35971-9
     (paper): 0-226-35972-7

Library of Congress Cataloging-in-Publication Data

Hughes, Everett Cherrington, 1897–
    On work, race, and the sociological imagination / Everett C.
  Hughes ; edited and with an introduction by Lewis A. Coser.
      p.   cm. — (The Heritage of sociology)
    Previously published essays by Hughes.
    Includes bibliographical references and index.
    1. Occupations. 2. Social classes. 3. Race relations.
  4. Sociology. 5. Hughes, Everett Cherrington, 1897–   . I. Coser,
  Lewis A., 1913–   . II. Title. III. Series.
  HT675.H82   1994
  305.8—dc20   93-40057
                                                        CIP

Contents

Introduction

Everett Cherrington Hughes
1897–1983

In the history of American sociology Everett C. Hughes played a unique role, mediating between the founding generation of the Chicago School and what has recently become known as the "Second Chicago School." His influence spread through provocative if low-keyed teachings as well as original papers of distinctive subtlety. Like one of his intellectual models, Georg Simmel, Hughes displayed a genius for discerning similarities of pattern among social phenomena of the most diverse sort, and for inventing constructs—mistakes at work, routinized emergency, bastard institutions, dilemmas and contradictions of status—that throw new light on everyday happenings by viewing them as instances of such general patterns.

Over the years Hughes pioneered in a number of substantive areas—most notably, the study of occupations and professions, and the relations between racial and ethnic groups—but his work mainly drew its distinction from being anchored in a few fundamental sociological queries. Again and again he asked about the basic processes in social life that accounted for social order and disorder. Fascinated by the kaleidoscope of social life, he sought to attend systematically to the institutional patterns that provide stability to social arrangements while remaining aware that they are vulnerable to influences that undermine stability and induce change. What he wrote about his mentor Robert Park also applied to himself: "[He] had no desire to form a system, yet he was primarily a systemic sociologist."[1] In the language of present-day sociology, one might suggest that what he systematically depicted was the interaction between human agency and social structure.

Like Park, Hughes's most powerful influence on the development

I have greatly profited from critical readings of an earlier draft of this introduction by Lee Braude, Arlene Daniels, Howard London, David Riesman, Elsie Schneewind, and Ida Simpson.

of sociology may have come through the impact he exerted on a number of talented students, for whom he served as an exemplar of playful yet steadfast curiosity about the social scene. For this reason, it is particularly important in assessing his legacy to take account of the type of human being he was—and, indeed, of the person whose constant companionship and intellectual stimulation helped to shape his mature work, his wife Helen.

The Man

Like many American sociologists of the first and second generations, Everett Hughes was a minister's son. When Everett was born, his father, the Reverend Charles A. Hughes, was a Methodist minister in Beaver, Ohio; later he preached in a number of other localities in that state. He was a strong believer in the Social Gospel, deeply committed to progressive causes, fighting both religious and racial intolerance. While his father probably strove to maintain some balance between faith and works, the son clearly gave priority to works.

Everett Hughes was proud of his family, paid attention to his family tree of both branches, and often illustrated a sociological point by reference to a story about one of his ancestors. All in all Hughes's recollections of his family give the strong impression that on both sides they belonged to the farming elite of Ohio: strongly religious, progressive, bent upon acquiring the advantages of higher education as soon as they became realistically available, first for the boys and then for the girls.

Hughes's family on both sides were among the early settlers in Ohio. His father's ancestors had originally come from Virginia but both sides of the family considered themselves proudly of Ohio stock. They all lived for several generations in small towns and settlements and almost all of them made their living farming the land. Most of them were not of a particularly scholarly disposition even though some, like Everett's grandfather, who had been a soldier in the Union army for more than three years, were ardent participants in matters theological or political in the informal discussion circles that prospered in much of nineteenth-century Ohio, in small-town and rural settlements. College education, at least for men, became the custom only in Everett's father's days. The latter, a country school teacher when he was married, only finished college when he was forty years of age. Women were not expected to go to college before several generations of men were already expected to do so. Everett's grandmother, as was the norm in her generation, did not go to college but six of her seven sons did.

That the young Everett would attend Wesleyan Methodist College after graduation from high school was not particularly astonishing. His family had already sent a number of its young men to that college and there were longstanding contacts between the college and the farming communities in which the Hugheses lived. Yet this son of a minister seems not to have shown any particular concern for matters religious but chose to concentrate on the learning of languages, Latin as well as French and German. It was most probably his command of these languages, as well as the wider field of learning in foreign tongues, that transformed the Methodist minister's son and Ohio farm boy in decisive ways and distinguished him and his career in later years from that of his agemates.

Having been a first-rate college student, the young Hughes might have been expected to embark on an academic career, especially since he evidently did not want to follow in his father's footsteps except for a short period after his graduation. But instead he embarked on what seemed then an atypical first career. Perhaps influenced by the Populist currents that still stirred the Middle West, he devoted the first postcollege years to teaching English to recent immigrants. He taught in the Green Bay area, helping recently arrived lumberjacks from Finland and Yugoslavia as well as from Italy and from the Ukraine to learn English so as to facilitate their first steps on the ladder of advancement in America. Later on he moved to live among the multiethnic work force of the Inland Steel Company in Chicago and in the company town of Pullman, Illinois, to continue the same work of English teaching to a multiethnic workforce. It was this experience, he later told his students, that made him realize that he had an ethnicity, too. After five years of such employment he entered the graduate Department of Sociology at the University of Chicago, but continued to work with the Park District, a job that let him keep contact with the city's many ethnic neighborhoods.

When Hughes entered the Chicago department in the early twenties, it was in a period of reorganization. Some members of the founding generation had died or retired; Albion Small was approaching retirement. William I. Thomas, perhaps the most illustrious member of the first generation, had been forced to retire because of a sexual indiscretion. A new generation was just beginning to take its place. Ellsworth Faris had been hired in 1919 to take over the social psychology courses that Thomas had taught. Park, whom Thomas had brought to Chicago just before the war to teach a course on "The

Negro in America," soon became a regular member of the department and, after Thomas, its leading figure. Before long Hughes's contemporaries—Herbert Blumer, Louis Wirth, and W. F. Ogburn—joined the department and helped consolidate its intellectual and organizational preeminence. Moreover, its association with the Department of Philosophy, especially with George Herbert Mead, further enhanced its status in the academy.

Of the many teachers at Chicago with whom Hughes studied, Park soon became his most important guide and model. It is touching to recall that even in his old age Hughes, who referred to all his other colleagues by their first or second name, never failed to refer to his mentor as *Professor* Park.

Park's career and lifestyle differed markedly from that of the minister's son from Ohio. Park spent most of his career in nonacademic pursuits, first as a muckraking journalist in a number of American cities and then, after a few years at Harvard and in Germany where he studied mainly with Simmel and Windelband, as secretary, speech writer, and travel companion for Booker T. Washington, President of the Tuskegee Institute. Only in 1914, at the age of fifty, did Park embark on an academic career in sociology, following a chance meeting with Thomas at a conference at Tuskegee.

Park never wrote a major work, but his occasional essays were influential—not to mention the textbook which he coedited with his junior colleague Ernest Burgess, *Introduction to the Science of Sociology*. Of decisive importance for his impact on Hughes, Park had the rare gift of inspiring students. The former newspaperman almost forced his students not to confine themselves to the library but to look at the world around them with the sociologically trained eyes of a sophisticated newspaperman. Not that he neglected theory—how could a student of Simmel and Windelband do that?—but he always insisted that without connection to the minutiae of social life theory was condemned to sterility. Park inspired his students to look at taxi dance girls and schoolmistresses, at real estate dealers and hoboes, at crowds and social movements, at marginal men and machine politicians. Since Hughes himself did not care for "people who were used to drinking their theory in straight philosophical draughts, unmixed with the empirical juices of life,"[2] he found Park an ideal mentor and model.

In some cases Park made his students so dependent on his guidance that they never produced much on their own after their dissertation. But others were inspired by his powerful intellect to create their own intellectual products after having been put on the road by their master.

This was emphatically the case with Everett Hughes. Even though he was probably Park's most beloved student, even though he often was not only the adoring disciple but also the constant companion of his mentor, and even though Park had attracted Hughes's future wife, Helen MacGill from her native Canada to Chicago—where she lived for a while before her marriage in Park's household—Hughes was never the obedient and uncritical follower of his mentor. Park, for example, wanted Hughes to write a dissertation on land use in Chicago; Hughes refused and wrote on the Chicago Real Estate Boards[3]—though later Park succeeded in persuading Helen Hughes to write an MA thesis on land use.

Many, though by no means all, of the themes on which Park wrote also engaged Hughes's thoughts and research interests. Social control, racial assimilation, social distance, social movements, and human migration: these and many other themes broached by Park were also to be found in the many-faceted work of Everett Hughes. Social status, social role, the nature of the self, are, as we shall see, at the roots of Park's as well as Hughes's core ideas, even though some of Park's interests, especially his work in human ecology, left Hughes indifferent.

What Hughes once said about Park might also apply to Hughes himself: "Park has left no *magnum opus*. He regarded his writings as prologomena to research, which would result in a more systematic knowledge of human social life. If he was tempted to write a treatise, he was diverted from it by his interest in ongoing social changes, in the events and problems of the day. If he was ever tempted to become an 'expert' on some particular social problem, he was held back by his conviction that every event had a place somewhere in the universal human processes and that no situation can be understood until one finds in it those universal qualities that allow one to compare it with other situations, however near or distant in time, place, and appearance."[4]

Having written his dissertation under Park, Hughes again engaged in a career move that differed from that of the other most gifted of his classmates. While Louis Wirth and Herbert Blumer stayed on at their alma mater and in time became major members of the Chicago department, Hughes accepted an appointment at McGill University in Montreal where, together with the Canadian sociologist Carl Dawson, he established the first Canadian Department of Sociology. His early sociological contributions, as we shall see, were largely inspired by the multilingual and multinational setting in which they originated. His first book grew of his work and life in Canada, *French Canada in Transition.*[5] It was the work of a man poised between French and Anglophone Canada and established his reputation as a student of ethnic relations and conflicts, of marginality and of the ever-threatened balance of national traditions and ethnic subordination. The study, which grew out of fieldwork of Everett and Helen Hughes in a small industrial city in Quebec, was the first major work of Hughes and established his reputation in the front ranks of multi-ethnic community studies. Hughes's interest in "marginal men" was surely stimulated by his own marginal status as an American, teaching in an English-speaking university in a French-speaking city in Canada.

When Hughes returned to the University of Chicago in 1938, moving in fairly quick steps from assistant professor to professor, he entered what was probably the most productive period in his life. In part this period of enhanced productivity may be explained by the fact that he now enjoyed daily intercourse with a galaxy of brilliant colleagues, while he had been relatively isolated and without much collegial stimulation in his Canadian years. Park had retired from Chicago in 1934 and none of his successors as the head of the department quite measured up to his status as the *primus inter pares* of the department, but Hughes joined a highly gifted band of academic brothers in thought.

The Chicago-based *American Journal of Sociology,* which until the 1930s was the most important ground-breaking and official journal of the American sociological fraternity lost some of its status when the American Sociological Society, previously dominated by the Chicago department, decided to establish its own journal in 1935 and to cut official ties with the Chicago department. Yet the *American Journal of Sociology,* edited for a while by both Everett and Helen Hughes, remained a prestigious publication, but it could no longer pretend to be *the* voice of American sociology.

While some of Hughes's younger colleagues, Herbert Blumer and Louis Wirth in particular, had been among his fellow students, and while Ernest Burgess and W. F. Ogburn had already been in the department in Park's days, its ranks were soon augmented in the fifties by a number of new appointments, mainly from Columbia, among whom Peter Blau and Peter Rossi were the most prominent. They brought to the department a research orientation which, while not hostile to the Chicago tradition of fieldwork studies, tended to reinforce the statistical approach to social phenomena which had hitherto mainly been presented by W. F. Ogburn. All in all, the Chicago department gained in breadth of interest and offering while it lost some of the inner cohesion that had marked it under Albion Small, W. I. Thomas, and Robert Park.

Hughes edited the *American Journal of Sociology* from 1952 to 1960 and chaired the department from 1952 to 1956. But one has the impression that this mild-mannered, gentle, and intensely private man did not muster the energy, and did not have the desire, to run the department in the forceful manner of Park or Thomas. Moreover, Hughes did not have the one-track mind that enabled some of his colleagues in sociology to concentrate entirely on their academic voca-tion. He did not want to sacrifice his love for baroque music or for modern novelists, such as Robert Musil or Heinrich Boell, or for recent African and Canadian writers, in order to become a super-chairman or super-editor. He got as much pleasure from literally culti-vating his own garden as from negotiating with deans about more funds for the department.

Even though, especially in his last years at Chicago, some of the most brilliant graduate students in the department tended to consider the fieldwork tradition that Hughes upheld with unrivaled brilliance somewhat old fashioned, Hughes trained a galaxy of young men and women who kept this tradition vibrantly alive. Howard Becker, Blanche Geer, Anselm Strauss, Joseph Gusfield, Fred Davis, Gladys and Kurt Lang, Eliot Friedson, and the most brilliant of them all, Erving Goffman, largely developed their native gifts under the loving and attentive guidance of Everett Hughes. (It is worth noting that Goffman, who is often seen as a kind of selfmade sociologist, owed a great deal of his initial stimulus to Hughes's influence. A German scholar has compiled a list of most-cited authors in the work of Goff-man and shows that Hughes is cited as often as Georg Simmel and almost as often as Emile Durkheim.)[6]

To profit from Hughes's teaching required some preparation and the acquisition of a third ear. Hughes was not a conventional teacher. His classes were not highly structured and logically built. Those of us, like my wife Rose Laub Coser and me, who had been trained by Robert K. Merton, whose every lecture was a beautifully constructed work of academic art, found it originally quite difficult to follow Hughes's utterly different mode of presentation. Somewhat like Georg Simmel, he was apt to move from one subject to the next by what seemed free association, he moved where the spirit dictated, starting to talk, say, about multiethnic contacts only to move after a minute or two to a story about one of his Ohio ancestors, to an account of some experience of Robert Park when working with Booker T.

Washington. He moved from large events to seemingly small matters and back again—all in a very few minutes. One's ear had to be closely attuned to his peculiar type of delivery. When I heard him for the first time in Chicago in 1948 I reported home that the man was utterly confused and confusing. When I heard him a second time, I reported that he was a sociological genius. One had to cultivate the ability to "edit out" much that at first seemed trivial and humdrum in his presentation in order to duly appreciate pearls of insight and wisdom such as: "The true *enfant terrible* is a person who knowingly uses the right words before the wrong combination of hearers."[7] Or: "The Catholic College is a city college; it gets a dental school and a law school before it gets a medical school; because there is no such thing as an evening medical school."[8]

Hughes's lectures were studded with observations and insights gathered in his own fieldwork and in that of his students, but it was also fed by what he learned during foreign travels, be it as an exchange professor or on private visits. He was a postdoctoral student in Germany just before the Nazis came to power, he returned to Germany at the end of the war as the first American exchange professor at the University of Frankfort and returned there several times after. He lectured at Kyoto and other Japanese universities as well as in India. He taught frequently in various Canadian universities, reestablishing contacts and friendships that had first been blossoming in his years at McGill. I mention these foreign contacts mainly because Hughes is often taken to be a somewhat provincial midwestern figure. He had deep roots on the Middle Border to be sure, but in the end much of the world was his oyster.

By 1960 Hughes was approaching retirement age at Chicago. I taught at the time at Brandeis University and it occurred to me that Brandeis, which at the time had no fixed retirement dates, might be able to attract Hughes to its ranks. I had met Hughes at the house of David Riesman in 1949, when I taught at the College of the University of Chicago, and had kept contact with him ever since. To my great joy, and that of the Sociology Department, Hughes accepted the offer of the Brandeis department and stayed there from 1961 to 1968. Being by then over 70 years of age it would have seemed that he had earned a well-deserved rest. Instead he joined the faculty of Boston College where he taught for another seven years. The Ohio son of a Methodist preacher taught, as he once jokingly remarked, at John D. Rockefeller's Baptist university, at a Jewish university, and finally at a Catholic college. At all of them he left a characteristic mark. At Brandeis, Gaye Tuchman, Michael Bodemann, and Barry Thorne, to just mention a few, became his devoted Ph.D. students. The very last of the students whose dissertations he supervised at Boston College was Howard London who did a study of a local community college.

Everett Cherrington Hughes died in Cambridge in his eighty-sixth year in the very house in which these lines are being written.

The Wife
Helen MacGill Hughes, 1903–1992

It is hardly customary, but it is high time that it become so, that when a male sociologist, married for a lifetime to another sociologist, is being honored and remembered, his wife and intimate collaborator be also remembered even if more briefly.

Helen MacGill was born in Vancouver in 1903. Her father was a liberal barrister and solicitor, her mother, an ardent feminist, a journalist, social reformer, and judge. Helen studied economics and German at the University of British Columbia, from where she graduated in 1925. The MacGills must surely have been in the vanguard of Vancouver's liberal social circles. Helen's sister Elsie became an engineer and the first woman to graduate in electrical engineering from the University of Toronto, and in aeronautical engineering from the University of Michigan.

Having first met Helen Hughes in Vancouver, Robert Park persuaded her in 1925 to become a graduate student in the Chicago Department of Sociology, the only woman among six or seven Laura Spelman Rockefeller Fellows. From the beginning of her studies Helen Hughes was very close to the Parks and for a while, before her marriage, lived in their house. Her MA thesis on land values in South Chicago was a careful illustration of Park's theory of urban invasion and succession.

In the summer of 1927 the two favored Park students, Helen and Everett Hughes, got married. When the Hugheses moved to McGill, where he finished his dissertation on the Chicago Real Estate Board, Helen began her own doctoral dissertation on a theme most congenial to Park, the former journalist, on *News and the Human Interest Story*. She worked on it with Park from 1927 to 1940. It was the last of the long series of dissertations that Park inspired.[9] It was published as a book in 1940 and has recently been republished forty-four years later.

While engaged in her own work, Helen also helped her husband in the work on his first book, *French Canada in Transition*.[10] From then on, as Arlene Kaplan Daniels has written: "Her career was fashioned around his."[11]

After the Hugheses returned to Chicago in 1938, Everett moved fairly quickly from Assistant to Full Professor. Helen came to realize the marginal position into which she was being pushed. She took five years off to devote to her two young daughters. In 1944 she was asked by the then editor of the *American Journal of Sociology* to become an assistant editor, a girl Friday, at the salary of $100 a month. (In later years the title changed but the salary hardly at all.) Altogether Helen Hughes had a seventeen-year stint at the *American Journal of Sociology*. Even though this was meant to be part-time work, she most probably did more work on it than any of the successive editors, including her husband.

Although she was offered other jobs by the University of Chicago Press, Helen Hughes preferred to work in the Sociology Department so as not to lose contact with her colleagues. In an autobiographical article published in 1975, nearing the end of her life, she summed it all up in a paper called: "Maid of All Work or Departmental Sister-in-Law, Faculty Wife Employed on Campus." The paper, it is worth noting, appeared in the *American Journal of Sociology*.[12]

Toward the end of her career Helen Hughes was elected President of the Eastern Sociological Society and Vice President of the American Sociological Association. She was one of the founders of Sociologists for Women in Society and edited its newsletter. All this gave her a good deal of pleasure. What measure of bitterness might still have been lodged in the recesses of her mind is hard to tell.

In the last stages of her career Helen Hughes edited a number of volumes intended to introduce high school students to the various areas of sociology, and also began to edit a series of studies on women's work in sociology. But her main work continued to be auxiliary to that of her husband. Their jointly written book *Where Peoples Meet*,[13] a liberal interpretation of and introduction to intergroup relations, was published under a contract that specified that two-thirds of the proceeds were to go to Everett Hughes and one-third to Helen. . . .[14]

The Work

There is no Hughesian social theory as there is a Weberian, Marxian, or Parsonian theory. Yet there is something distinctive about Hughes's thought, something akin to the sociologist he perhaps most admired after Park, Georg Simmel. Both men have often been described as unsystematic sociologists, notwithstanding the fact that several scholars have demonstrated that Simmel's writings contain a great deal of systematic theory and that devoted students of Hughes have often claimed the same for him. Yet there is also an elusive quality to their work, represented by Ortega y Gasset's loving description of Simmel as a philosophical squirrel—jumping from one nut to another, performing splendid exercises as it leaps from branch to branch, and rejoicing, so it would seem, in the sheer gracefulness of its acrobatic leaps—a quality that manifests itself in Hughes's work no less than Simmel's.[15]

Hughes did not develop his ideas through a linear progression of thought. Rather, his style was to move from an initial observation to another suggested by the first. He himself once characterized his style as proceeding largely by free association. "In my work," he wrote, "I have relied a great deal on free association, sometimes on a freedom of association that could seem outrageous to the defenders of some established interest or cherished sentiment. Wright Mills must be given credit for the phrase *sociological imagination*. The essence of the sociological imagination is free association, guided but not hampered by a frame of reference internalized not quite into the unconscious. It must work even in one's dreams, but be where it can be called up at will."[16]

One could add to what Hughes says about himself that he proceeded by what Kenneth Burke has called "perspective by incongruity," a notion which Burke defined, referring to Oswald Spengler, as follows: "When we apply a word usually applied to one setting and transferring its use to another setting," it is a "perspective by incongruity," since "it is established by violating the 'proprieties' of the word in its previous linkages."[17] Applying perspectives by incongruity is a subversive enterprise because it undermines the habitual sequences of ideas; but it is also creative of a new mode of thinking since it introduces perspectives that are ordinarily suppressed or unnoted.

I don't know whether Hughes ever read Burke's *Permanence and Change* in which he discusses the above notion. The book appeared first in 1936, at which time it caused some discussion in intellectual and academic circles. I am inclined to think that we have in Hughes a case of independent discovery. One example among many possible ones must suffice. In a study of "Mistakes at Work," Hughes compares various institutions and their reaction to mistakes at work by

self and others. At first blush the theme sounds humdrum, but the
reader is brought up short by the very first paragraph:

> The comparative student of man's work learns about doctors by studying
> plumbers; and about prostitutes by studying psychiatrists. This is not to
> suggest any degree of similarity greater than chance expectations between
> the members of these pairs, but simply to indicate that the student starts
> with the assumption that all kinds of work belong in the same series,
> regardless of their places in prestige or ethical ratings. . . . We seek for the
> common themes in human work. . . . Both the physician and the plumber
> do practice esoteric techniques for the benefit of people in distress. The
> psychiatrist and the prostitute must both take care not to become too
> personally involved with clients who come to them with rather intimate
> problems. (This volume, p. 79)

In his other comparative studies of work and occupations, Hughes
adduces a novel and illuminating perspective which is not related
to the Burkean notion. He suggested not incongruity but divergent
definitions of the situation in what would seem to be a common
enterprise. Here again one example may have to suffice.

When we take a sick child to the hospital's emergency room and
in our anxiety wish that the child be treated immediately, we often
become distressed when the resident in charge treats our precious
child as if it were just one case among many. Hughes may have observed this in a hospital setting when one of his daughters was ill. But
what would only have made most of us furious stimulated Hughes's
sociological imagination. He puts his thoughts on the subject so well
that I feel I must quote him at some length:

> In many occupations the workers or practitioners (to use both a lower
> and a higher status term) deal routinely with what are emergencies to the
> people who receive the services. This is a source of chronic tension between
> the two. For the person with the crisis feels that the other is trying to
> belittle his trouble. . . . [The practitioner's] very competence comes from
> having dealt with a thousand cases of what I like to consider my unique
> trouble. The worker thinks he knows from long experience that people
> exaggerate their troubles. He therefore builds up devices to protect himself
> to stall people off. . . . [Moreover, he has to keep his cool for the sake of
> objectivity, so] there may indeed be in the minds of the receivers of emer-
> gency services a resentment that something so crucial to them can be a
> matter for a cooler and more objective attitude. (This volume, p. 66)

And thus Hughes coined the concept of *routinized emergency*.[18]
What Hughes suggests here, and in a good many of his essays, is

that we can gain as much or even more purchase on illuminating insights if we try to abstract from some of the concrete problems proper to a specific organization, occupation, or profession, if we focus on what they have in common rather than on their particular problems and structural characteristics. One of my personal experiences with Hughes may serve us well here.

At the Ph.D. examinations at Brandeis at which we served together, while my own questions were, I fear, fairly standard, Hughes's had a special quality. Here is one example:

ECH: What do a dwarf and a giant have in common?
Candidate: No answer.
ECH: Both are freaks, of course, my good fellow.

I submit that most of us, in the unlikely event that we would have offered such an insight, would have followed the candidate's embarrassed silence with a mini-lecture on the process of abstraction and its power to encompass many concrete data, the potent virtues of logical reasoning, and *tutti quanti*. Hughes eschewed such fancy notions and used the categories of his midwestern common sense wherever and whenever they served as well as abstract formulations.

Perhaps the most cogent characterization of the overall drift of Hughes's thought came from the late Ely Chinoy when he wrote that "the steadfast search for ever broader levels of generalization coupled with intense interest and personal concern with the people and problems studied" was at the root of Hughes's approach to sociology. I do not recall a single doctoral examination in which Hughes did not close by asking the candidate: "Under what other conditions and in what other situations would you expect phenomena similar to those that you have written about to tend to occur."[19]

Like Georg Simmel, Hughes was primarily a writer of essays. Although he wrote books on a French Canadian town on race relations (with others) and on medical education,[20] they do not seem to me to fully exemplify the brilliance of insight and perception that their author displayed in his numerous essays. This preference for the essay form stemmed, I believe, from the restlessness of Hughes's ever-alert mind. There was so much to observe in the human comedy that struck the alert observer, there were so many generalizations to be made, there was so much need to bring some order into the seeming disorder of social life. Given the myriad of impressions that crowded upon one if one only opens one's eyes, it was just too confining and restrictive to explore just a few phenomena in detail.

Isaiah Berlin once quoted a fragment of the Greek poet Archilocus which says: "The fox knows many things, but the hedgehog knows one big thing." He interpreted this to mean that there is one type of person "who relates everything to a single central vision, one system less or more coherent . . . and, on the other side, those who pursue many ends, often unrelated and even contradictory, connected, if at all, only in some *de facto* way. . . . They entertain ideas that are centrifugal rather than centripetal, their thought is scattered or diffused, moving on many levels, seizing upon the essence of a vast variety of experiences. . . . The first kind of personality belongs to the hedgehogs, the second to the fox."[21] Talcott Parsons was a prototypical hedgehog, Everett Hughes a prototypical fox. While Parsons pursued one big problem, the quest for what accounted for social order, proceeding so to speak from above, trying to identify on the capstones of the social edifice the normative glue that held the social structure together, Hughes scanned the ordinary surface of social life, its many eddies and currents, the moves and countermoves of human actors as they strove through competition and conflict, through strife and accommodation, to arrive at a livable human order. While Parsons was mainly concerned with lofty institutions, Hughes concentrated on the drama of daily life.

Ida Harper Simpson put the matter well when she wrote: "How institutions come into being, survive or fail to survive is the question that guides Hughes's study of society. The working of the processes are generalized through comparative study of all kinds of institutions from the lowly to the lofty and from the legitimate to the illegitimate. Research design built upon assumptions of modalities leave out the atypical. Hughes sees the study of these as essential to understanding the variant forms of institutional life. The kind of institution with which one begins study matters little from a theoretical point of view. . . . Research strategy, however, points to the lowly ones as the best starting points. They are less able to clothe themselves with cultural elaborations to shield their inner workings, and their members, being humble, are less likely than members of lofty institutions to seduce sociologists to take their point of view. Study of the lofty institutions might best be guided by findings on the lowly ones."[22]

While Parson's gaze was almost exclusively fixed on the theoretical works of those of his predecessors who could help him construct his imposing social edifice, Hughes mostly spanned the world of ordinary human beings, be it in his own environment or elsewhere, in order to wrest from them the secret of how they manage to live together in their always precarious effort to create a livable social environment.

Hughes was a widely read man, in command of the scholarly, but also the literary, work in a number of languages. But at bottom what interested him most of all were human beings, males and females, whites and African Americans, financiers and criminals, neurologists and prostitutes—the entire array of hundreds of human types who together compose the kaleidoscope that we call the social order.

Among the many instruments Hughes uses to study the human infinite variety, fieldwork surely took pride of place. As David Riesman has said: "He was the star to pull the wagon of fieldwork through the mud of dailiness."[23]

This collection highlights Hughes's contributions to the sociology of work, occupations, and professions, not only because he wrote frequently and searchingly in these areas, but also because he was the first sociologist to pay them sustained attention. He was the first to my knowledge who gave courses on these subjects at the Chicago department or elsewhere. I have also included papers on race relations because these, building on the prior work of Park, laid the groundwork for much of the work of first-generation African-American sociologists such as Franklin Frazier, St. Clair Drake, and Horace Cayton, all of them intellectual products of the Chicago department. But I am especially fond of the miscellaneous papers I have here grouped under the rubric "The Sociological Imagination." These papers, I would argue, show most directly the brilliancy of Everett Hughes's mind. Here is the sociological fox at his best. What Arlene Daniels, in a splendid paper from which I have borrowed a great deal, has called Hughes's "radical perspective"[24] is perhaps best exemplified in the last section of this volume, but it pervades the other writings as well.

I had first planned to provide in the concluding pages of this introductory essay a selective dozen or so of quotations to illustrate Hughes's observational acuity, his illuminating perceptions, and the powers of a synthesizing mind. I finally decided not to do so. The attentive reader will find dozens of such quotable quotes in even this relatively small gathering of Hughes's perceptions, wit, and wisdom. But I cannot refrain from quoting just three from a not-very-well-known essay. These will have to stand for the brilliance of countless others. They may also be of particular relevance to the readers of this volume who will be mainly teachers or students:

- The apprentice is what the master used to be, and hopes to become what he is.[25]
- Much of man's learning has come from that symbiosis in which a man's hobby is subsidized by drudgery.[26]
- Perspective then is the way . . . in which the artist relates close things to those in the distance. And this is what students are constantly doing.[27]

The man who could write down such observations was no ordinary member of the sociological tribe; he marched at the very head of the procession.

Notes

1. "Robert E. Park," in T. Raison, ed., *The Founding Fathers of Social Science.* Ermondsworth, England: Penguin 1969, p. 169.

2. Everett C. Hughes, *The Sociological Eye,* with a new introduction by David Riesman and Howard Becker, New Brunswick, N.J., Transaction Books, 1984, p. 106.

3. Everett C. Hughes, *The Chicago Real Estate Board: The Growth of an Institution,* Society for Social Research, 1931. Reprinted, edited by Lewis A. Coser and Walter Powell, Arno Press, 1979.

4. Ibid., p. 548.

5. Everett C. Hughes, *French Canada in Transition,* Chicago, University of Chicago Press, 1943, reprinted 1963.

6. Robert Hettlage and Karl Lenz, ed., *Erving Goffman—ein soziologischer Klassiker der zweiten Generation,* Paul Haupt, Bern and Stuttgart, 1991, pp. 60–61.

7. Everett C. Hughes, *Students' Culture and Perspectives: Lectures on Medical and General Education,* University of Kansas Law School, Lawrence, Kansas, 1961, p. 29.

8. Ibid., p. 43.

9. Helen MacGill Hughes, *News and the Human Interest Story,* Introduction by Robert Park, Chicago, University of Chicago Press, 1940.

10. Everett C. Hughes, *French Canada in Transition,* Chicago, University of Chicago Press, 1943, reprinted 1963.

11. Arlene Daniels, "Helen MacGill Hughes 1903–1992," *Footnotes,* August 1992.

12. *American Journal of Sociology,* 78, 4 (1975), pp. 770 ff.

13. Everett and Helen MacGill Hughes, *Where Peoples Meet: Racial and Ethnic Frontiers,* New York, The Free Press, 1952.

14. I am deeply in debt to an impressive paper on both Hugheses by Susan Hoecker-Drysdale, "Sociologists in the Vineyard: The Careers of Everett Cherrington Hughes and Helen MacGill Hughes." It is as yet unpublished but should not remain so.

15. Jose Ortega y Gasset, "In Search of Goethe from Within," *Partisan Review* XVI (1949), p. 1166.

16. *The Sociological Eye,* p. xvi.

17. Kenneth Burke, *Permanence and Change,* 1936, New York, New Republic, p. 119.

18. For a creative development of these notions, though without the mention of Hughes's work, see: Barry Schwartz, "Waiting, Exchange, and Power: The Distribution of Time in Social Systems," *A.J.S.* 79, 4 (1974), pp. 841–70.

19. Ely Chinoy, review of "The Sociological Eye," *Sociological Quarterly* 13, 4 Fall 1972, p. 565.

20. Howard S. Becker, Blanche Geer, Everett C. Hughes, and Anselm Strauss, *Boys in White,* Chicago, University of Chicago Press, 1961.

21. Isaiah Berlin, *The Hedgehog and the Fox,* New York, Mentor Books, 1957, pp. 7–8.

22. Ida Harper Simpson, "Continuities in the Sociology of Everett C. Hughes," *Sociological Quarterly* 13, 4 (Fall 1972), p. 548.

23. David Riesman, "The Legacy of Everett Hughes," *Contemporary Sociology* 12, 5 (September 1983), p. 481.

24. Arlene Kaplan Daniels, "The Irreverent Eye," *Contemporary Sociology* 1, 5 (September 1972), pp. 402–7.

25. Everett C. Hughes, *Students' Culture and Perspectives: Lectures on Medical and General Education*, University of Kansas Law School, Lawrence, 1961, p. 23.

26. Ibid., p. 23.

27. Ibid., p. 17.

I

WORK

1

The Study of Occupations

Any occupation in which people make a living may be studied sociologically. Many have been so studied in recent years, especially those which are undergoing changes in techniques and social organization and in their social and economic standing. Sometimes the study is instigated by those in the occupation; sometimes by people not in it but affected by it. The motive may be immediate practical advantage; it may be greater understanding and general social advantage. Sociology has much to gain from such studies, provided that those who undertake them make and keep a sociological bargain with those who support them and those who allow themselves to be studied. The maximal gain can be reached, however, only when the sociologist keeps clearly in mind his ulterior goal of learning more about social processes in general.

In the following pages, we are frankly preoccupied with this ulterior goal of learning about the nature of society itself from the study of occupations.

The Labor Force

Modern industrial and urban societies and economies, no matter what the political systems under which they operate, are characterized by a wholesale mobilization of people away from traditional and familial activities into more formally organized work activities. These activities are named and categorized in payrolls, organization charts, and union-management contracts, and in income-tax, licensing, and social-security legislation.

In the sense that they work at some times in their lives in this system of things, more people are engaged in occupations than in other kinds of societies and at a greater variety of occupations. In

Chapter 20 of *Sociology Today*, edited by Robert K. Merton, Leonard Broom, and Leonard S. Cottrell, Jr., © 1959 by Basic Books, Inc. Publishers, New York. Reprinted by permission.

industrial countries, the census more and more serves the end of informing government and business about the actual and potential labor force and about the actuarial problems of providing for people who are not at work, whether because of age, physical condition, lack of the skills needed in a changing technology, or simply because they live in the wrong place. Race, sex, marital status, and other characteristics formerly determined civil estate quite directly; now it is work that counts (although it has always been a great determiner of status), and the other characteristics take their importance by virtue of their influence on one's place in the labor force.[1]

It also seems that everyone who is not too young, too old, too sick, or too burdened with household duties is rather expected to have an occupation in the sense indicated. In Soviet Russia, this expectation has become compulsion; a man may not stay away from his work without a doctor's certificate, and the physician who gives such certificates too freely is called on the carpet.[2] In this country, those who look to our national resources have lately added womanpower to the list, not because women did not work in the past and are now expected to do so, but because they have become mobilized away from the household and into the labor force in greater proportion and for longer periods of their lives than previously.[3]

I leave to others the task of counting the occupations in industrial economies and the changing numbers of people engaged in each of them, and the tiresome business of fitting the many occupations into a small enough number of categories to permit crowding them into tables. I can think of no set of categories that has been given such heavy sociological work to do, both theoretical and practical, as those of occupations in census tables. Measures of social stratification and of mobility, both territorial and social, are based upon them, as are international comparisons. They are used as independent variables against which to weigh differences of political opinion, taste, religion, and many other things. One is tempted to ask whether they are equal to the burden; it is a question on which many people are very competently breaking their heads.

Work and Leisure

Oddly enough, at a time when nearly everyone is being drawn into the labor force, the proportion of a man's daily, weekly, annual, and life time that he is expected to devote to work is falling so drastically that the days of leisure in each seven may become nearly equal to the days of work. Already the waking hours spent away from work are, for many people, more than those spent at work, even on working days. At the same time, a new concept has been introduced, that of underemployment. It refers not to hours, weeks, and months of idleness so much as to the supposed underuse of human effort; the standard of efficient use applied is that of an economy which, like ours, provides great amounts of capital per worker and thus allows great per-man-hour production. The underemployed man may put forth great effort, but his product is small. It is as if the famed Protestant ethic had been transferred from the individual to the system; it is the machinery which is supposed to put in seven days a week and almost, if not quite, 52 weeks a year. The machine-tenders can take it easier at work, although they are expected to keep their eyes and ears piously glued to the "media" so that they may keep their consumption up to expectation. For, as G. Tarde said in his *Psychologie économique,*[4] a return to the early evangel, with its belief in the vanity of human desires, would be the death of modern industry.

Although the great masses of people who are occupied are taking it easier, a minority appears to be bound to the tireless wheels of the machines. Those who manage the machines and the organization required to keep them and their products moving appear to require an extra dose of a certain brand of the Protestant ethic, a brand which does not leave time for prayer or other solitary and idiosyncratic activities. The new distribution of work and leisure in the life of the individual, and as between people in various positions in our society and economy; the new concepts, values, and expectations with respect to them, and to the levels and kinds of effort expected or required of people in the various positions; these are fundamental problems of society and of occupations. The change of balance between work and leisure has given new emphasis and a new turn to studies of leisure. The demand for men of unlimited ambition and drive to fill certain of the positions in our economy of abundance has, in its turn, given a new impulse to studies of social mobility into the higher ranks of management.

The Division of Labor

Division of labor, one of the most fundamental of all social processes, finds one of its most explicit expressions in occupations. The phrase, however, is but a poor term for differentiation of function in a social whole. It is poor because it emphasizes the division and neglects the integration, the relations among the functions so divided or differentiated. All organization of behavior consists of differentiation of function. Economic division of labor is but a special case, or a special aspect of it.

An occupation, in essence, is not some particular set of activities; it is the part of an individual in any ongoing system of activities. The system may be large or small, simple or complex. The ties between the person in different positions may be close or so distant as not to be social; they may be formal or informal, frequent or rare. The essential is that the occupation is the place ordinarily filled by one person in an organization or complex of efforts and activities. Sociologically speaking, the division of labor is only incidentally technical. It consists, not of ultimate components of skill or of mechanical or mental operations, but of the actual allocation of functions to persons. Individual components of motion or action are combined in ways that sometimes appear fearful and wonderful to a mechanically oriented or rational and detached mind. The logic of the division and combination of activities and functions into occupations and of their allocation to various kinds of people in any system is not to be assumed as given, but is in any case something to be discovered. Likewise, the outward limits of a system of division of labor are not to be assumed but are to be sought out. Analysis of systems whose limits have not been determined can be very deceiving.

Homans[5] has recently emphasized exchange as a basic social process, the analysis of which might bring us closer to a sound general theory of social behavior. Although this is not an entirely novel idea, it is an important one and especially pertinent to the analysis of division of labor. Where there is differentiation of function, there is exchange—and exchange not merely of money, goods, or tangible and easily described services. Durkheim's book, let us remember, is entitled *De la division du travail social*—on the division of social labor. And although it may be true that more and more kinds of exchange tend to have an expression in money, it is also true that it is very difficult to keep money exchanges free of other kinds.

One of the problems of the purest markets is to limit exchanges to the purely economic. Glick has recently found this to be so in the market in egg futures.[6] The rules and signals for buying and selling are made explicit so that the dealers will not be able to give private information or to exchange favors on the floor. I mention this case only to emphasize that the division of labor involves many kinds of exchange, many of them not at all apparent, and that several kinds may go on at once. This is true of occupations as well as of those differentiations of functions found in families and other systems of relationship. In many occupations, the exchanges occur on at least two levels. There is exchange between a person and the various others with whom he interacts in his occupational role. It is of this exchange that Henderson wrote in "Physician and Patient as a Social System."[7] It is also described in studies of industrial relations, and especially of the informal relations among people in the same work situation. One must remember, however, that much interaction occurs in formally defined relationships and that much involves persons not in personal contact with one another. The other level is that of exchanges between the occupation and the society in which it occurs; they underlie those characteristic features of certain occupations, license and mandate.

License and Mandate

An occupation consists in part in the implied or explicit *license* that some people claim and are given to carry out certain activities rather different from those of other people and to do so in exchange for money, goods, or services. Generally, if the people in the occupation have any sense of identity and solidarity, they will also claim a *mandate* to define—not merely for themeselves, but for others as well—proper conduct with respect to the matters concerned in their work. They also will seek to define, and possibly succeed in defining, not merely proper conduct but even modes of thinking and belief for everyone individually and for the body social and politic with respect to some broad area of life which they believe to be in their occupational domain. The license may be merely technical; it may, however, extend to broad areas of behavior and thought. It may include a whole style of life, or it may be confined to carrying out certain technical activities which others may not carry out—at least not officially or for a reward. The mandate may be small and narrow, or the contrary.

License, as an attribute of an occupation, is usually thought of as specific legal permission to pursue the occupation. I am thinking of something broader. Society, by its nature, consists in part of both allowing and expecting some people to do things which other people are not allowed or expected to do. Most occupations—especially those considered professions and those of the underworld—include as part of their being a license to deviate in some measure from some common modes of behavior. Professions, perhaps more than other kinds of occupation, also claim a broad legal, moral, and intellectual mandate. Not only do the practitioners, by virtue of gaining admission to the charmed circle of the profession, individually exercise a license to do things others do not do, but collectively they presume to tell society what is good and right for it in a broad and crucial aspect of life. Indeed, they set the very terms of thinking about it. When such a presumption is granted as legitimate, a profession in the full sense has come into being. The nature and extent of both license and mandate, their relations to each other, and the circumstances and conflicts in which they expand or contract are crucial areas of study, not merely for occupations, but for society itself. Such licenses and mandates are the prime manifestation of the *moral* division of labor—that is, of the processes by which differing moral functions are distributed among the members of society, as individuals and as categories of individuals. These moral functions differ from one another in both kind and measure. Some people seek and get special responsibility for defining values and for establishing and enforcing sanctions over a certain aspect of life; the differentiation of moral and social functions involves both the area of social behavior in question and the degree of responsibility and power.

Since this is the aspect of occupations to which I give most emphasis in this paper, I will illustrate it in a manner which I hope will stimulate discussion and research.

Many occupations cannot be carried out without guilty knowledge. The priest cannot mete out penance without becoming an expert in sin; else how may he know the moral from the venial? To carry out his mandate to tell people what books they may or may not read and what thoughts and beliefs they must espouse or avoid, he must become a connoisseur of the forbidden. Only a master theologian can think up really subtle heresies; hence Satan is of necessity a fallen angel. A layman would be but an amateur with a blunderbuss where a sharpshooter is wanted. The poor priest, as part of the exchange involved in his license to hear confessions and to absolve, and his mandate to tell us what's what, has to convince the lay world that he does not yield to the temptations of his privileged position; he puts on a uniform and lives a celibate existence. These are compensating or counter-deviations from the common way of dressing and living; they would not be admired, or perhaps even tolerated, in people who have no special function to justify them. The priest, in short, has both intellectual and moral leeway, and perhaps must have them if he is to carry out the rest of his license. He carries a burden of guilty knowledge.

The lawyer, the policeman, the physician, the reporter, the scientist, the scholar, the diplomat, the private secretary, all of them must have license to get—and, in some degree, to keep secret—some order of guilty knowledge. It may be guilty in that it is knowledge that a layman would be obliged to reveal, or in that the withholding of it from the public or from authorities compromises the integrity of the man who so withholds it, as in the case of the policeman who keeps connections with the underworld or the diplomat who has useful friends abroad. Most occupations rest upon some bargain about receiving, guarding, and giving out communications. The license to keep this bargain is of the essence of many occupations.

The prototype of all guilty knowledge is, however, a different, potentially shocking, way of looking at things. Every occupation must look relatively at some order of events, objects, or ideas. These things must be classified, and seen in comparative light; their behavior must be analyzed and, if possible, predicted. A suitable technical language must be developed in which one may talk to his colleagues about them. This technical, therefore relative, attitude must be adopted toward the very people whom one serves; no profession can operate without license to talk in shocking terms behind the backs of its clients. Sometimes an occupation must adopt this objective, comparative attitude toward things which are very dear to other people or which are the object of absolutely held values and sentiments. I suppose that this ultimate license is the greatest when the people who exercise it, being guardians of precious things, are in a position to do great damage. (No one is in so good a position to steal as the banker.)

Related to the license to think relatively about dear things and absolute values is the license to do dangerous things. I refer not to the danger run by the steeplejack and the men who navigate submarines, for that is danger to themselves. (Even so, there is a certain disposition to pay them off with a license to run slightly amok when the one comes down and the other up to solid ground.) I speak, rather, of the license of the doctor to cut and dose, of the priest to play with men's salvation, of the scientist to split atoms; or simply of the danger that advice given a person may be wrong, or that work done may be unsuccessful or cause damage.

License of all these kinds may lie at the root of that modicum of aggressive suspicion which most laymen feel toward professionals, and of that raging and fanatical anger which burns chronically in some people and which at times becomes popular reaction. Many antivivisectionists, according to Hughes,[8] do not love beasts more but love doctors less, suspecting them of loving some parts of their work too much. It is a chronic protest. Of course there are people who believe that they have suffered injury from incompetent or careless work or that they have been exploited by being acted upon more for the professional's increase of knowledge or income than for their own well-being.

Herein lies the whole question of what the bargain is between those who receive a service and those who give it, and of the circumstances in which it is protested by either party. Of equal or greater sociological significance is the problem of a general questioning of license or mandate. Social unrest often shows itself precisely in such questioning of the prerogatives of the leading professions. In time of crisis, there may arise a general demand for more conformity to lay modes of thought and discourse.

One of the major professional deviations of mind, a form of guilty knowledge, is the objective and relative attitude mentioned above. One order of relativity has to do with time; the professional may see the present in longer perspective. The present may be, for him, more crucial in that it is seen as a link in a causative chain of events; the consequences of present action may be seen as more inevitable, rippling down through time. The emergency, in this sense, may appear greater to the professional than to the layman. In another sense, it appears less crucial, since the professional sees the present situation in comparison with others; it is not unique, and hence the emergency is not so great as laymen see it.

Something like this seems to lie in the attack upon the Supreme Court following its decisions on civil rights and upon professors who insist on freedom to discuss all things in this time of Cold War. They are thought to be playing legal and academic tunes while the Communists plaster us with firebombs. In time of crisis, detachment appears the most perilous deviation of all, hence the one least to be tolerated. Their deviation, in these cases, consists in a drastic reversal of what many layman consider the urgent as against the less urgent aspects of our situation. And it arises from their license to think in different terms.

Militant religious sects give us an instructive illustration. They ordinarily, in Christianity at least, consist of people convinced that they are all in imminent danger of damnation. So long as they remain militant sects, they are in chronic crisis. It is perhaps not without sociological significance that they do not tolerate a clergy, or much differentiation of function at all. It is as if they sense that professionalizing inevitably brings some detachment, some relative and comparative attitude. In a large society the clergy are generally more ardent than the laity; a sect might almost be defined as a religious group in which the opposite is true. Inquisitions to the contrary, it is probable that the professional clergy tend to be more tolerant than ardent lay-men. Although it may seem paradoxical to suggest it, one may seri-ously ask under what circumstances religious people tolerate a profes-sional clergy.

The typical reform movement is an attempt of laymen to redefine values and to change action about some matter over which some occupation (or group of occupations or faction within an occupation) holds a mandate. The movement may simply push for faster or more drastic action where the profession moves slowly or not at all; it may be a direct attack upon the dominant philosophy of the profession, as in attempts to change the manner of distributing medical care. The power of an occupation to protect its license and to maintain its mandate and the circumstances in which licenses and mandates are attacked, lost, or changed are matters for investigation. (And one must not overlook movements within a profession.) Such work is study of politics in the fundamental sense—that is, in the sense of studying constitutions. For constitutions are the relations between the effective estates which *constitute* the body politic. In our society, some occupations are among the groups which most closely resemble what were once known as estates. While there has been a good deal of study of the political activities of occupational groups, the subject has been somewhat misunderstood as a result of the strong fiction of political neutrality of professions in our society. Of course, a certain license to be politically neutral has been allowed some occupations, but the circumstances and limits of such neutrality are again a matter for study. Special attention should be given to the exchanges implied and to the circumstances, some of which we have mentioned, in which the license is denied, and the ways in which it is violated and sub-verted, from within or without.

One can think of many variations of license and mandate, and of the relations between them. School teachers in our society have little license to think thoughts that others do not think; they are not even allowed to think the nastier thoughts that others *do* think. Their man-date seems limited to minor matters of pedagogy; it does not include definition of the fundamental issues of what children shall be taught. Educational policy is given into their hands very grudgingly, although they have a good deal of power by default. Mandate by default is itself a matter for study. The underworld, to take another example, has a considerable license to deviate; in fact, members get paid to help respectable people escape the norms of everyday life. But the license is not openly admitted. The manner in which the people of the underworld find spokesmen and the nature of the exchanges in-

volved have often been discussed as a pathology of politics. The full
circle of exchanges is seldom analyzed with an eye to learning something significant about the very nature of social exchanges. Study of
the license of artists and entertainers could also yield much knowledge
concerning the degrees of conformity possible in a society and the
consequences of trying to reduce deviation to something like zero.
For these occupations seem to require, if they are to produce the very
things for which society will give them a living of sorts (or, in some
cases, unheard-of opulence), at least some people who deviate widely
from the norms more or less adhered to and firmly espoused by other
people. Their license is, however, periodically in a parlous state, and
there seems no guarantee that it will not, at any moment, be attacked.
There has recently been a case which turns upon whether poetic license includes speaking for an enemy country in time of war.

Occupations and Social Matrices

If an occupation is a more-or-less standardized one-man's part in
some operating system, it follows that it cannot be described apart
from the whole. A study of occupations, then, becomes in part a study
of the allocation of functions and the consequent composition of any
given occupation.[9]

Although an occupation may conceivably consist of but one activity
in a narrow and mechanical sense, it takes an extremely rationalized
organization to keep it so. Most occupations consist of a number, a
bundle, of activities. Some may be bundled together because they
require similar skills; others, simply because they can conveniently be
done at one place, or because taken alone they do not occupy a man's
full time; still others, because they are, or seem to be, natural parts
of a certain role, office, or function. The physician's repertoire, for
example, includes technically unrelated activities, bound together by
the demands of his basic function. Only in those specialties which can
be practiced without personal contact with patients can physicians
group their activities on strictly technical lines. One might, indeed,
try to scale occupations according to the dominance of technical as
against role factors in determining combinations of activities.

The extreme of technically rational division and grouping of activities, under conditions of constant and aggressive invention of new
machines and forms of organization, would lead to continual destruc-
tion and reforming of occupations.[10] The problems of adjusting self-
conceptions and social roles in such a case have been much studied

lately. The opposite of this would be a system of strongly traditional and entrenched occupations whose activities, whether bound together by technical considerations or not, are considered to belong rightfully and naturally together.

This leads us to the distinction between historic and less historic occupations. A historic occupation is historic, not because its chief activity is an old one but because it has long had a name, a license, and a mandate, a recognized place in the scheme of things. In the extreme case, a historic occupation has a strong sense of identity and continuity; a galaxy of historic founders, innovators, and other heroes, the saints or gods of the trade; and a wealth of remembered historic or legendary events, which justify its present claims. The aspirant to such a trade is expected to acquire a strong sense of belonging to an historic estate, somewhat set off from other men. New occupations, like new families, seek a heroic genealogy to strengthen their claims to license and mandate. Occupations vary greatly in the degree to which they become the master determinants of the social identity, self-conception, and social status of the people in them.

In an occupation which is strongly historic, one would expect the combination of activities also to have a certain historic quality, reinforced by a traditional logic. Historic or not, occupations vary greatly in their autonomy in determining what activities are their duty and prerogatives. One would, however, expect occupations of long standing to resist attempts, especially of outsiders, to determine the content of their work or the rules governing it.

The various activities which make up an occupation are, of course, given varying values both by the people inside and by others. Sometimes the name of the occupation expresses an emphasis upon one rather than other activities; note the use of "preacher," "priest," and "pastor" in referring to clergy of various denominations, and the insistence of some gynecologists upon being called gynecological surgeons. Some one activity may be symbolically valued beyond its importance in the present complex of activities. Changes in technology, economics, and organization may change the balance between the named symbolic activity and others; in extreme cases, the symbolic activity may be lost or dropped from the repertory of the occupation while the name persists.

Nursing is a striking example of such a series of shifts. The word has a certain connotation in the lay mind; it refers to a role and an attitude, but also to certain comforting activities considered consonant with the role. The elaboration of the organization of hospitals, clinics, and public-health agencies, combined with great technological changes in medicine and an immense increase in the demand for medical services, has led to a great reshuffling of functions in the whole medical system. Doctors need much more technical help than before; the system also requires much more administrative activity. A host of new occupations has arisen. The physician has passed along many activities to the nurse; the nurse has in turn passed along many of hers to other occupations. The result has been upward mobility of the nurse, since a good number of the new occupations stand below her in the hierarchy and since there are some posts of high prestige, income, and authority to which nurses alone may aspire. But there has been a certain dissociation of the occupation called nursing from the activities traditionally associated with it in the lay mind. The case is not peculiar, but it is so clear cut as to allow sensitive observation.

Every occupation has some history which may in part be described in terms of changes in the bundle of activities, in the values given them, and in the total system of which the occupation is a part. Changes may occur in ownership and control over access to appropriate tools (pulpits, operating rooms, law libraries, stages and properties, Univacs and laboratories), methods of payment and exchange, the formal authority and status systems in which work is done, the terms of entry to the occupation, and competition among individuals, occupations, and whole complexes of goods and services for the patronage of consumers. Of course, these same matters are crucial to study of an occupation at present; but sociologists have to be reminded of the pertinence of history rather more than of present doings.

I hope I have not put so many things into the last few paragraphs that the main points will be overlooked: namely, that the items of activity and social function which make up any occupation are historical products. The composition of an occupation can be understood only in the frame of the pertinent social and institutional complex (which must in turn be discovered, not merely assumed). The allocating and grouping of activities is itself a fundamental social process.

The Work Situation

I should at this point mention work situations as systems of interaction, as the setting of the role-drama of work, in which people of various occupational and lay capacities, involved in differing complexes of *Lebenschancen*, interact in sets of relationships that are social as well as technical. Some of the best work in contemporary sociology[11] is being done in such settings and is giving us new knowledge of reciprocal expectations of role performance, definition of roles, group solidarity, and development and definition of reference groups. We are by this time alerted to the value of work situations as posts for observing the formation of groups and the generation of social rules and sanctions. I am not sure that we are using the findings of such observation vigorously enough in building our theories of social control and of the larger legal and political processes.

Let me conclude with some remarks on the individual and his occupation and his career. Career, in the most generic sense, refers to the fate of a man running his life-cycle in a particular society at a particular time. The limitations put upon his choice of occupation by his own peculiarities (sex, race, abilities, class, wealth, access to and motivation for education, and access to knowledge of the system itself) in interaction with the "times" have been the object of many studies. Not all the problems of logic and method involved in such studies have been adequately attacked or solved.

Occupations vary in their stength as named reference-groups, as the basis for full and lasting self-identification and firm status. They vary also in their demand for full and lasting commitment and in the age and life-phase at which one must decide to enter training for them. Some occupations are more visible to young people than are others, and effective visibility varies also by class and other social circumstances. The inner workings of the best known cannot be seen by outsiders. Add to this the fact of changes in even the most historic occupations, and it is evident that young people must choose their occupations, as they do their wives, largely on faith (if, indeed, they choose at all). The career includes not only the processes and sequences of learning the techniques of the occupation but also the progressive perception of the whole system and of possible places in it and the accompanying changes in conceptions of the work and of one's self in relation to it. A good deal of work is being done on these matters; the phrase *adult socialization* is being applied to some of the processes involved.[12]

The processes are complicated by the fact that some occupations, strong as their symbols of common identity (their license and mandate) may be, are inwardly very heterogeneous. Within medicine, there is wide choice of specialties; each of them is not merely a unit of technical work but a position in the huge and complex system of health institutions. They offer alternative career lines, some of them mutually exclusive from an early stage. These career lines are variously ranked within the profession itself as well as outside; the people in each of them have their own ethos and sometimes their own variant system of relative values concerning many things in medicine. They differ, for example, in their notions of what knowledge and skills should be taught in medical schools. How these factors act upon and are reacted to by students who are in the process of choosing their specialties is discussed in a current paper.[13] A part of the individual's career may be the making of the finer decisions concerning his hoped-for place within an occupational system, the projecting of his self-image in the direction of one rather than others of the available models of mature members of his occupation.

Career involves, at each stage, choices of some rather than other activities in one's economy of effort. A career consists, in one sense, of moving—in time and hence with age—within the institutional system in which the occupation exists. Ordinarily, career is interpreted as progress upward in the system, but a man can make progress in a number of ways. He may become more skillful at the basic activities of the occupation; the increase of skill may be rewarded by increase of income, security, and prestige among his fellows. If his occupation is practiced directly with customers or clients, he may get more of them and better ones. However, progress and advancement also consist in part of change in the proportions of time and effort devoted to various activities, and even in rather complete change of organizational functions or role.

Sometimes the greater success is paid for by a complete abandonment of the activities symbolically most closely associated with the occupation, a consequent loss of skill in those activities, and passage from identification with the basic colleagueship to some other. This is a career contingency of much importance to the individual's self-conception. It often creates severe guilt. We might expect the severity of such crises to vary with the sense of commitment and the strength of the colleague-group as a significant other for its members. Some occupations appear intense, others weak and indifferent, in commitment. In some there is a casual attitude toward particular activities and perhaps a full acceptance of the right of employers to determine just what work one shall do. In others, there is a rich culture and a strong sense among the members of being different from other people. There are songs and lore about logging, railroading, and going to sea. In these occupations there are strong feelings about who really shares in the dangers and fate of the group, and who consequently has a right to the name. Jazz musicians, who live life wrong-end to—for their night is day, and other people's pleasure is their work—have a similarly strong sense of who is and who is not one of them. Some of the professions also have a sense of identity and a tendency to be self-conscious about who is a true member of the group.

Today, there are great numbers of people in occupations which are, in fact, products of modern industrial and business technology and organization and in which there appears to be little sense of belonging to a closed circle of people with a peculiar fate. The sense of identification of such people with their work, or with classes and categories of people at work, is a matter for study. Many of them are said to be alienated both from their work fellows and from society. Not the least problem of such people is the balance between work and leisure—not merely as proportions of their lifetimes, years, weeks, and days, but in terms of their importance and meaning. This is also, in the broad sense, a problem of career, of a man and his work seen in the perspective of his ongoing life and life chances. We may then think of man and his work, of careers, as an immense area of problems, embracing a great many of the problems of formation of social personality and of adjustment of individuals to their social surroundings. Careers in various occupations are patterned in varying degree. In the narrowest sense, career—as Mannheim wrote—is a predictable course through a bureaucracy.[14] But the patterns, the possible positions and sequences in work systems, themselves change. And each human career is worked out in some particular historical phase. Ours is a rapidly changing phase, which means that careers and career contingencies are changing, too. This gives the study of careers, and of other facets of occupations and work, a certain timeliness and excitement that adds to their basic relevance for study of social and social-psychological processes.

Notes

1. See Evelyn M. Kitagawa, *The Family as a Unit in the Work Force: A Review of the Literature*, Population Research and Training Center, University of Chicago, 1956.

2. Mark G. Field, "Structured Strain in the Role of the Soviet Physician," *Amer. J. Sociol.*, 53:5 (1953), 493–502.

3. National Manpower Council, *Womanpower*, Columbia University Press, 1957.

4. Paris, 1902, Vol 1, p. 186. Tarde's chapters on the economic role of desires and beliefs are good reading for those who are working on a theory of consumption and leisure.

5. George C. Homans, "Social Behavior as Exchange," *Amer. J. Sociol.*, 53 (1958), 597–606.

6. Ira O. Glick, "Futures Trading: A Sociological Analysis," unpublished Ph.D. dissertation, University of Chicago, 1957. See also Max Weber, "Die Börse" (1894), in *Gesammelte Aufsätze zur Soziologie und Sozialpolitik*, Tübingen. J. C. B. Mohr, 1924, pp. 256–322.

7. L. J. Henderson, "Physician and Patient as a Social System," *N.E.J. Med.*, 212 (1935), 819–23.

8. Helen Hughes, "The Compleat Anti-vivisectionist," *Sci. Mon.*, N.Y., 65:6 (1947), 503–7.

9. Throughout this paper, but especially in what follows, it would be hard for me to distinguish what is, at least in some small sense, my own combining of ideas and what I owe to my colleagues in recent studies, Howard S. Becker, Blanche Geer, and Anselm Strauss. I am sure that many of my former students and other colleagues will have reason to think that I am borrowing liberally from their work.

10. Georges Friedmann has been the leading student of this problem. See his *Où Va le Travail Humain?* Paris, Gallimard, 1950; *Problèmes Humains du Machinisme Industriel*, Paris, Gallimard, 1946. He has also written a fundamental criticism called "La thèse de Durkheim et les formes contemporaines de la division du travail." *Cahiers Internationaux de Sociologie*, 19 (1955) 45–48.

11. See Erving Goffman, *Presentation of Self in Society*, University of Chicago Press, 1956.

12. Howard S. Becker and Anselm Strauss, "Careers, Personality, and Adult Socialization," *Amer J. Sociol.*, 72 (1956), 253–63. See also Robert K. Merton, George Reader, and Patricia Kendall (eds.), *The Student Physician: Introductory Studies in the Sociology of Medical Education*, Harvard University Press, 1957.

13. Kurt W. Back and Bernard S. Philips, "Public Health as a Career of Medicine: Specialization within a Profession," paper read at the annual meetings of the American Sociological Society, 1957.

14. Karl Mannheim, "Über das Wesen und die Bedeutung des wirtschaftlichen Erfolgsstrebens," *Archiv für Sozialwissenschaft and Sozialpolitik*, 63:3 (1930), 449–512.

2

Professions

Professions are more numerous than ever before. Professional people are a larger proportion of the labor force. The professional attitude, or mood, is likewise more widespread; professional status, more sought after. These are components of the professional trend, a phenomenon of all the highly industrial and urban societies; a trend that apparently accompanies industrialization and urbanization irrespective of political ideologies and systems. The professional trend is closely associated with the bureaucratic, although the queen of the professions, medicine, is the avowed enemy of bureaucracy, at least of bureaucracy in medicine when others than physicians have a hand in it.

A profession delivers esoteric services—advice or action or both—to individuals, organizations, or government; to whole classes or groups of people or to the public at large. The action may be manual; the surgeon and the bishop lay on their hands, although in the one case manual skill is of the essence, while in the other it need not be great because the action is symbolic. (Yet some priests and religious healers become very effective in their manner of laying hands on the heads of people who seek confirmation or comfort.) Even when manual, the action—it is assumed or claimed—is determined by esoteric knowledge systematically formulated and applied to problems of a client. The services include advice. The person for or upon whom the esoteric service is performed, or the one who is thought to have the right or duty to act for him, is advised that the professional's action is necessary. Indeed, the professional in some cases refuses to act unless the client—individual or corporate—agrees to follow the advice given.

The nature of the knowledge, substantive or theoretical, on which advice and action are based is not always clear; it is often a mixture of several kinds of practical and theoretical knowledge. But it is part of the professional complex, and of the professional claim, that the

Reprinted by permission from *Daedalus*, Journal of the American Academy of Arts and Sciences, Boston, Mass., Vol. 92, No. 4, 1965.

practice should rest upon some branch of knowledge to which the professionals are privy by virtue of long study and by initiation and apprenticeship under masters already members of the profession.

The Oxford Shorter Dictionary tells us that the earliest meaning of the adjective "professed" was this: "That has taken the vows of a religious order." By 1675, the word had been secularized thus: "That professes to be duly qualified; professional." "Profession" originally meant the act or fact of professing. It has come to mean: "The occupation which one professes to be skilled in and to follow. . . . A vocation in which professed knowledge of some branch of learning is used in its application to the affairs of others, or in the practice of an art based upon it. Applied specifically to the three learned professions of divinity, law, and medicine; also the military profession." From this follows later the adjective "professional," with the meanings now familiar.

Professionals *profess*. They profess to know better than others the nature of certain matters, and to know better than their clients what ails them or their affairs. This is the essence of the professional idea and the professional claim. From it flow many consequences. The professionals claim the exclusive right to practice, as a vocation, the arts which they profess to know, and to give the kind of advice derived from their special lines of knowledge. This is the basis of the license, both in the narrow sense of legal permission and in the broader sense that the public allows those in a profession a certain leeway in their practice and perhaps in their very way of living and thinking. The professional is expected to think objectively and inquiringly about matters which may be, for laymen, subject to orthodoxy and sentiment which limit intellectual exploration. Further, a person, in his professional capacity, may be expected and required to think objectively about matters which he himself would find it painful to approach in that way when they affected him personally. This is why it is unfair to ask the physician to heal himself, the priest to shrive himself, or the teacher to be a perfect parent. A professional has a license to deviate from lay conduct in action and in very mode of thought with respect to the matter which he professes: it is an institutionalized deviation, in which there is a certain strain toward clear definition of situations and roles.

Since the professional does profess, he asks that he be trusted. The client is not a true judge of the value of the service he receives; furthermore, the problems and affairs of men are such that the best of professional advice and action will not always solve them. A central feature, then, of all professions, is the motto—not used in this form, so far as I know—*credat emptor*. Thus is the professional relation distinguished from that of those markets in which the rule is *caveat emptor*, although the latter is far from a universal rule even in the exchange of goods. The client is to trust the professional; he must tell him all secrets which bear upon the affairs in hand. He must trust his judgment and skill. In return, the professional asks protection from any unfortunate consequences of his professional actions; he and his fellows make it very difficult for anyone outside—even civil courts—to pass judgment upon one of their number. Only the professional can say when his colleague makes a mistake.

The mandate also flows from the claim to esoteric knowledge and high skill. Lawyers not only give advice to clients and plead their cases for them; they also develop a philosophy of law—of its nature and its functions, and of the proper way in which to administer justice. Physicians consider it their prerogative to define the nature of disease and of health, and to determine how medical services ought to be distributed and paid for. Social workers are not content to develop a technique of case work; they concern themselves with social legislation. Every profession considers itself the proper body to set the terms in which some aspect of society, life, or nature is to be thought of, and to define the general lines, or even the details, of public policy concerning it. The mandate to do so is granted more fully to some professions than to others; in time of crisis it may be questioned even with regard to the most respected and powerful professions.

These characteristics and collective claims of a profession are dependent upon a close solidarity, upon its members constituting in some measure a group apart with an ethos of its own. This in turn implies deep and lifelong commitment. A man who leaves a profession, once he is fully trained, licensed, and initiated, is something of a renegade in the eyes of his fellows; in the case of the priest, even in the eyes of laymen. It takes a rite of passage to get him in; another to read him out. If he takes French leave, he seems to belittle the profession and his former colleagues. To be sure, not all occupations called professions show these characteristics in full measure. But they constitute the highly valued professional syndrome as we know it. Professions come near the top of the prestige-ratings of occupations.

Many occupations, some new, some old, are endeavoring so to change their manner of work, their relations to clients and public, and the image which they have of themselves and others have of them, that they will merit and be granted professional standing. The new ones may arise from the development of some scientific or technological discovery which may be applied to the affairs of others. The people who "process" data for analysis by computers are a recent example. Some of the specialties within medicine are due largely to the invention of some diagnostic instrument, or to an extension of biological or chemical knowledge. After the virus came the virologist, who works alongside the bacteriologist and the person who knows about fungi—together they are the microbiologists, who work with microscopes, and lately with the electronic one. Other new professions or specialties (and specialties follow much the same course of development as professions themselves) may arise from some change in society itself. As impersonal insurance replaced the older, more personal ways of spreading the risk of death, injury, illness, unemployment, and loss of property, actuarial knowledge was of necessity developed, and a new profession arose. The professional social worker is a product of social changes. In an epoch of great technological and organizational change, new techniques and new social demands work in some sort of interaction to produce new esoteric occupations.

Perhaps the way to understand what professions mean in our society is to note the ways in which occupations try to change themselves or their image, or both, in the course of a movement to become "professionalized" (a term here used to mean what happens to an occupation, but lately used to refer also to what happens to an individual in the course of training for his occupation). Courses and seminars entitled Professions, Occupations, or Sociology of Work—which I have been holding for more than twenty-five years—invariably attract many people from outside sociology. As often as not, they want to write a paper to prove that some occupation—their own—has become or is on the verge of becoming a true profession. The course gives them a set of criteria for their demonstration. Librarians, insurance salesmen, nurses, public relations people, YMCA secretaries, probation officers, personnel men, vocational guidance directors, city managers, hospital administrators, and even public health physicians have been among them.

These people are serious, often quite idealistic. The changes they want to bring about or to document are directed to the same *terminus ad quem*, but the starting points lie in different directions. The insurance salesmen try to free themselves of the business label; they are not selling, they are giving people expert and objective diagnosis of their risks and advising them as to the best manner of protecting themselves. They are distressed that the heads of families do not confide in them more fully. The librarians seek to make themselves experts on the effects of reading, on bibliography and reference, rather than merely custodians and distributors of books; in schools and colleges, librarians want status as members of the teaching staff. They insist that they are, or must become, jointly with social psychologists, investigators of communications. That is their science, or one of their sciences. People in business management work at developing a science of management which could presumably be applied to any organization, no matter what its purpose. The social workers earlier were at pains to prove that their work could not be done by amateurs, people who brought to their efforts naught but good will; it required, they said, training in casework, a technique based on accumulated knowledge and experience of human nature and its operation in various circumstances and crises. Their first goal was to establish the position of the professional and to separate it from the amateur friendly visitor or reformer. The nurse, whose occupation is old, seeks to upgrade her place in the medical system. Her work, she says, requires much more general education than formerly, and more special knowledge; as medicine advances, the physicians delegate more and more technical functions to the nurse, who delegates some of her simpler functions to practical nurses, aides, and maids. The nurse wants a measure of independence, prestige, and money in keeping with her enlarged functions, as she sees them. The YMCA secretary wants his occupation recognized not merely as that of offering young men from the country a pleasant road to Protestant righteousness in the city, but as a more universal one of dealing with groups of young people. All that is learned of adolescence, of behavior in small groups, of the nature and organization of community life is considered the intellectual base of his work. The vocational guidance people have trouble in bringing the teaching profession to recognize that theirs is a separate complex of skills, presumed to rest on psychology. The public health men have a double problem. They must convince other physicians that their work—which is generally not the diagnosing and treating of patients—is really medicine. They must also combat the belief of physicians that they should do for fees some of what the public health people do for a fixed salary.

In these examples appear the main themes of professionalization. Detachment is one of them; and that in the sense of having in a particular case no personal interest such as would influence one's action or advice, while being deeply interested in all cases of the kind. The deep interest in all cases is of the sort that leads one to pursue and systematize the pertinent knowledge. It leads to finding an intellectual base for the problems one handles, which, in turn, takes those problems out of their particular setting and makes them part of some more universal order. One aspect of a profession is a certain equilibrium between the universal and the particular. The priest who would fix his attention entirely on the universal aspects of religious behavior might find himself indifferent as to which religion he would attach himself to; and thus, a renegade and a heretic. Churches do not encourage such circulation of the elite. Great corporations, too, although they may seek men who know the science of management, want an executive's curiosity about and love of the universal aspects of human organization tempered with a certain loyalty and commitment to his employer. I suppose there may be a professional man so free-sweeping in his interests that he does not mind what client he serves and what aspects of the client's affairs he deals with. He would be a rarity—a rich outcast or a poor idealist.

The balance of the universal and the particular in a profession varies, but there is always some measure of both, with an appropriate equilibrium between detachment and interest. The balance between universal and particular is related to that between the theoretical and the practical. Branches of learning are not always very directly related to the ordinary business of life. If some occupations become professions by developing an intellectual interest, others do it by becoming more practical. A large number of chemists are now employed by industries. Psychologists are seeking and obtaining legislation giving them monopoly over the name and making it an offense for anyone to "practice" psychology without it. Some sociologists, especially those who do research by the "project" for "clients," would do likewise. Perhaps one should distinguish between professions in essence, such as medicine or engineering, which pursue knowledge to improve practice; and professions by accident, such as, say, archaeology, where the practices are merely the means to increasing knowledge. In both cases, the people engaged may make their living by their activities. There appears to be a trend in certain fields of knowledge for this distinction to disappear and for the learned societies to become professional guilds concerned with problems of practice, employment, licensing, and distribution of their services. Many learned societies show strain between the intellectuals and the professionalizers.

This strain, incidentally, is found in some degree in all professions. A physician may be too devoted to research; a lawyer too concerned with comparative law; a social worker overcurious about the roots of human behavior. In fact, inside most professions there develops a tacit division of labor between the more theoretical and the more practical; once in a while conflict breaks out over issues related to it. The professional schools may be accused of being too "academic";

the academics accuse other practitioners of failure to be sufficiently intellectual.

Another set of themes in professionalizing movements has to do with a change of status of the occupation in relation to its own past, and to the other people—clients, public, other occupations—involved in its work drama. Changes sought are more independence, more recognition, a higher place, a cleaner distinction between those in the profession and those outside, and a larger measure of autonomy in choosing colleagues and successors. One necessary validation of such changes of status in our society is introduction of study for the profession in question into the universities. It may be as an undergraduate program, leading to a Bachelor's degree with a major in the theory and practice of the occupation. A large proportion of the university undergraduates in this country are in such professional courses. Other professions seek to have a Master's degree made the standard professional qualification; so it is in social work, hospital administration, business administration, laboratory technology, librarianship, and many others. The Master's degree is also used as qualification for a professional or administrative elite in occupations for which the basic preparation is a Bachelor's degree. The Ph.D. or some substitute, such as the Doctor of Education, is also used as qualification for higher administrative and teaching positions in professional agencies and schools.

The older professions, law and medicine, have long been established in the universities; at present in this country, they can keep their aspirants in college for four years and in professional school for three or four years after that. Indeed, so sure are they of their place that they tend to encourage undergraduates to pursue what lines of study they will, so long as their achievements are high. One way in which an occupation—or a college—can document its high status is by being able to take its pick of the young people about to enter the labor market, and then to keep them in school a long time before admitting them into the charmed circle.

Some combination of scholastic aptitude, ambition, and financial means is required to accomplish this educational aim. The ambition must have been fostered in some social setting, generally in the middle-class family, although occasionally in a working-class family with the aid of a sponsoring schoolteacher who sets sights high. The financial means may come from the aspirant's family, a discounting in advance of the income to be made in the profession, or from an investment in talent by government, industry, or the foundations. The latter is of

increasing importance in allowing people to continue in higher professional training, especially for work thought to be of use to defense
or related industrial development. It is probably effective only when
reinforced by the expectations of good income and high prestige.

Not all occupations which aspire to professional standing can
promise enough of either of these ingredients to get the most talented
and then to keep them in school as long as do medicine, law, and the
sciences. Characteristically they seek to improve their position in both
recruitment and the education system: in the earlier phases of their
move toward professionalism, the people in an occupation may have
to earn their way slowly and painfully to higher education, and the
professional school may have difficulty in getting itself accepted in
universities. It may take an operation bootstrap to get a corps of
people in the occupation academically qualified to teach succeeding
generations and grant them professional degrees.

This competition for status is accompanied by a trend toward prolonging the professional training at both ends: at the beginning by
multiplying prerequisites for entry to professional school, at the finish
by prolonging the course and the various apprentice or internship
programs. This is held in check by the fact that many of the would-be
professions cannot offer enough future income and prestige to get
people early and keep them long in school. Parents of less income
and education also press their children to seek security in known
middle-level occupations. This pressure may also work against the
movement to lift professional requirements.

Old and new alike, the professions cherish their recruits once they
get them. Having picked their candidates with great care, medical
schools, for instance, gnash their teeth and tear their hair over a sheep
lost from the fold. They wonder what they have done wrong to make
the lamb stray. They make it clear to the professional recruit that he
owes it to himself, the profession, and the school to stick with his
choice. Has it not been discovered by all the tests that this is the one
right outlet for his talents? Is it not his duty to use his talents for his
country in the best possible way? Have not the profession and the
professional school made a great investment in him? Has he the right
not to give full return on it? The day has passed when the youngsters
entering professional school are told to look well at their neighbors
in the classroom, for few of them will be there next year. The theme
is mutual commitment, reinforced by students' auxiliaries sponsored
by the professional associations, and by the use of such terms as
"student-physician," which stress that the student is already in the
professional family. One owes allegiance for life to a family.

Thus we have a high degree of competition among the professions for talent, combined with a great feeling of possessiveness over the recruits as soon as they have crossed the threshold. The professional student is, to some extent, already an organization man.

But that is not the only respect in which the modern professional is an organization man. Professions are more and more practiced in organizations. The *Freie Berufe* in Germany were considered free not merely because they were worthy of free men, but because those who followed them had no employer. Even the *freier Gelehrte*, or independent scholar, once he had acquired the right to teach, received his income in fees from his clients, the students. The university merely gave him his validation and his forum, as the court gives lawyers a playing field and a referee for their contest. The true professional, according to the traditional ideology of professions, is never hired. He is retained, engaged, consulted, etc., by some one who has need of his services. He, the professional, has or should have almost complete control over what he does for the client.

Especially in medicine, the protest against working in organizations and for salary is very strong. Yet in this country, more than in England, where there is a national plan of medical practice, physicians work in organizations. A decade ago it was reported that for every physician in the United States, there were between four and five people in the related or paramedical professions. There are more now; many people in the medical systems are in nonmedical work such as accounting, housekeeping, engineering and maintenance, and actuarial work for medical insurance schemes. An increasing proportion of physicians are in specialties; the specialist characteristically must work with other physicians. Some specialties never get the first call from an ailing patient; they are reached only after one or more referrals. Some specialties are, like pathology and anaesthesiology, practiced only in hospitals or clinics. All physicians now work at least a year for salary as interns; many work for a salary for several years as residents. In some specialties—those far from the first call of ailing people—work for an organization, possibly for salary, is the rule. An increasing number of lawyers work in large firms where duties and cases are assigned, not completely chosen by the individual practitioner himself. The firm operates as a referral system and allows the individual lawyer enough cases of one kind to permit him to specialize. Many lawyers have but one client, a company; and when there is but one client, it becomes in fact an employer.

Law and medicine—the models which other professions try to approximate—in spite of nourishing free practice of the individual for a number of clients with a minimum of institutional apparatus, are in fact far along the road to practice in complicated organizations which intervene in many ways between them and their clients. Engineers, applied scientists, and people in most of the newer professions nearly all work in organizations with others of their own profession, and with many people of related occupations. Indeed, it becomes hard to say who is the client in many cases; in the case of medicine, is it the insurance company or the patient? In the school, is it the child, the parent, the community at large, or some class of people within it? In social work, is it the agency—which pays—or the so-called client, who is worked upon not always of his own free will? It is characteristic of modern professions that they do work in such institutional settings, often with capital goods which they do not own and with a great variety of people. Professional ideology prefers a two-party arrangement: the professional and his client. It prefers the client who can speak for himself and pay for himself. This is not the prevailing arrangement, nor is it likely to be.

Thus arise a great number of problems for professions. The problem of finding a clientele becomes that of finding a place in a system of organizations. The problem of colleague relationships becomes that of determining who, in a complex organization of many professions, are indeed one's colleagues, and in what degree. The problem of freedom becomes one of distinguishing between one's obligations to the person, if it be such a case, on which one performs some action or to whom one gives some advice, and to one's employer or organization. For example, does the college physician report the secrets of his student-patient to the dean and, if so, in what situations? There is also a problem of authority; what orders does one accept from an employer, especially one who is not a member of one's own profession and whose interests may not always be those of the professional and his clients?

The other side of this coin is that the employer, even in business, finds himself dealing with an increasing number of professional (staff) people, who will not be ordered about as freely as line people. Indeed, Robert Maynard Hutchins once said:

> . . . business may eventually be organized like a university, with the staff claiming a kind of academic freedom, participating in the formation of policy, and enjoying permanent tenure. When that happens the university administrators of America will derive a certain grim satisfaction from the struggles of those captains of industry who have had the habit of complaining about the mismanagement of universities.[1]

As the professions become more organized, business organizations become more professionalized. The result is the development of new patterns of organization. If the professional man giving staff services to business or industry sets a certain pattern of freedom not common among the employees of business, he has also lost a certain kind of freedom which inhered in the private practice of professions for clients of whom enough were solvent to assure him a good income and a fitting style of life.

But it may be possible that under present conditions the private practitioner of a profession does not have so much freedom, or at least not the same kinds of freedom as his colleague working in some sort of larger organization. In theory, the private practitioner is free to move at will; in fact, it is very chancy for a man established in practice in a given community to move. Reputations among the common run of clients are local and may depend upon conformity with local customs and beliefs concerning nonprofessional matters. The man who works in an organization may develop a wider reputation, even a national one: he may improve his lot by moving from time to time. He may be freer of social pressures. The man who practices privately may, in fact, be the choreboy of his clients, doing only those things which they want in a hurry and which do not warrant the seeking out of a better-known or more specialized practitioner, firm, or other organization. He may thus have little or no choice of what kinds of work he will do. The man in the larger organization may apply himself to some line of work and become so proficient in it that he need not accept any work not to his taste. Perhaps the man in the organization may not pick his client, but he can often pick his problems. It may perhaps be that a few men at the very top of a profession can practice privately and as they wish, because of a great reputation throughout the profession and among sophisticated and affluent clients; while the bulk of people in private and "solo" practice will be choreboys without much reputation among clients and without any among their more specialized colleagues.

In between these two extremes there may be—and I believe there are—a large and increasing number of competent people who work in organized settings. They will, in order to be successful, develop reputations among their colleagues and will be, in case the profession is such as to demand it, known as effective with clients. They will work out new systems of relationships, which may be much the same in business, government agencies, universities, hospitals, and clinics, and other kinds of organizations; among the relationships to be worked out are those of the balance between obligations to one's professional colleagues, both in and out of one's present organization, and the organizations in which one works. New formulae of freedom and control will be worked out. The people in organizations will be—although in some sense bureaucrats—the innovators, the people who push back the frontiers of theoretical and practical knowledge related to their professions, who will invent new ways of bringing professional services to everyone, not merely to the solvent or sophisticated few. Indeed, I think it likely that the professional conscience, the superego, of many professions will be lodged in that segment of professionals who work in complicated settings, for they must, in order to survive, be sensitive to more problems and to a greater variety of points of view.

On the other hand, the professionals will become more sensitive to outside opinion; and, like other organized groups, they will hire public relations people to perform for them the esoteric service of creating a satisfactory public image in the press, on television, and in the schools, where young people learn about the careers open to them. It is all a rather confusing prospect. The professions will, in any case, be a large and influential element in our future, and in that of all societies which go the road of industrialization and urbanization; the organizational structures in which they will work will very likely resemble one another, no matter what the prevailing political ideologies in various countries of the same degree of industrialization.

In the meantime, there are large parts of the world which are not far along this road. In some of them there is an oversupply of professional people and an undersupply, or some lack of balance in the supply, of related professions. A recent paper reports that whereas in this country there are several nurses for each physician, in India there are seven physicians for one nurse. Oversupply means, of course, only more than can be supported by an economy. Lack of demand may be due to lack of money or to lack of acceptance of the very definition of wants to which a profession caters. It is generally both money and sophistication which are lacking. What will be the course of the rise of demand for medicine, education, legal protection, and social services in the now poor and nonindustrial countries? It will not be the same course as in the older industrial countries, for the latter had no models to go by; people of the now-developing countries know, or soon will know, that such personal services exist and are widely available in the older industrial economies. They will hardly pass through the same stages of professional practice, organization, and distribution of services as we did.

Many of the institutions of a modern society depend upon an adequate supply of professionals who perform services for corporate bodies: people to plan and build water systems, communications, roads, industrial plants; people to train others in various trades and techniques and to organize public services. Professionals who do these things have, in the past, come to a new country from abroad as employees or representatives of colonial powers, business concerns, or missionary agencies. They have not always sought native recruits or successors; nor have they always given full recognition to local colleagues where there have been some. We are evidently in a new situation with respect to the deploying of professional people over the world. It is not clear who will sponsor such a deployment, what sort of reception professionals from abroad will get in new nations, or how professionals from the highly urban and industrial countries will fit work abroad into their careers.

Again we face the problem of the relation of the particular, the culture-bound, aspect of professions to the universal aspect. The professional may learn some things that are universal in the physical, biological, or social world. But around this core of universal knowledge there is likely to be a large body of practical knowledge which relates only to his own culture. The physician may recognize the rhythm of the beat of an East Indian woman's heart, yet lack the slightest knowledge of how to get her to accept his diagnosis of what ails her and his advice about how to live with it. Furthermore, the physician—or other professional—may have become so accustomed to his own society's particular way of practicing, of payment, of dividing labor with others that he will not and cannot adapt himself to these particularities of another society, especially a preindustrial and not highly literate one. An interlude in another part of the world might interrupt the accumulation of reputation, seniority, and money so essential to his career at home; whatever he might learn in practice of his profession abroad might or might not be applicable to his future work at home. While professions are, in some of their respects, universal, in others they are closely ethnocentric. In many professions, careers are contained within a single economy and society. One of the interesting developments of the future will be new patterns of international exchange of professional knowledge and professional institutions.

Notes

1. "The Administrator," in R. B. Heywood (ed.), *The Works of the Mind* (Chicago: University of Chicago Press, 1947), pp. 135–56.

3

Social Role and the Division of Labor

All of the many ways in which the work of human beings is studied lead back at some point to the obvious, yet infinitely subtle, fact of the division of labor. What is a job description if not a statement of what one worker, rather than another, does or is supposed to do? Similar reference to division of labor lies implicitly in study of the number and migrations of the labor force, of motive and effort, of basic capacities and the learning of skills, and in analysis of the price of labor, services, and goods.

The division of labor, in its turn, implies interaction; for it consists not in the sheer difference of one man's kind of work from that of another, but in the fact that the different tasks and accomplishments are parts of a whole whose product all, in some degree, contribute to. And wholes, in the human social realm as in the rest of the biological and in the physical realm, have their essence in interaction. Work as social interaction is the central theme of sociological and social psychological study of work.

Social role, the other term in my title, is useful only to the extent that it facilitates analysis of the parts played by individuals in the interaction which makes up some sort of social whole. I am not sure that I would put up much of an argument against the objection that it is not a very useful term, provided the objector has a better one to refer to the same complex of phenomena. I would argue vociferously, however, if the objector implies either that social interaction is not an ever-present and crucial feature of human work, or that the social-psychological description of a division of labor implied by the term social role is of less importance than a description in terms of techniques. I would mention to the objector that even those who work in solitude are often interacting with a built-in father or with God himself, who is known to be worse than any flesh-and-blood slavedriver; and that those who toil upward in the night while their companions

Reprinted by permission of the publisher from the *Midwest Sociologist*, Vol. XVII. Spring, 1956. Copyright 1956. Midwest Sociological Society.

sleep may quite simply be seeking access to an as yet unknown, but more admired, set of companions or colleagues.

I will not define or further belabor these terms, social role and the division of labor, but rather illustrate some of their dimensions from those kinds of work which consist in doing something for, or to, people. I say *for* or *to* people intentionally, but not cynically. Any child in any school will sometimes believe that something is being done *to* him rather than *for* him; the boy in a reform school nearly always thinks so. The patient in a mental hospital is often convinced that things are being done *to* him *for* someone else; although it may be in the nature of his illness so to believe, he may nevertheless often be right. Even the person suffering from tuberculosis, although he knows he is ill and willingly undergoes treatment, considers that many of the rules of society and of the hospital, and even some parts of the treatment, are done *to* him, rather than *for* his benefit. Even in short-term illnesses, the patient may view as indignities some of the things allegedly done for his recovery. At the least, he may think they are done for the convenience of those who work in the hospital rather than for his comfort. These are but some of the simpler ambiguities in those kinds of work called personal or professional services. Perhaps it is well to recall that the opposite of service is disservice, and that the line between them is thin, obscure, and shifting.

In many of the things which people do for one another, the *for* can be changed to *to* by a slight over-doing or by a shift of mood. The discipline necessary to that degree of order and quiet which will allow study in a classroom can easily turn into something perceived by the children as perverse and cruel; their perceptions may be truer than the teacher's own self-perception. Wherever a modicum of power to discipline by tongue or force is essential to one's assigned task, the temptation to overuse it and even to get pleasure from it may be present, no matter whether one be a teacher, an attendant in a mental hospital, or a prison guard. The danger of major distortion of relationship and function within the framework of a formal office lurks wherever people go or are sent for help or correction: the schoolroom, the clinic, the operating room, the confessional booth, the undertaking parlor all share this characteristic. Whatever terms we eventually may use to describe social interaction at work must be such that they will allow these subtle distortions of role or function to be brought to light and related to whatever are their significant correlates in personalities or situations.

Another feature of the kinds of work in question lies in the peculiar ambiguities with respect to what is seen as honorable, respectable,

clean, and prestige-giving as against what is less honorable or respectable, and what is mean or dirty. The term *profession* in its earlier and
more restricted usage referred to a very few occupations of high learning and prestige, whose practitioners did things for others. Law and
medicine are the prototypes. Yet both of them have always required
some sort of alliance, or, at least, some sort of terms with the lowliest
and most despised of human occupations. It is not merely in Dickens's
novels that lawyers have truck with process-servers, informants, spies,
and thugs. What the learned lawyers argue before an Appellate Court
(and I hear that the cases for textbooks used in law schools are almost
all from Appellate Courts) is but a purified distillate of some human
mess. A lawyer may be asked whether he and his client come into
court with clean hands; when he answers, "yes," it may mean that
someone else's hands are of necessity a bit grubby. For not only are
some quarrels more respectable, more clean, than others; but also
some of the kinds of work involved in the whole system (gathering
evidence, getting clients, bringing people to court, enforcing judgments, making the compromises that keep cases out of court) are
more respected and more removed from temptation and suspicion
than others. In fact, the division of labor among lawyers is as much
one of respectability (hence of self concept and role) as of specialized
knowledge and skills. One might even call it a moral division of labor,
if one keeps in mind that the term means not simply that some lawyers, or people in the various branches of law work, are more moral
than others; but that the very demand for highly scrupulous and respectable lawyers depends in various ways upon the availability of
less scrupulous people to attend to the less respectable legal problems
of even the best people. I do not mean that the good lawyers all
consciously delegate their dirty work to others (although many do).
It is rather a game of live and let live; a game, mind you, hence
interaction, even though it be a game of keeping greater than chance
distances.

As the system of which the lawyer's work is part reaches down
into the nether regions of the unrespectable and outward to the limbo
of guile and force, which people may think necessary but do not
admire, so the physician's work touches the world of the morally and
ritually, but more especially of the physically, unclean. Where his
work leaves off, that of the undertaker begins; in some cultures and
epochs they have shared the monopoly of certain functions and certain
occult arts. The physician has always had also to have some connection (even though it be again the connection of competition or of
studied avoidance) with the abortionist, with the "quacks" who deal

with obscure and "social" diseases, as well as with the lesser occupations which also treat physical and mental troubles: the midwife, who has in certain places and times been suspected of being willing to do her work a bit prematurely; the blood-letter, who has at times been also the lowly barber; the bonesetter, who in mediaeval Italy was also the smith; and the masseur and keeper of baths, who is often suspected of enjoying his work too much. If the physician has high prestige—and he has had it at various times in history, although perhaps never more so than now—it is not so much *sui generis,* as by virtue of his place in the particular pattern of the medical division of labor at the time. Two features of that division of labor at present are (1) that the level of public confidence in the technical competence and good faith of the medical system is very high and (2) that nearly all of the medical functions have been drawn into a great system of interlocking institutions over which physicians have an enormous measure of control. (Only abortion remains outside, and even that can be said only with some qualification.)

It is also a division of labor notorious for its rigid hierarchy. The ranking has something to do with the relative cleanliness of functions performed. The nurses, as they successfully rise to professional standing, are delegating the more lowly of their traditional tasks to aides and maids. No one is so lowly in the hospital as those who handle soiled linen; none so low in the mental hospital as the attendant, whose work combines some tasks that are not clean with potential use of force. But if there is no system in which the theme of uncleanliness is so strong, likewise there is none in which it is so strongly compensated for. Physical cleanliness of the human organism depends upon balances easily upset; the physicians and his coworkers operate at the margins where these balances are, in fact, often upset. To bring back health (which is cleanliness) is the great miracle. Those who work the miracle are more than absolved from the potential uncleanliness of their tasks; but those who perform the lowly tasks without being recognized as among the miracle-workers fare badly in the prestige rating. And this gives us a good case for rubbing in the point that the division of labor is more than a technical phenomenon; that there are infinite social-psychological nuances in it.

Actually, in the medical world there are two contrary trends operating simultaneously. As medical technology develops and changes, particular tasks are constantly downgraded; that is, they are delegated by the physician to the nurse. The nurse in turn passes them on to the maid. But occupations and people are being upgraded, within certain limits. The nurse moves up nearer the doctor in techniques and devotes more of her time to supervision of other workers. The practical nurse is getting more training, and is beginning to insist on the prerogatives which she believes should go with the tasks she performs. New workers come in at the bottom of the hierarchy to take over the tasks abandoned by those occupations which are ascending the mobility ladder. Others come in outside the hierarchy as new kinds of technology (photography, electronics, physics) find a place in the medical effort. Satisfactory definitions of role for these new people are notoriously lacking, and that in a system in which rigidly defined roles and ranks are the rule. Here we have indeed a good case for illustrating the point that a role definition of a division of labor is necessary to complement any technical description of it. And the question arises of the effect of changes in technical division upon the roles involved. Sometimes a desired change of role is validated by a change in technical tasks (the nurses are an excellent example). Sometimes a change in technical division creates a role problem, or a series of them. I think we may go further and say that when changes of either kind get under way the repercussions will be felt beyond the positions immediately affected, and may indeed touch every position in the system. Some roles in a division of labor may be more sensitive to changes in technique than are others. It seems probable, for instance, that some aspects of the basic relationships of nurse, physician, and patient will not be greatly altered by the shifting of technical tasks from one to the other and from both of them to other people in the medical system. (I purposely included the patient, for he has a part in the medical division of labor, too.)

There will probably always be in this system, as in others, someone whose role it is to make ultimate decisions, with all the risks that go with them and with all the protections necessary. This is the role of the physician. He has and jealously guards more authority than he can, in many cases, actually assume. There will probably always be in the system, complementary to this position, another of the right-hand man order; a position which defers to the first but which, informally, often must exceed its authority in order to protect the interests of all concerned. The nurse occupies this position. When the doctor isn't there, she may do some necessary thing which requires his approval—and get the approval when he comes back. She is the right-hand man of the physician, even and perhaps especially when he isn't there. The nurse also sometimes fires furnaces and mends the plumbing, i.e., she does tasks of people below her or outside the role hierarchy of medicine. It hurts her, but she does it. Her place in the division of labor is essentially that of doing in a responsible way whatever necessary things are in danger of not being done at all. The nurse would not like this definition, but she ordinarily in practice rises to it. I believe that, if we were to take a number of systems of work in which things are done for people, we could dig out a series of roles or positions which could be described in some such way, and could see the consequences for the roles of changes in technique and in other roles in the system. And I would defend the term *role* as a fair starting term in such an enterprise; for it suggests a part in a whole act involving other people playing, well or badly, their expected parts.

I have been saying, in various rather indirect ways, that no line of work can be fully understood outside the social matrix in which it occurs or the social system of which it is part. The system includes, in most and perhaps in all cases, not merely the recognized institutional complex but reaches out and down into human life and society. As in the case of law and even in medicine, there are usually some connections which we cannot easily, or do not willingly, follow out. There are also ambiguities and apparent contradictions in the combinations of duties of any one occupation or position in an occupational system.

One of the commoner failures in study of work is to overlook part of the interactional system. We speak of the physician and patient as a social system (as did the late Dr. L. J. Henderson in an article by that name), or at most include the nurse; or we speak of teacher and pupil, lawyer and client, and the like. Certainly in some occupations there is some basic relation such as these; a relation which is partly reality, partly stereotype, partly ideal nostalgically attributed to a better past or sought after in a better future. Perhaps the commonest complaint of people in the professions which perform a service for others is that they are somehow prevented from doing their work as it should be done. Someone interferes with this basic relation. The teachers could teach better were it not for parents who fail in their duty or school boards who interfere. Psychiatrists would do better if it were not for families, stupid public officials, and ill-trained attendants. Nurses would do more nursing if it were not for administrative duties, and the carelessness of aides and maintenance people. Part of the complained-of interference is merely institutional. The institutional matrix in which things are done for people is certainly becoming more complex in most professional fields; there are more and more kinds of workers in a division of labor ever changing in its boundaries between one person's work and another's. But it is not so much the numbers of people who intervene that seems to bother the professional most; it is rather the differing conceptions of what the work really is or should be, of what mandate has been given by the public, of what it is possible to accomplish and by what means; as well as of the particular part to be played by those in each position, their proper responsibilities and rewards. Compared to the restrictions, resistances, and distortions of purpose, assignments, and efforts in a school, a mental hospital, a social agency or a prison, the much studied restriction of production in a factory is simplicity itself. In the factory, there is at least fair consensus about what the object produced shall be. There is often no such consensus in institutions where things are done for or to people.

Every one, or nearly every one of the many important services given people by professionals in our times, is given in a complex institutional setting. The professional must work with a host of nonprofessionals (and the professionals ordinarily are short-sighted enough to use that pejorative term ad nauseam). These other workers bring into the institutional complex their own conceptions of what the problem is, their own conceptions of their rights and privileges, and of their careers and life-fate. The philosophy—of illness, crime, reform, mental health, or whatever—which they bring in is often that of another class or element of the population than that to which the professional belongs or aspires. Like most humans, they do not completely accept the role-definitions handed down from above, but in communication among their own kind and in interaction with the people served, treated, or handled, work out their own definition. They build up an ethos, and a system of rationalizations for the behavior they consider proper, given the hazards and contingencies of their own positions. The proper study of the division of labor will include a look at any system of work from the points of view of all the kinds of people involved in it, whether their position be high or low, whether they are at the center or near the periphery of the system. And those who seek to raise standards of practice (and their own status) in the occupations and institutions which do things for people would do well to study, in every case, what changes in the other positions or roles in the system will be wrought by changes in their own, and what problems will be created for other people by every new solution of one of their own problems.

4

Work and Self

There are societies in which custom or sanctioned rule determine what work a man of a given status may do. In our society, at least one strong strain of ideology has it that a man may do any work which he is competent to do; or even that he has a right to the schooling and experience necessary to gain competence in any kind of work which he sets as the goal of his ambition. Equality of opportunity is, among us, stated very much in terms of the right to enter upon any occupation whatsoever. Although we do not practice this belief to the full, we are a people who cultivate ambition. A great deal of our ambition takes the form of getting training for kinds of work which carry more prestige than that which our fathers did. Thus a man's work is one of the things by which he is judged, and certainly one of the more significant things by which he judges himself.

Many people in our society work in named occupations. The names are tags, a combination of price tag and calling card. One has only to hear casual conversation to sense how important these tags are. Hear a salesman, who has just been asked what he does, reply, "I am in sales work," or "I am in promotional work," not "I sell skillets." School teachers sometimes turn schoolteaching into educational work, and the disciplining of youngsters and chaperoning of parties into personnel work. Teaching Sunday School becomes religious education, and the Y.M.C.A. secretary is "in group work." Social scientists emphasize the science end of their name. These hedging statements in which people pick the most favorable of several possible names for their work imply an audience. And one of the most important things about any man is his audience, or his choice of the several available audiences, to which he may address his claims to be someone of worth.

These remarks should be sufficient to call it to your attention that a man's work is one of the more important parts of his social identity, of his self, indeed, of his fate, in the one life he has to live, for there

Reprinted by permission of the publisher from J. H. Rohrer, and Muzafer Sherif, eds. *Social Psychology at the Crossroads.* Copyright 1951, Harper & Row, Publishers, Inc.

is something almost as irrevocable about choice of occupation as there is about choice of a mate. And since the language about work is so loaded with value and prestige judgments, and with defensive choice of symbols, we should not be astonished that the concepts of social scientists who study work should carry a similar load, for the relation of social-science concepts to popular speech remains close in spite of our efforts to separate them. The difference is that the value-weighting in popular speech is natural and proper, for concealment and ego-protection are of the essence of social intercourse. But in scientific discourse the value-loaded concept may be a blinder. And part of the problem of method in the study of work behavior is that the people who have the most knowledge about a given occupation (let us say medicine), and from whom therefore the data for analysis must come, are the people in the occupation. They may combine in themselves a very sophisticated manipulative knowledge of the appropriate social relations, with a very strongly motivated suppression, and even repression, of the deeper truths about these relationships, and, in occupations of higher status, with great verbal skill in keeping these relationships from coming up for thought and discussion by other people. This is done in part by the use of and insistence upon loaded value words where their work is discussed.

May I, to illustrate the point that concepts may be blinders, tell you briefly of my own experience in the study of occupations. Maybe one reason we social scientists fall into their trap so easily is that many such occupations have higher status than our own.

My first essay into the field was a study of the real estate agents in Chicago. These highly competitive men were just at that point in their journey toward respectability at which they wished to emphasize their conversion from business-minded suspicion of one another to the professional attitude, with confidence in each other and with a demand for confidence from the public. I started the study with the idea of finding out an answer to this familiar question, "Are these men professionals?" It was a false question, for the concept "profession" in our society is not so much a descriptive term as one of value and prestige. It happens over and over that the people who practice an occupation attempt to revise the conceptions which their various publics have of the occupation and of the people in it. In so doing, they also attempt to revise their own conception of themselves and of their work. The model which these occupations set before themselves is that of the "profession": thus the term profession is a symbol for a desired conception of one's work and, hence, of one's self. The movement to "professionalize" an occupation is thus collective mobility of some among the people in an occupation. One aim of the movement is to rid the occupation of people who are not mobile enough to go along with the changes. There are two possible kinds of occupational mobility. One is individual. The individual makes the several choices, and achieves the skills which allow him to move to a certain position in the occupational, and thus—he hopes—in the social and economic hierarchy. His choice is limited by several conditions, among which is the social knowledge available to him at the time of crucial decision, a time which varies for the several kinds of work.

The other kind of occupational mobility is that of a group of people in an occupation, i.e., of the occupation itself. This has been important in our society with its great changes of technology, with its attendant proliferation of new occupations and of change in technique and social relation of old ones. Now it sometimes happens that by the time a person has the full social knowledge necessary to the smartest possible choice of occupations, he is already stuck with one and in one. How strongly this may affect the drive for professionalization of occupations, I don't know. I suspect that it is a motive. At any rate, it is common in our society for occupational groups to step their occupation up in the hierarchy by turning it into a profession. I will not here describe this process. Let me only indicate that in my own studies I passed from the false question "Is this occupation a profession?" to the more fundamental ones, "What are the circumstances in which the people in an occupation attempt to turn it into a profession, and themselves into professional people?" and "What are the steps by which they attempt to bring about identification with their valued model?"

Even with this new orientation the term *profession* acted as a blinder. For as I began to give courses and seminars on occupations, I used a whole set of concepts and headings which were prejudicial to full understanding of what work behavior and relations are. One of them was that of the "code of ethics," which still tended to sort people into the good and the bad. It was not until I had occasion to undertake study of race relations in industry that I finally, I trust, got rid of this bias in the concepts which I used. Negro industrial workers, the chief objects of our study, performed the kinds of work which have least prestige and which make least pretension; yet it turned out that even in the lowest occupations people do develop collective pretensions to give their work, and consequently themselves, value in the eyes of each other and of outsiders.

It was from these people that we learned that the common dignifying rationalization of people in all positions of a work hierarchy except the very top one is, "We in this position save the people in the next higher position above from their own mistakes." The notion that one saves a person of more acknowledged skill, and certainly of more acknowledged prestige and power, than one's self from his mistakes appears to be peculiarly satisfying. Now there grow up in work organizations rules of mutual protection among the persons in a given category and rank, and across ranks and categories. If one uses the term "code of ethics" he is likely not to see the true nature of these rules. These rules have of necessity to do with mistakes, for it is in the nature of work that people make mistakes. The question of how mistakes are handled is a much more penetrating one than any question which contains the concept "professional ethics" as ordinarily conceived. For in finding out how mistakes are handled, one must get at the fundamental psychological and social devices by which people are able to carry on through time, to live with others and with themselves, knowing that what is daily routine for them in their occupational roles may be fateful for others, knowing that one's routine mistakes, even the mistakes by which one learns better, may touch other lives at crucial points. It is in part the problem of dealing routinely with what are the crises of others. The people in lower ranks are thus using a powerful psychological weapon when they rationalize their worth and indispensability as lying in their protection of people in higher ranks from their mistakes. I suppose it is almost a truism that the people who take the larger responsibilities must be people who can face making mistakes, while punctiliousness must remain in second place. But this is a matter which has not been very seriously taken into account, as far as I know, in studies of the social drama of work.

Of course, the rules which people make to govern their behavior at work cover other problems than that of mistakes. Essentially the rules classify people, for to define situations and the proper behavior in situations one has to assign roles to the people involved. Thus among the most important subject matter of rules is setting up of criteria for recognizing a true fellow-worker, for determining who it is safe and may even be necessary to initiate into the in-group of close equals, and who must be kept at some distance. This problem is apt to be obscured by the term "colleague-ship," which, although its etymology is perfect for the matter in hand, carries a certain notion of higher status, of respectability. (In pre-Hitler Germany the Social-Democratic workers called one another "Comrade." The Christian trade-unions insisted on the term "Colleague.")

Allow me to mention one other value-laden term which may act as a blinder in study of the social psychology of work, to wit, "restriction of production." This term contains a value assumption of another kind—namely, that there is someone who knows and has a right to determine the right amount of work for other people to do. If one does less, he is restricting production. Mayo and others have done a good deal to analyze the phenomenon in question, but it was Max Weber who—forty years ago—pointed to "putting on the brakes," as an inevitable result of the wrestling match between a man and his employer over the price he must pay with his body for his wage. In short, he suggested that no man easily yields to another full control over the effort, and especially over the amount of physical effort he must daily exert. On the other hand, there is no more characteristically human phenomenon than determined and even heroic effort to do a task which one has somehow taken as his own. I do not mean to make the absurd implication that there could be a situation in which every man would be his own and only taskmaster. But I think we might understand the social interaction which determines the measure of effort if we are to keep ourselves free of terms which suggest that it is abnormal to do less than one is asked by some reasonable authority.

You will have doubtless got the impression that I am making the usual plea for a value-free science, that is, for neutrality. Such is not my intention. Our aim is to *penetrate more deeply* into the personal and social drama of work, to understand the social and social-psychological arrangements and devices by which men make their work tolerable, or even make it glorious to themselves and others. I believe that much of our terminology, and hence, of our problem setting, has limited our field of perception by a certain pretentiousness and a certain value-loading. Specifically we need to rid ourselves of any concepts which keep us from seeing that the essential problems of men at work are the same whether they do their work in the laboratories of some famous institution or in the messiest vat room of a pickle factory. Until we can find a point of view and concepts which will enable us to make comparisons between the junk peddler and the professor without intent to debunk the one and patronize the other, we cannot do our best work in this field.

Perhaps there is as much to be learned about the high-prestige occupations by applying to them the concepts which naturally come to mind for study of people in the most lowly kinds of work as there is to be learned by applying to other occupations the conceptions developed in connection with the highly valued professions. Furthermore, I have come to the conclusion that it is a fruitful thing to start study of any social phenomenon at the point of least prestige. For, since prestige is so much a matter of symbols, and even of pretensions—however well merited—there goes with prestige a tendency to preserve a front which hides the inside of things; a front of names, of indirection, of secrecy (much of it necessary secrecy). On the other hand, in things of less prestige, the core may be more easy of access.

In recent years a number of my students have studied some more or less lowly occupations: apartment-house janitors, junk men, boxers, jazz musicians, osteopaths, pharmacists, etc. They have done so mainly because of their own connections with the occupations in question, and perhaps because of some problem of their own. At first, I thought of these studies as merely interesting and informative for what they would tell about people who do these humbler jobs, i.e., as American ethnology. I have now come to the belief that although the problems of people in these lines of work are as interesting and important as any other, their deeper value lies in the insights they yield about work behavior in any and all occupations. It is not that it puts one into the position to debunk the others, but simply that processes which are hidden in other occupations come more readily to view in these lowly ones. We may be here dealing with a fundamental matter of method in social science, the matter of finding the best possible laboratory animal for study of a given series of mechanisms.

Let me illustrate. The apartment-house janitor is a fellow who, in making his living, has to do a lot of other people's dirty work. This is patent. He could not hide it if he would. Now every occupation is not one but several activities; some of them are the "dirty work" of that trade. It may be dirty in one of several ways. It may be simply physically disgusting. It may be a symbol of degradation, something that wounds one's dignity.

Finally, it may be dirty work in that it in some way goes counter to the more heroic of our moral conceptions. Dirty work of some kind is found in all occupations. It is hard to imagine an occupation in which one does not appear, in certain repeated contingencies, to be practically compelled to play a role of which he thinks he ought to be a little ashamed morally. Insofar as an occupation carries with it a self-conception, a notion of personal dignity, it is likely that at some point one will feel that he is having to do something that is *infra dignitate*. Janitors turned out to be bitterly frank about their physically dirty work. When asked, "What is the toughest part of your job," they answered almost to a man in the spirit of this quotation: "Garbage. Often the stuff is sloppy and smelly. You know some fellows can't look at garbage if it's sloppy. I'm getting used to it now, but it almost killed me when I started." Or as another put it, "The toughest part? It's the messing up in front of the garbage incinerator. That's the most miserable thing there is on this job. The tenants don't co-operate—them bastards. You tell them today, and tomorrow there is the same mess over again by the incinerator."

In the second quotation it becomes evident that the physical disgust of the janitor is not merely a thing between him and the garbage, but involves also the tenant. Now the tenant is the person who impinges most on the daily work activity of the janitor. It is the tenant who interferes most with his own dignified ordering of his life and work. If it were not for a tenant who had broken a window, he could have got his regular Saturday cleaning done on time; if it were not for a tenant who had clogged a trap, he would not have been ignominiously called away from the head of his family table just when he was expansively offering his wife's critical relatives a second helping of pork-chops, talking the while about the importance of his job. It is the tenant who causes the janitor's status pain. The physically disgusting part of the janitor's work is directly involved in his relations with other actors in his work drama.

By a *contre coup*, it is by the garbage that the janitor judges, and, as it were, gets power over the tenants who high-hat him. Janitors know about hidden love-affairs by bits of torn-up letter paper; of impending financial disaster or of financial four-flushing by the presence of many unopened letters in the waste. Or they may stall off demands for immediate service by an unreasonable woman of whom they know from the garbage that she, as the janitors put it, "has the rag on." The garbage gives the janitor the makings of a kind of magical power over that pretentious villain, the tenant. I say a kind of magical power, for there appears to be no thought of betraying any individual and thus turning this knowledge into overt power. He protects the tenant, but, at least among Chicago janitors, it is certainly not a loving protection.

Let your mind dwell on what one might hear from people in certain other occupations if they were to answer as frankly and bitterly as did the janitors. I do not say nor do I think that it would be a good thing for persons in all occupations to speak so freely on physical disgust as did these men. To do so, except in the most tightly closed circles, would create impossible situations. But we are likely to overlook the matter altogether in studying occupations where concealment is practiced, and this gives a quite false notion of the problems which have to be faced in such occupations, and of the possible psychological and social by-products of the solutions which are developed for the problem of disgust.

Now the delegation of dirty work to someone else is common among humans. Many cleanliness taboos, and perhaps even many moral scruples, depend for their practice upon success in delegating the tabooed activity to someone else. Delegation of dirty work is also a part of the process of occupational mobility. Yet there are kinds of work, some of them of very high prestige, in which such delegation is possible only to a limited extent. The dirty work may be an intimate part of the very activity which gives the occupation its charisma, as is the case with the handling of the human body by the physician. In this case, I suppose the dirty work is somehow integrated into the whole, and into the prestigious role of the person who does the work. What role it plays in the drama of work relations in such a case is something to find out. The janitor, however, does not integrate his dirty work into any deeply satisfying definition of his role that might liquidate his antagonism to the people whose dirt he handles. Incidentally, we have found reason to believe that one of the deeper sources of antagonisms in hospitals arises from the belief of the people in the humblest jobs that the physicians in charge call upon them to do their dirty work in the name of the role of "healing the sick," although none of the prestige and little of the money reward of that role reaches the people at the bottom. Thus we might conceive of a classification of occupations involving dirty work into those in which it is knit into some satisfying and prestige-giving definition of role and those in which it is not. I suppose we might think of another classification into those in which the dirty work seems somehow willfully put upon one and those in which it is quite unconnected with any person involved in the work drama.

There is a feeling among prison guards and mental-hospital attendants that society at large and their superiors hypocritically put upon them dirty work which they, society, and the superiors in prison and hospital know is necessary but which they pretend is not necessary. Here it takes the form, in the minds of people in these two lowly occupations, of leaving them to cope for twenty hours, day in and day out, with inmates whom the public never has to see and whom the people at the head of the organization see only episodically. There is a whole series of problems here which cannot be solved by some miracle of changing the social selection of those who enter the job (which is the usual unrealistic solution for such cases).

And this brings us to the brief consideration of what one may call the social drama of work. Most kinds of work bring people together in definable roles; thus the janitor and the tenant, the doctor and the patient, the teacher and the pupil, the worker and his foreman, the prison guard and the prison, the musician and his listener. In many occupations there is some category of persons with whom the people at work regularly come into crucial contact. In some occupations the most crucial relations are those with one's fellow-workers. It is they who can do most to make life sweet or sour. Often, however, it is the people in some other position. And in many there is a category of persons who are, so to speak, the consumers of one's work or services. It is probable that the people in the occupation will have their chronic fight for status, for personal dignity with this group of consumers of their services. Part of the social psychological problem of the occupation is the maintenance of a certain freedom and social distance from these people most crucially and intimately concerned with one's work.

In a good deal of our talk about occupations we imply that the tension between the producer and consumer of services is somehow a matter of ill-will or misunderstandings which easily might be removed. It may be that it lies a good deal deeper than that. Often there is a certain ambivalence on the side of the producer, which may be illustrated by the case of the professional jazz musicians. The musician wants jobs and an income. He also wants his music to be appreciated, but to have his living depend upon the appreciation does not entirely please him. For he likes to think himself and other musicians the best judges of his playing. To play what pleases the audience—the paying customers, who are not, in his opinion, good judges—is a source of annoyance. It is not merely that the listeners, having poor taste, demand that he play music which he does not think is the best he can do; even when they admire him for playing in his own sweet way, he doesn't like it, for then they are getting too close—they are impinging on his private world too much. The musicians accordingly use all sorts of little devices to keep a line drawn between themselves and the audience; such as turning the musicians' chairs, in a dance hall without platform, in such a way as to make something of a barrier. It is characteristic of many occupations that the people in them, although convinced that they themselves are the best judges, not merely of their own competence but also of what is best for the people for whom they perform services, are required in some measures to yield judgment of what is wanted to these amateurs who receive the services. This is a problem not only among musicians, but in teaching, medicine, dentistry, the arts, and many other fields. It is a chronic source of ego-wound and possibly of antagonism.

Related to this is the problem of routine and emergency. In many occupations, the workers or practitioners (to use both a lower and a higher status term) deal routinely with what are emergencies to the people who receive the services. This is a source of chronic tension between the two. For the person with the crisis feels that the other is trying to belittle his trouble; he does not take it seriously enough. His very competence comes from having dealt with a thousand cases of what I like to consider my unique trouble. The worker thinks he knows from long experience that people exaggerate their troubles. He therefore builds up devices to protect himself to stall people off. This is the function of the janitor's wife when a tenant phones an appeal or a demand for immediate attention to a leaky tap; it is also the function of the doctor's wife and even sometimes of the professor's wife. The physician plays one emergency off against the other; the reason he can't run right up to see Johnny who may have the measles is that he is, unfortunately, right at that moment treating a case of the black plague. Involved in this is something of the struggle mentioned above in various connections, the struggle to maintain some control over one's decisions of what work to do, and over the disposition of one's time and of one's routine of life. It would be interesting to know what the parish priest thinks to himself when he is called for the tenth time to give extreme unction to the sainted Mrs. O'Flaherty who hasn't committed a sin in years except that of, in her anxiety over dying in a state of sin, being a nuisance to the priest. On Mrs. O'Flaherty's side there is the danger that she might die unshriven, and she has some occasion to fear that the people who shrive may not take her physical danger seriously and hence may not come quickly enough when at last her hour has come. There may indeed be in the minds of the receivers of emergency services a resentment that something so crucial to them can be a matter for a cooler and more objective attitude, even though they know perfectly well that such an attitude is necessary to competence, and though they could not stand it if the expert to whom they take their troubles were to show any signs of excitement. I have not worked out in any full or systematic way all of the problems of this routine vs. emergency drama. Nor, for that matter, have I worked out systematically any of the problems mentioned in this discussion. My aim has been to call attention to certain problems which lie, it seems to me, on the margin between sociology and psychology, problems on which people of these two disciplines should be working jointly.

5

The Humble and the Proud:
The Comparative Study of Occupations

This paper takes as its point of departure two earlier statements of mine concerning *Sociology of Work*. Almost two decades ago I wrote:

> We need to rid ourselves of any concepts which keep us from seeing that the essential problems of men at work are the same whether they do their work in the laboratories of some famous institution or in the messiest vat room of a pickle factory (Rohrer and Sherif, 1951:318).

and more recently, in a personal communication concerning studies of medical and college students:[1]

> The ideas grew out of study of lowly factories and humble occupations— which is the right place to start, for everything happens in them and people don't try to cover up the seamy side so much as in more mobile pursuits.

Both these sentences refer to method. Both, as do most statements concerning sociological method, express a social rhetoric. For such statements are written at a given moment in the history of the world, in a given place, at a certain point in the development of the science of sociology, and by a given person. That person sees things from a certain perspective; he speaks in the hope that others will accept his perspective and use it in their work. A critic complained that the title *Boys in White* (1961) downgraded medical students; we should have called them men. We called them boys because it seemed to us that, after having been treated like men in the last years of college, they were treated like boys in medical school. *Making the Grade* (1968), even without an "s" on grade, suggests that students misdirect their academic efforts; the book tries to tell why they direct them as they do. Titles, statements of method, and choice of problems for study

Reprinted by permission of the publisher from *The Sociological Quarterly*, Vol. XI, No. 2, 1970. Copyright 1970, Midwest Sociological Society.

are all a kind of social rhetoric; one hopes his rhetoric will call attention to neglected aspects of reality, correct biases, and so change methods of study that better findings and theories will result.

Why did we give such titles to those two books? Behind that lies the deeper question: why did we make the kind of study which would naturally be reported under these titles? Why did I make those two statements which I quoted earlier? Would I make the same statement now to students and colleagues going out to study people at their work?

Empirical Beginnings in the Sociology of Work

In the late 1930s, throughout the 1940s, and into the 1950s, several of us at the University of Chicago were engaged in studies of industry.[2] In 1939, I began to teach a course on professions. People from various departments of the university and from many occupations came into the course; many of them wanted to write about the efforts of their own occupation to have itself recognized as a profession. It is said that our image of the devil—the Christian devil, that is—is based on the testimony in ecclesiastical courts of people possessed. From the claims and hopes of people in the many occupations seeking professional status, we learned what the concept means to people. I soon changed the name of the course to "The Sociology of Work," both to overcome to some extent the constant preoccupation with upward mobility of occupations and also to include studies of a greater variety of occupations and problems. A good many students wrote papers on the occupations of their fathers, their kin, and even on their own. Some of the papers were developed into more systematic studies and were presented as theses. The occupations considered included—I write them down as they come to me—janitors, junk dealers (and how they come to engage in the recovery industry), furriers, funeral directors, taxi drivers, rabbis, school teachers, jazz musicians, mental hospital attendants, osteopaths, city managers, pharmacists, and YMCA secretaries. Others studied lawyers, physicians, and the clergy, as well as the newer professions or the newer specialties in these older professions. We studied workers, union leaders, and management in a variety of industries. As the war wore on, industry wanted more workers and some of them were willing to consider hiring Negroes, women, and even the Japanese (our enemy). That gave occasion to learn something about acceptance and rejection of new kinds of colleagues by workers in industry, as well as by management and the professions. We also got clues about how levels and directions of effort and production are determined in both lowly and proud kinds of work. Those who perform services, it turned out, prefer some customers, clients, patients, or even sinners, to others. Some tasks in any occupation are preferred over others; some are jealously guarded, while others are gladly delegated to those they consider lesser breeds, such as women or Negroes, either inside or outside the occupation (profession). The contingencies which face people as they run their life-cycle, their career at work, turned out to be a constant theme. The great variety of students and of occupations and work situations studied stimulated the search for and the finding of common themes. Some of these common themes I put into an *Outline for Sociological Study of an Occupation* which was used by a whole generation of students.

The historic circumstance was that large numbers of graduate students were coming to Chicago to study sociology. They had come from a variety of ethnic backgrounds, and wrote about them, being at once proud and a little ashamed, most certainly self-conscious! They strove to be both emancipated from and loyal to their backgrounds. In Robert E. Park's time and later in the courses of Louis Wirth and Herbert Blumer they recognized in themselves "the marginal man." The new courses on work and industry perhaps made them more aware of the occupations that lay in their family (and ethnic) backgrounds; occupations to which they had become marginal. Social mobility generally takes the form of abandoning one's father's occupation. If these students started their sociological analysis on the humbler occupations, it was by accident. They started where they were—or had been. They should have been struck into pillars of salt. Those students were not alienated from their milieux; emancipated, yes, but not alienated. Sociology written by the emancipated is different from sociology written—or acted—by the alienated. Emancipation is a very delicate balance between detachment and involvement.

An Emerging Comparative Frame of Reference

If those students—who studied janitors, factory workers, furriers, and the like—compared the lowly with the proud, it was not a degrading of the noble, but an ennobling of what some might have considered less than noble. As these studies went on, many of these students, as well as myself, became convinced that if a certain problem turned up in one occupation, it was nearly certain to turn up in all. We were skeptical when someone said, for instance, that in their favorite occupation there was no "restriction of production," no exclusion of some people from the intimacy and protection of colleagueship, no favoring of some clients or customers over others, no codes of behavior with supporting informal sanctions, no secrecy, no sense of rank. The thing was to discover in what form the problem turned up, how serious it was, and how it was handled. Our aim was to discover patterns of interaction and mechanisms of control, the things over which people in a line of work seek to gain control, the sanctions which they have or would like to have at their disposal, and the bargains which were made—consciously or less consciously—among a group of workers and between them and the other kinds of people in the drama of their work. There is no absolute virtue in studying one kind of work rather than another, if the inward frame of one's mind is comparative. The essence of the comparative frame is that one seeks differences in terms of dimensions common to all the cases. If one becomes overenamored of a particular occupation, he is likely to describe it in terms which suggest that it is not comparable to others. If he seeks common dimensions, the differences between occupations become clearer, and more impressive.

Even at the time of which I am speaking, there were many institutions and many people of various disciplines studying the problems of industrial and professional work. Any student of such matters would be aware of the early work of Werner Sombart on the source of the modern industrial labor force (1927); of Henri de Man on the loss of joy in work (1929); of Max Weber's long—and untranslated— monograph on the sources and adaptation of the labor force of modern industry (1908), and his other one on the psychophysics of industrial work (1908–09);[3] and of Carr-Saunders' book on *The Professions* (1933)—to mention just a few of the classics in the field. The industrial and postindustrial world has become self-conscious about its labor force, about education for work, and about recruitment in various kinds of work, as well as about the unemployables of city and rural slums. There are endless new problems demanding attention. The economists appear to have lost interest in problems of the organization of work, the motivation of workers, and, to some extent, in the distribution of goods and services. People called sociologists and social psychologists have picked up these problems.

The Encompassing System of Work Organization

It is not my purpose to talk of the state of such studies, but instead I will turn to an aspect of the study of professional work which was not fully developed in the earlier studies. We were inclined to look at the occupation as an entity, thus neglecting somewhat, but not completely, the general system of which it is part. Professions are, in a measure greater than ever, parts within larger wholes. Each profession seeks a monopoly; it does so in part by limiting its activities and the area of its responsibilities and tasks, while delegating purposely or by default many related tasks and responsibilities to other occupations. Within the profession itself, specialization marks out limited fields and creates a division of labor internal to the profession.

No profession fulfills all the wants in its general field; nor does it serve the wants of all its potential clients equally. The most complete professional—but not economic—monopoly I can think of in our society is that of the undertaker. No one escapes him; but even he is engaged in a special activity in the great field of birth, health and disease, and death. The core of his activity is the urgent and necessary disposal of human remains. His domain is slightly confused by the new transplanting surgery. It is expanded by his exploitation of some of the deepest of human sentiments and of some of the tragi-comic aspects of the culture of the survivors. Around an almost irreducible core the undertaker creates—an interaction with his clients—a body of wants and then seeks to satisfy them. I take the undertaker simply as an example to suggest that the activities of a profession must be seen in the larger setting and in terms of its place among other occupations and activities. If some occupations are more proud and others more humble, there are differences of prestige within any given occupation as well. It may be that the prouder or more prestigious the occupation, as measured by its position on the scales used by students of that phenomenon, the greater the differences within it. I suspect that the very fact of a profession being high in prestige gives some of those within it the power to make the most of the symbolic value of their name and to monopolize—or oligarchize—the facilities necessary to practice as they wish and the positions of power and prestige in their work system. As this elite develops, by contre-coup (backlash) there may develop within the profession a sort of lower-middle class which, in professional matters, will oppose the will of the elite, although they will not completely oppose them; what prestige this lower middle has within the profession depends upon their recognizing in some measure the standards of qualification set up by the elite. They might be called the fundamentalists of the trade, upholding to the letter some conception of their work which they believe was laid down by some founding father- or mother-hero—human, demigod, or divine. Still lower in the scale there may be people who, though legitimate in qualification, so far fail that they are hardly in the colleagueship of the profession at all, and they work in their own way outside it. There are in medicine, law, in the academic profession and the clergy, a number of levels—not merely points on a scale but clusters of practicing members.

The Naming Function of Professionals

To understand them one must understand the system, including the clients and their wants. Persons and organizations have problems; they want things done for them—for their bodies and souls, for their social and financial relations, for their cars, houses, bridges, sewage systems; and they want things done to the people they consider their competitors or their enemies. What they want done no doubt has some existence apart from the system of services within which the professions operate. But we scarcely know what their problems would be; that is, in what circumstances they would think they had problems, how they would define the problems, to whom they would turn for help, what they would offer in return for it, what they would consider good service, and what recourse they would have if the service were not satisfactory. For it is in the course of interaction with one another and with the professionals that the problems of people are given definition. Pains and complaints are the lot of the human (and other) species. But, diseases are inventions; they are definitions of conditions and situations. The humans who suffer may or may not accept the professionals' definition of what ails them and their recommendations of what to do. Shame and guilt may be generated without benefit of professionals, but sin and absolution from it have become professional in definition; clients accept or reject in varying degree the professional definition and the professional cure. If belief is general, and supported by political power, the professionals have strong sanctions in their hands. If a given system of religious beliefs is generally accepted and is supported by political power, religion and law become one system. The professionals of religion can make lack of belief not merely heresy, but a crime; the priest is supported by the instruments of the law—by courts and police. Political beliefs may be equally mandatory, as in certain countries; political piety, political guilt and sin take on the quality of the corresponding religious phenomena in a society of one mandatory religion; in both cases the bodies of the guilty may be burnt just in case the fires of hell are not really as hot as they are said to be (an odd bit of unbelief on the part of the professionals of religion; there is always a bit of skepticism in professional belief).

The lawyer, by his efforts on behalf of his client against his client's opponents, has a hand in defining the law. He may defend those who live by setting up a counterlaw and a countersystem of protection—as do the leaders of organized crime. But the lawyer's monopoly over his function is practically complete, and the completeness consists in the power of the state to enforce what the courts—the lawyers' institution—decide are proper grievances and proper remedies.

As for education, the power of the academic to say who is learned has been great. He dispenses a powerful instrument—a set of prerogatives, of access to positions and goods. But without a strong prevailing professional definition of learning, what boy ever would have sought to learn to write doggerel verse in school Greek with vowels pronounced in the English way?[4] Certainly it was not by direct application of this bizarre skill that the man earned his place in the world. The ability and the willingness to acquire it made him a member of a select group who were given access to careers demanding high ability, no doubt, but little direct use of that particular kind of learning. The society of learned men had to prove themselves in various activities, and many of them got great pleasure from their classical studies. But the whole system was an artifact. It had a beginning and has come to an end, or nearly so. Other kinds of learning have become legitimate and new professionals foster them. Some of them are of immediate utility, such as in keeping books, in making engines run, in going to the moon and back; the line from academic learning to its application is often long and complicated, and highly institutionalized.

As society changes, the problems of people and institutions change. The changes in professional recognition, definition, and management of the wants which arise from those changes are by no means direct and immediate. What are the relations between changing problems, the definition of personal and collective wants arising from them, and the inward structure of professions, including the place of their elites in leading the way to new definitions and new ways of distributing their services? These are questions to be studied in a great variety of cases. In a rather rambling way, I have been saying that *professionals do not merely serve; they define the very wants which they serve.* Thus, the old dictum that the professions fulfill the basic wants or desires of people and society is much too simple. We must start from the assumption that even with respect to biological wants, the serving professions are in constant interaction with the people they serve, but in contact with and responsive to some kinds of people more than others, and with society at large, in varying degree, initiating changes and responding to them. Often the response is resistance, sometimes active innovation. We know far too little about these processes.

The professions—occupations of high prestige—work only on those wants which are defined as legitimate. In medicine, some diseases or troubles are more respectable than others; some (e.g., venereal diseases) are not respectable at all. The desire to be cured of them is considered legitimate, and in our time it has become permissible to talk about them and to undertake programs of prevention; it is still not common, however, for people to gain great prestige from having cured prestigious patients of them.

To want to bring a pregnancy to premature end—abortion—has not been considered legitimate, but many women have felt this want most urgently. I believe I would be right in stating that there has never been a society in which there were not some people willing to satisfy this want. One might rank pregnancies from those ardently wanted to those most desperately not wanted, from blessing through neutrality to nuisance to catastrophe. We have seen in our time a tremendous change of attitude toward the legitimacy of abortion. In England changes in the law appear to have created a great international demand. Some physicians have in the past few weeks been struck from the rolls in London for having allegedly drummed up abortion clients from abroad. Thus has an illegitimate want become at least formally legitimate; but that does not mean that those who satisfy the want will gain positions of prestige in the medical system. But to the extent that abortion does become an accepted part of medical practice, one may suppose that the illegitimate abortionist will disappear. The latter have been of many kinds. Some have been apostles of freedom, courageously running the risk of prison and loss of standing in the name of delivering women from their chains. Others have practiced abortion somewhat cautiously on patients referred to them in various ways either by respectable physicians or by respectable women who knew somebody who knew somebody who went to Dr. So-and-So. Women without medical license (the midwife and the granny) have also filled this want, for patients with little or no access to the middle-class referral circle, but also sometimes for the lady in distress. And always there has been, and no doubt will be, the decision as to who is a legitimate case—who has a right to ask for abortion. Class, age, marital status, the pains which threaten if a child is born of the pregnancy—these and other variables will no doubt determine whether a physician will accept a patient for abortion, even if the law allows. The legitimacy of the want—and of the service to fulfill it—thus seems to lie partly in the nature of the difficulty, but also partly in the person, in his status, and the source of his troubles, and partly in the state of society. The boundaries of legitimate want, and of legitimate professional services are not fixed, but tend to vary with time, person, and circumstance. Within the limits of the legitimate, some activities, some services, and services to some clients are more respectable and lend more prestige to the professional than do others.

At the margins of the legitimate and beyond it some professionals operate, as well as persons in other occupations, without professional standing, some even outside the law. Also within the limits of the legitimate and the respectable, the procedures become so numerous and complicated that the profession at the center of the system must delegate a great deal of its work to people in other occupations. This is certainly and noticeably so in matters of health and medicine, where the so-called paramedical professions and occupations have multiplied with resulting problems of authority, the making of decisions, and the allocating of functions to the many members of the medical and health system. Also the specialties of the medical profession themselves tend each to have their own philosophy of medical practice, their own research emphases, and their own notions of the best way to distribute their therapeutic and preventive services. Finally, as the system becomes more complicated, as more kinds of people are involved in it, it becomes crucial to find out how innovations are made and how they become legitimate, if they do.

We may also ask whether there is any field of human wants in which the professional definition is fully accepted by everyone. Perhaps there is always a raw edge where professional definition and practice do not utterly match wants and active demands. There will perhaps always be doomed people who will not accept the professional judgment of their ailment; people who will be curious about things the educational establishment thinks there is no need to be curious about. On these raw edges there may occur what one might call amateur experimenting, experimenting without license or mandate. The mandate of the professional establishment may thus be questioned.

Something of this kind is occurring in the field of education—that of teaching and learning. It is the field in which the professionals are divided into probably the greatest number of discontinuous ranks, each with its own license and mandate. It is the field in which there is probably the greatest range in the measure of authority used in course of performing the service; there is everything from complete dictatorship of the teacher (give me the answer I want or be damned), to egalitarian relations between teacher and learning (both being eager learners), to dictatorship of the pupil. There is always involved in it the relation between generations, as well as relationships between social statuses. The system has depended upon the young—the to-be-taught—internalizing the teaching generations' image of the society into which the young were to be initiated and their concept of the knowledge, skills, and personal traits which would be useful and should be satisfying. Apparently a large number of the younger generation does not see the future through the same glasses as their teachers, and those whom they believe the teachers represent. Perhaps for the first time in history, the young take a gloomier view of the future than do their elders. Certainly their concept of social time and distance—of the relation of learning to action in social matters—is different from that on which modern education has been built.

I believe that the lesson of that earlier advice about the humble and the proud has been pretty well learned. Furthermore, many young people now seek emancipation from their parents' pride, not from their humility. The rhetoric of our time should emphasize study of the whole settings in which particular occupations (professional and nonprofessional) occur, with attention to the shifting boundaries between them and the kind of cooperation required for any one of them to perform effectively; to the shifting boundaries between the professional systems and the clienteles they serve; and finally, to the development of new definitions of wants growing out of constant social interaction and change. In the course of doing such study, we might learn more about the fate of professional mandates—and pride including our own.

Notes

1. When Becker, Geer, Strauss, and I had completed the study of a medical school, reported in *Boys in White* (1961), we were asked to study the undergraduate life of the same university and the result was *Making the Grade: The Academic Side of Student Life* (1968). The bulk of the fieldwork on both studies was done by Howard S. Becker and Blanche Geer. Anselm Strauss had a hand in the study of the medical school, doing

the "dirty work" of staying up all night with interns and residents. Marsh Ray was a member of the field team in the study of undergraduates. I was the entrepreneur of both studies, a role which very soon passed to my coworkers, Geer and Becker. They also did the bulk of the writing.

2. W. Lloyd Warner, Robert J. Havighurst, Burleigh Gardner, Frederick Harbison, William F. Whyte, and I were members of a Committee on Human Relations in industry. Many graduate students worked with us, as well as other members of the staff. Among the students of sociology who had a hand in the various projects in industry or in study of occupations were: Robert Dubin, Harold Wilensky, Harvey L. Smith, Melville Dalton, Edward Gross, Robert W. Habenstein, Edith Lentz, Donald Roy, the late Mozell Hill, William Hale, David Solomon, Orvis Collins, Lee Rainwater, and David Moore. There were others at the peak of the enterprise, and also some later. The peak in the study of occupations came later than that of industrial studies. Some members of the committee continued to work together, but on somewhat different projects.

3. Weber's works on science as a profession and on politics as a profession are much better known as are his many references to functionaries and professionals in the body of his *Economy and Society* which is now available in full and in English (1968).

4. Ong (1969:627–30) states this point in that portion of his *Daedalus* article entitled "The Atrophy of Puberty Rites." I had not seen his article when I wrote this paper. I recommend it to social scientists, not to make them smile knowingly at the plight of the poor teachers of Greek, but to make them take thought about their own puberty rites.

References

Becker, Howard S., Blanche Geer, and Everett C. Hughes. 1968. *Making the Grade: The Academic Side of Student Life*. New York: John Wiley and Sons.

Becker, Howard S., Blanche Geer, Everett C. Hughes, and Anselm Strauss. 1961. *Boys in White*. Chicago: University of Chicago Press.

Carr-Saunders, A. M., and P. A. Wilson. 1933. *The Professions*. London: Macmillan.

de Man, Henri. 1929. *Joy in Work*. Cedar Paul (trans.). London: George Allen & Unwin, Ltd.

Hughes, Everett C. 1951. "Work and the Self." Pp. 313–23 in John Rohrer and Muzafer Sherif (eds.), *Social Work at the Crossroads*. New York: Harper & Brothers.

Ong, W. 1969. "Crisis and Understanding in the Humanities." *Daedalus* 98 (Summer): 617–40.

Sombart, Werner. 1937. "Capitalism." Pp. 195–208 in *Encyclopaedia of the Social Sciences*. Vol. 11. New York: Macmillan.

———. 1927. "Die Anpassung der Bevölkerung an die Bedürfnisse des Kapitalismus." Pp. 363–469 in Werner Sombart. *Das Wirtschaftsleben im Zeitalter des Hochkapitalismus*. München: Duncker & Humblot.

Weber, Max. 1968. *Economy and Society: An Outline of Interpretive Sociology* (complete translation of *Wirtschaft und Gesellschaft*). Guenther Roth (trans.). Towata, New Jersey: Bedminster Press, Inc.

————. 1924. "Auslese und Anpassung (Berufswahl und Berufschicksal) der Arbeiterschaft der Geschlossenen Grossindustrie (1908)," pp. 1–60; also, "Zur Psychophysik der Industriellen Arbeit (1908–09)," pp. 61–225 in Max Weber, *Gesammelte Aufsätze zur Soziologie und Sozialpolitik,* Tübingen: Mohr, 1924.

6

Mistakes at Work

The comparative student of man's work learns about doctors by studying plumbers; and about prostitutes by studying psychiatrists. This is not to suggest any degree of similarity greater than chance expectation between the members of these pairs, but simply to indicate that the student starts with the assumption that all kinds of work belong in the same series, regardless of their places in prestige or ethical ratings. In order to learn, however, one must find a frame of reference applicable to all cases without regard to such ratings. To this end, we seek for the common themes in human work. One such theme is that of routine and emergency. By this I mean that one man's routine of work is made up of the emergencies of other people. In this respect, the pairs of occupations named above do perhaps have some rather close similarities. Both the physician and the plumber do practice esoteric techniques for the benefit of people in distress. The psychiatrist and the prostitute must both take care not to become too personally involved with clients who come to them with rather intimate problems. I believe that in the study of work, as in that of other human activities and institutions, progress is apt to be commensurate with our ability to draw a wide range of pertinent cases into view. The wider the range, the more we need a fundamental frame of reference.

Another theme in human work is the problem of mistakes and failures. It, too, is found in all occupations. The more times per day a man does a given operation, the greater his chance of doing it wrong sometimes. True, his skill may become so great that his percentage of errors is nearly zero. It is common talk in the medical profession that certain surgical operations really ought not to be done at all, except *in extremis,* by men who do not have the opportunity to do them literally by the hundreds every year. In a large and favorably known hospital, the interns and residents—who are there to learn by practice—complain that the leading members of the surgical staff take all the interesting cases, not merely out of charity, but to keep their level

From the *Canadian Journal of Economics and Political Science,* Vol. XVII, August, 1951, pp. 320–27.

of skill up to the point of least risk for the few patients who can pay
a really high fee. This reduces the opportunities of the interns and
residents to acquire skill. One may speak of a calculus of the probability of making mistakes, in which the variables are skill and frequency
of performance. It is obvious that there are many possibilities. One
who never performs a given action will never do it wrong. But one
who has never tried it could not do it right if he were on some occasion
compelled to try. This is the position of the layman with reference to
many skills. Some skills require more repetition than others for the
original learning and for maintenance. In some, even the most proficient make many failures, while in others the top level of skill is close
to perfection. Occupations, considered as bundles of skills, are subject
to the contingencies contained in all combinations of these factors of
learning and of maintaining skill, and, correlatively, subject to variations in the probability that one will sometimes make mistakes. These
are matters in which experimental and vocational psychologists are
much interested and on which they are doing significant work.

But there are other factors in this problem of mistakes and failures.
Some mistakes are more fateful than others, either for the person who
makes them, for his colleagues, or for the persons upon whom the
mistakes are made. Those who train students for research which requires receiving the confidences of living people and getting and keeping entrée to groups and institutions of various sorts are aware of this
problem. (We are at present working on a project to discover how to
train students to a high level of skill in social observation with the least
risk of damage to all concerned.) In occupations in which mistakes are
fateful and in which repetition on living or valuable material is necessary to learn the skills, it is obvious that there is a special set of
problems of apprenticeship and of access to the situations in which
the learning may be done. Later on, when the neophyte is at his work,
there arises the problem of his seeming always to have known how,
since the very appearance of being a learner is frightening. At any
rate, there are psychological, physical, social, and economic risks in
learning and doing one's work. And since the theoretical probability
of making an error someday is increased by the very frequency of the
operations by which one makes one's living, it becomes natural to
build up some rationale to carry one through. It is also to be expected
that those who are subject to the same work risks will compose a
collective rationale which they whistle to one another to keep up their
courage, and that they will build up collective defenses against the lay
world. These rationales and defenses contain a logic that is somewhat
like that of insurance, in that they tend to spread the risk psychologi-

cally (by saying that it might happen to anyone), morally, and financially. A study of these risk-spreading devices is an essential part of comparative study of occupations. They have a counterpart in the devices which the individual finds for shifting some of the sense of guilt from his own shoulders to those of the larger company of his colleagues. Perhaps this is the basis of the strong identification with colleagues in work in which mistakes are fateful, and in which even long training and a sense of high calling do not prevent errors.

Now let us approach the subject from the side of the person who, since he receives the services, will suffer from the mistakes when they are made. In a certain sense, we actually hire people to make our mistakes for us. The division of labor in society is not merely, as is often suggested, technical. It is also psychological and moral. We delegate certain things to other people, not merely because we cannot do them, but because we do not wish to run the risk of error. The guilt of failure would be too great. Perhaps one reason why physicians do work gratis for each other's families is to keep completely free from the economic necessity of treating people with whom they are so closely involved that mistakes would be too hard to face.

Sometimes a person requires an assurance that can be had only by being in a strictly lay frame of mind. Belief in the charisma of skill is a lay, rather than a professional, attitude. The professional attitude is essentially statistical; it deals in probabilities. But there are matters about which we prefer to think in absolutes. In dealing with such matters we delegate the relative way of thinking to another, who becomes our agent. He runs our risks for us. We like to believe him endowed with charisma. Ray Gold, who studied some of the building trades, found that the housewife likes to believe that the plumber she calls in is perfect, not merely *relatively* good. He keeps the mysterious entrails of her precious house in order. How much more does one want to believe absolutely in one's dentist, lawyer, physician, and priest. (There are of course other nontechnical factors involved in delegation of tasks. Some work is *infra dignitate*. Some is necessary, but shady, or forbidden by one's particular taboos and aversions.)

Now this does not mean that the person who delegates work, and hence, risk, will calmly accept the mistakes which are made upon him, his family, or his property. He is quick to accuse; and if people are in this respect as psychiatrists say they are in others, the more determined they are to escape responsibility, the quicker they may be to accuse others for real or supposed mistakes.

In fact, I suppose that we all suspect just a little the objectivity of those to whom we delegate the more fateful of our problems. We suspect them for that very experimental spirit which we know is, in some degree, necessary to hardy and progressive skill in meeting our crises. Thus there is probably always some ambivalence in our feelings towards the people whom we hire to make our mistakes, or at least to run the risk of making them. The whole problem or set of problems involved in delegating work—and risks—to others is one on which there is not much to be found in the anthropological, sociological, or psychological literature. For each occupation that one studies one should, I believe, seek to determine just what it is that is delegated to the persons in the occupation and what are the attitudes and feelings involved on both sides.

We now have before us the problem and the characters. The characters are the people who, because they do something often and for others, run the risk of making mistakes and of causing injury; and those other people who, for technical, economic, psychological, moral, or status reasons, delegate some of their tasks and problems to others and who therefore may have mistakes made upon them and at their expense. These are not really two kinds of people, but are the same people in different roles. The relation of these two roles is part of the personal adjustment of everyone who works. The problem is the reduction and absorption of the risk of failure on both sides, and of the kinds of conflicts within and between persons, which arise from the risk of error, mistakes, and failures.

As soon as we go into these problems we are faced with another: that of defining what a failure or mistake is in any given line of work or in a given work operation. This leads to still another which turns out to be the significant one for the social drama of work: Who has the right to say what a mistake or a failure is? The findings on this point are fairly clear; a colleague-group (the people who consider themselves subject to the same work risks) will stubbornly defend its own right to define mistakes, and to say in the given case whether one has been made.[1] Howard S. Becker has found that professional jazz musicians will do considerable injury to themselves rather than let any layman, even the one who is paying their wages, say that a musician is playing badly or even that he has struck the wrong note. An orchestra leader who would even relay a layman's complaint to a member of his band would be thought already on the road to becoming a "square," one of those outsiders who do not understand jazz music. Now you may say that jazz music is so lacking in any canons of correctness that there is no such thing as a single false note within the larger noise. It is all a matter of individual opinion. There is no clear and objective standard by which a judgment can be made.

But how clear is it in other lines of work? When one starts comparing occupations in this regard one finds that in most of them it is very difficult to establish criteria of success or failure, and of mistakes as against proper execution of work. The cases where all parties to the work drama would agree are few indeed. In factories which make precision parts the criteria are finely measured tolerances, but usually there is an informally agreed upon set of tolerances which are slightly looser than those in the book. Workmen and inspectors are continually at odds over the difference, even when the workmen want the parts they make to be workable. This is a case of the clearest kind of criterion. In medicine the criteria of success and failure are often far from clear. Dr. Bruno Bettelheim recently stated that psychotherapists do not discuss together their successes and failures because there are no standards to go by; that is why, he said, they spend so much time discussing whether their historical reconstructions of the troubles of their patients are correct or not. Health is, after all, a relative matter. Most people are interested in making the old body do as long as possible; this makes medicine quite a different matter from the automobile industry (where the garage man makes his work easier by persuading you the old car isn't worth mending).

Even where the standards may be a little clearer than in medicine and education, the people who work and those who receive the product as goods or services will have quite different degrees and kinds of knowledge of the probabilities and contingencies involved. The colleague-group will consider that it alone fully understands the technical contingencies, and that it should therefore be given the sole right to say when a mistake has been made. The layman, they may contend, cannot even at best fully understand the contingencies. This attitude may be extended to complete silence concerning mistakes of a member of the colleague-group, because the very discussion before a larger audience may imply the right of the layman to make a judgment; and it is the *right* to make the judgment that is most jealously guarded.

In some occupations it is assumed that anyone on the inside will know by subtle gestures when his colleagues believe a mistake has been made. Full membership in the colleague-group is not attained until these gestures and their meaning are known. When they are known, there need not be conscious and overt discussion of certain errors even within the colleague-group. And when some incident makes an alleged failure or mistake a matter of public discussion, it is perhaps the feeling that outsiders will never understand the full context of risk and contingency that makes colleagues so tight-lipped. And if matters have gone to such a point that mistakes and failures

are not freely discussed even within the trusted in-group, public discussion may be doubly feared; for in addition to questioning the prerogative of in-group judgment, the outside inquisitor lifts the veil from
the group's own hidden anxieties, the things colleagues do not talk
about even among themselves. This may be the source of the rather
nervous behavior of schoolteachers when my colleagues and I report
to them—at their own request—some of the things we are finding
out about them.

One of the differences between lay and professional thinking concerning mistakes is that to the layman the technique of the occupation
should be pure instrument, pure means to an end, while to the people
who practice it, every occupation tends to become an art. David Riesman,[2] who was once a clerk to Justice Brandeis, and an assistant in
the office of the District Attorney of New York, tells of the wonderful
briefs which young lawyers draw up for presentation to lower court
judges who can scarcely read them, much less judge the law that is
in them. The ritual of looking up all the past cases, and the art of
arguing out all possibilities are gone through, even when the lawyer
knows that the decision will be made upon a much simpler—perhaps
also a much sounder—basis. What is more, the ritual and the art are
respected, and the men who perform them with brilliance and finesse
are admired. The simple client may be dazzled, but at some point he
is also likely to think that he is being done by the whole guild of
lawyers, including his own, the opposing counsel, and the court. In a
sense, the art and cult of the law are being maintained at his expense.
The legal profession believes, in some measure, in the cult of the law.
The individual case is thought of not merely as something to be decided, but as part of the stream of observance of the cult of the law.

And here we come to the deeper point of Dr. Bettelheim's remark
concerning his own colleagues, the psychotherapists. A part of their
art is the reconstruction of the history of the patient's illness. This
may have some instrumental value, but the value put upon it by the
practitioners is of another order. The psychotherapists, perhaps just
because the standards of cure are so uncertain, apparently find reas-
surance in being adept at their art of reconstruction (no doubt accompanied by faith that skill in the art will bring good to patients in the
long run).

Another example of these ways of thinking is to be found in social
work. This profession is said to make a distinction between successful
and professional handling of a case. The layman thinks of success as
getting the person back on his feet, or out of his trouble. The social
worker has to think of correct procedure, of law, of precedent, of the

case as something which leaves a record. She also appreciates skillful interviewing, and perhaps can chuckle over some case which was handled with subtlety and finish, although the person never got "well" (whatever that would be in social work).

In teaching, where ends are very ill-defined—and consequently mistakes are equally so—where the lay world is quick to criticize and blame, correct handling becomes ritual as much as or even more than an art. If a teacher can prove that he has followed the ritual, the blame is shifted from himself to the miserable child or student; the failure can be and is put upon them.

Ritual is also strongly developed in occupations where there are great unavoidable risks, as in medicine. In such occupations the ritual may, however, be stronger in the second and third ranks of the institutions in which the work is done. Thus, in medicine, the physician, who stands at the top of the hierarchy, takes the great and final risks of decision and action. These risks are delegated to him, and he is given moral and legal protection in taking them. But the pharmacist, who measures out the prescribed doses, and the nurse, who carries out the ordered treatment, are the great observers of ritual in medicine. Pharmacists are said often to become ritualistic wipers and polishers, flecking infinitely small grains of dust from scales on which they are only going to weigh out two pounds of Paris green. The ritualistic punctiliousness of nurses and pharmacists is a kind of built-in shock-absorber against the possible mistakes of the physician. Indeed, in dramatizing their work, these second-rank professions explicitly emphasize their role as saviors of both patient and physician from the errors of the latter. And here again we get a hint of what may be the deeper function of the art, cult, and ritual of various occupations. They may provide a set of emotional and even organizational checks and balances against both the subjective and the objective risks of the trade.

I suspect that it is a rare occupation whose practitioners develop no criteria of good work, and no concept of mistake or failure other than as a simply defined successful conclusion of the given case or task. Usually the professional judgment will contain explicit or implicit references to an art, a cult, and a ritual. The function of the art, cult, and ritual is not so much to bring the individual case to an early successful conclusion as to relate it to the ongoing occupation itself, and to the social system in which the work is done. In most occupations, a man can be judged as quite wrong by his colleagues for an action which the lay client might consider very successful indeed. The quack, defined functionally and not in evaluative terms, is the man who continues through time to please his customers but not his colleagues. On the contrary, a man may be considered by his colleagues to have done a piece of work properly and without error, even when the client may accuse him of error, mistake, or failure.

In these remarks I have mentioned two concepts of great importance for study of the universal work drama. One is the concept of role; the other, that of social system. A person, asked what his work is, can answer in two ways. He can say *what* he does: I make beds, I plumb teeth. Or he can say *who* he is: I am the person who does so and so. In the latter case he is naming his role. A large part of the business of protecting one's self from the risks of one's own work mistakes lies in definition of role; and in some occupations, one of the rewards is definition of one's role in such a way as to show that one helps protect people from the mistakes of others. Now, roles imply a system of social arrangements. Most work is done in such systems. Part of the function of these systems is to delegate, to spread, or, in some cases, to concentrate, the risk and the guilt of mistakes; and also to spread and to allocate the losses which result from them. The details of these matters are better left until they have been worked out more fully.

This one example of sociological analysis prompts some remarks concerning the academic division of labor with reference to human work. In the historical and conventional division of academic labor, work has belonged to the economists, as do voters and kings to the political scientist, and fun and vice to the sociologist. The historian handled anything which had been written down on paper or other material long enough ago for the author, his characters, and all the relatives of both to be so long dead that no one would bring a libel suit. Indeed, it was better if they were in danger of being forgotten, for the historian's fame depended on rediscovering them. But his mandate allowed him to tell all about his characters—their work, their politics, and their gambols. The anthropologist went about the earth on one-man expeditions discovering people who didn't write and hadn't been written about. Since he was alone in the field and since his reputation depended upon his being the first there, he looked at everything from hair texture and the shape of shin bones to religion, art, kinship, crime, and even the technique and organization of work, and the distribution of the products of labor.

Now the division of academic labor, like other human arrangements, is as much the result of social movements as of logic. Some persons in, or on the periphery of, academic life are seized, from time to time, with a new preoccupation. They pursue it and their successors nourish it. The third generation will have refined out of it some pure essence which will be called a social science; but they will not ordinarily have yielded to anyone else the original liquor from which their essence was distilled. Thus, the pure essence of economic reasoning was abstracted from preoccupation with all sorts of things having to do with the material and moral welfare of man, as may be seen in Adam Smith's *The Wealth of Nations*. Since the quantities which would appear in place of the letters in economic equations—if some economist were to be so impure as to make such a substitution— would include the price of the labor used in manufacturing and distributing those goods which are produced in sufficient quantities to fit the formulae, it is quite natural that work should have been one of the preoccupations of the economist. Indeed, it was natural that economists should extend their interest to whatever might affect the price and supply of labor: migration, the birth-rate, religion and philosophy, laws, trade unions, politics, and even mental and physical capacities, although the latter have become the psychologists' claim to entry into the factory. Economists have been interested in those distractions from labor which have more lately been the concern of the sociologist, but which Daniel Defoe, who never heard of sociology, commented upon in *The True-Born Englishman:*

> *The lab'ring poor, in spight of double pay*
> *Are sawcy, mutinous and beggarly*
> *So lavish of their money and their time*
> *That want of forecast is the nation's crime*
> *Good drunken company is their delight*
> *And what they get by day, they spend by night.*

If the occupation of the economist be economic reasoning, in ever more sophisticated formulae, human work continues to be one of his *pre*-occupations. And this illustrates the fate of each branch of social science; that while it refines and purifies its theoretical core, its logic, it can never free itself from the human mess. Wallowing there, each purist will find himself in the company of others who, although they seek to create a different pure product of logic, must extract it from this same mess. It might be of some use, in these days of the cult of collaboration between the social disciplines, for us to understand the social movements out of which the various social sciences have come, and the consequent development in each not merely of a central and distinguishing logic, but of a large periphery or halo of preoccupation with institutions and events. It is, I believe, treading upon a preempted area of events and institutions that brings accusation of academic trespass, rather than borrowing its fundamental logic. Thus a sociologist should stay out of factories because the economist was there first. The economist should stay out of the family. Neither of them should be caught in an insane asylum, which is the domain of psychiatrists.

But, to the extent that there is some logic in the academic division of labor, representatives of each discipline will be found studying not merely some one institution but any events which yield to effective analysis by their particular logic. Economics will cease to be merely— if it ever was—the science of markets; anthropology, of primitive peoples; education, of what happens in schools; sociology, of families, churches, play-grounds, settlement houses, and prisons.

Human work, including the institutions in which people work for a living, has become one of the lively frontiers on which social scientists meet. Without belaboring the point, I refer you to V. W. Bladen for an acute analysis of what is happening among economists, anthropologists, and sociologists on this frontier.[3] Work, I submit, is in all human societies an object of moral rule, of social control in the broadest sense, and it is precisely all the processes involved in the definition and enforcement of moral rule that form the core problems of sociology.

Notes

1. The colleague-group does not in all cases succeed in getting and keeping this right. Perhaps they do not always want the full responsibility of convicting one another of error and of applying sanctions. It would be more correct to say that a kind of jurisprudence of mistakes is an essential part of the study of any occupation. Professor Norman Ward has suggested that a study of the official *error* in baseball would throw light on the processes involved.

2. "Toward an Anthropological Science of Law and the Legal Profession," *The American Journal of Sociology*, LVII (September, 1951), pp. 121–35.

3. "Economics and Human Relations," *The Canadian Journal of Economics and Political Science*, Vol. 14 (August, 1948), pp. 301–11.

II

RACE AND STATUS

7

The Study of Ethnic Relations

Since so many people are making a desperate effort (perhaps the last before they meet their Maker) to understand and modify the relations between peoples, ethnic groups, and races, it is appropriate to note some of the biases and false assumptions that vitiate well-intentioned study and discussion of these relations. The relations between French and other Canadians are not one of the desperate cases. Quite the contrary. The points I have to make, however, apply to the Canadian case as well as to those that threaten the peace of the world.

I have already used the term *ethnic group,* a colorless catch-all much used by anthropologists and sociologists; it is a term likely to be taken up by a larger public, and consequently likely to take on color that will compel the sociologists to get a new one, for it is one of the risks of our trade that our words lose the scientifically essential virtue of neutrality as they acquire the highly desirable virtue of being commonly used. The anthropologists will probably not have to change, since they study people who cannot read. To return from this digression, which does have a point for the subject in hand, what is an ethnic group? Almost anyone who uses the term would say that it is a group distinguishable from others by one, or some combination, of the following: physical characteristics, language, religion, customs, institutions, or "cultural traits." This definition is, however, exactly wrong-end to. Its wrongness has important consequences, not only for study of intergroup relations, but for the relations themselves. An ethnic group is not one because of the degree of measurable or observable difference from other groups: it is an ethnic group, on the contrary, because the people in it and the people out of it know that it is one; because both the *ins* and the *outs* talk, feel, and act as if it were a separate group. This is possible only if there are ways of telling who belongs to the group and who does not, and if a person learns early, deeply, and usually irrevocably to what group he belongs. If it is easy to resign from the group, it is not truly an ethnic group.

Dalhousie Review, Vol. XXVIII, No. 4, Jan., 1948. Reprinted by permission of the *Dalhousie Review.*

These points should be clear and dear to any English-speaking Canadian. By the kind of measures usually used, the English-speaking part of the Canadian people would be considered a colony of Great Britain or a part of the United States. About all the evidence to prove that Canadians are a separate ethnic group is a little extra virtue and the fact that they export their Aimee Semple McPhersons, Tex Guinans, Norma Shearers, Pidgeons, and Masseys—and buy them back at the box office. Yet Canadians are Canadians just as naturally as Englishmen are Englishmen, and they never yield to the temptations to belong to other nations. Well, hardly ever.

To be sure, the living of a common life and the facing of common problems—conditions that lead to the growth of an ethnic group, nationality, and even a race—will almost certainly encourage the development of a peculiar language, at least of peculiar turns of expression and meaning, and of some unique customs and institutions. Some of these peculiar traits will become the dear symbols of the group's distinction from others; their value for group solidarity may exceed their measurable degree of uniqueness. The essential fact remains, however, that the cultural traits are attributes of the group, and not that the group is the synthesis of its traits.

What difference does this error make? It warps study both of groups and also of the relations between them. When I first went from Chicago to McGill University, I took with me the conventional notions of studying the assimilation and acculturation (to use both the sociologists' and the anthropologists' lingo) of European immigrants in North America. I looked up all the studies I could find of what was happening to the French Canadians. In the census I sought figures on the number of French Canadians who speak English. Now the assumption was that French Canadians are being gradually assimilated to the English-Canadian culture and world, and that the trait of language was the index thereof. If a French Canadian spoke English, he was presumably less French. It took me a long time to discover that the French Canadian who speaks English best is generally pretty stoutly French in sentiment and way of living, and that sometimes one who speaks but little English has often suffered severe lesions in the integrity of his French culture and loyalty. Eventually I learned that one of the commonest errors of English Canadians is to take the use of English, a tweed coat, or something else considered an expression of Englishness, as evidence that some French Canadian they meet is about to resign from his group. Later, when they discover that he is more French than they have thought, they decide that he has reverted. In fact, the English Canadians have simply learned more about him. A certain withdrawal of cordiality often results. The misunderstanding arises from the error of considering that individual cultural traits are the measure of a man's belonging to an ethnic group, and of the solidarity of the group itself. This error is usually accompanied by the hidden assumption that the individual traits are, or ought to be, disappearing and that one fine day they will be gone—and the French-Canadian people will no longer exist. This is misjudgment, of course, in line with the common tendency to regard one's own group as immortal and the other as relatively a passing thing. It might, incidentally, be interesting to speculate upon what will have become of English Canadians as an ethnic entity by the time French Canadians have disappeared as one.

An additional consequence or expression (I will not try to be too nice about deciding which) of this point of view is the judging of a group's right to exist on the basis of the quality of its cultural peculiarities, called for this purpose "cultural contributions." An English-Canadian teacher of French in a Canadian university used to maintain—in a stout Ontario twang—that since French Canadians had corrupted the French language into a "patois" and since they had made no worthy contributions to French literature and culture, they had no right to hold out from the English-Canadian language and culture. This argument could cut both ways. Whether in the Canadian case it cuts either way is not at issue. Before deciding the case of any people, one would have to agree upon some canons of linguistic and literary aesthetics and upon some standards by which to determine when a contribution to culture has been made. Need I dwell upon the difficulty of getting such agreement from people of two cultures?

Thus far I have myself contributed to another and graver error, that of implying that one can study the relations between groups by analyzing only one of the groups concerned. It takes more than one ethnic group to make ethnic relations. The relations can be no more understood by studying one or the other of the groups than can a chemical combination by study of one element only, or a boxing bout by observation of only one of the fighters. Yet it is common to study ethnic relations as if one had to know only one party to them. Generally the person who studies such relations is a member of one of the groups involved. One might suppose that he would assume that he knows his own group and would therefore study the other.

That is not quite what happens. Most studies turn out to deal with whichever of the groups is considered the minority. The student who is himself of the minority wants to make his group known and appreciated by the dominant group; one who is of the dominant group is likely to assume that he knows his own and that the problem is, after all, one of how the minority will adjust to the dominant group. In conducting a seminar on race and cultural contacts, I have found that the majority of students propose projects that are simply studies of some minority group, with the word *problem* attached: the Nisei problem, the Flemish problem, the French-Canadian problem. In the resulting reports, the dominant group gets off with a drubbing because of its prejudices, although it may be shown that there is hope of a more "liberal" attitude's arising in some hearts. The wounds and virtues of the minority are exposed to view and their relics to veneration. The *relations*, however, are never studied. Since it is generally true that members of a minority have a more lively experience of the dominant group than members of the latter have of the minority, more can perhaps be learned about the inter-group relations by studying the minority than by studying the dominant group. This might give some justification for starting with the minority, but not for leaving the matter there, as is often done. Even that would not be so bad, if the study were pushed into all realms of life and experience, and not limited to political and economic relations. Much is to be learned about intergroup relations by probing to the depths of personal experience, by discovering through what experiences the individual learns both the realities and the fictions of his position as a member of an ethnic group. To what literature can one turn to study this aspect of French-English relations in Canada?

But whether a student studies one or all the groups in a situation— and he should study all—he must study *relations* if that is what he claims he wants to know. If he puts the emphasis on relations, he will find out fairly easily what kind of things he will have to know about the groups themselves in order to understand the relations. He will learn, for instance, that study of folklore, as such, is not study of intergroup relations; but he will also become sensitive to the hints of group loyalty and aggression in tales and songs. He will sit up and listen to a French-Canadian folksong in which, long ago, the rich old man whom the pretty young maid does not want to marry was turned into a *maudit anglais*. He will turn to the folklorist, who will be able to tell him more of the history of the song and who will correct his impressions—as one of the several excellent French-Canadian folklorists will probably do to my interpretation of the above song. He will also learn, however, to discipline his own passion for curio and antique hunting by keeping his eye firmly on the objective of studying relations. He will find his curiosity about both groups greatly enlivened and his eye sharpened, but he will not try to be a specialist in all matters concerning the group and will turn willingly to others for their specialized knowledge.

Now the way to keep this disciplining objective in mind is to start quite consciously with an assumption; namely, that if the groups in question have enough relations to be a nuisance to each other it is because they form a part of a whole, that they are in some sense and in some measure members of the same body. With this idea firmly in mind, one can set about finding out what the whole is and what is the part of each in the whole. In doing this, one will almost certainly not fall into the errors so far considered, and will avoid another one: that of studying only the conscious surface of the relations between groups—their quarrels, opinions, propaganda, and counter-propaganda. Among the respects in which the two groups are parts of a larger whole may be some of which people are not ordinarily aware and of which, if they are aware of them, they do not ordinarily think in ethnic terms at all. This conception will also keep one from thinking that either of the groups has so independent an existence that it could be studied without reference to other groups around it.

Almost anyone will agree that the French-Canadian people has become what it is, not merely by virtue of what its ancestors brought with them from France, but also because of its long contact with Anglo-American life and civilization. I refer not to anglicisms in its speech, its love of baseball, or other English or North American customs which it may have adopted, but to its very peculiarities. French Canada has never had to swallow its own spit. Its balance of population has long been maintained by spilling the excess into a continent until recently thirsty for settlers and industrial labor. Its malcontents and heretics have been able to find companions and a place to exercise their peculiar talents somewhere in North America. How much relief from inner pressure of number and of psychological and social tension French Canada has been afforded by being part of something much larger than herself, no one can say. Nor can I prove, although I think it is so, that the failure of the continent to continue this function of absorption for French Canada is partly responsible for the current brand of more bitter nationalism and nationalist in Quebec.

I stress the functions that the rest of Canada and North America perform for Quebec, not to reinforce any feelings that other Canadians may have about French Canada's debt to the English-speaking world, but to prepare for the kill. There has been some study of the economic, demographic, and political functions of French Canada in the development of Canada as a whole, but not much of her cultural and deeper psychological functions in the development of the rest of the Canadian people. During the war, the two-thirds vote of French-Canadians against conscription served beautifully to obscure the one-third vote of other Canadians against it. In those years, I frequently heard my United States compatriots most unjustly and ignorantly criticize the magnificent Canadian war effort. How often I heard English-Canadians, instead of answering with the eloquent facts, defensively impugn the patriotism of their French-Canadian fellow citizens! The temptation was great. Indeed, the critic often suggested this way out himself, since he usually wanted to think well of the Canadian. Proving oneself a good fellow on the other fellow's terms, however, does not generally increase the other fellow's respect for the group to which one belongs; and in this case it may be doubted whether Canada was well served. The presence of a minority whose sentiments vary from one's own, either in direction or intensity, is a wonderful salve to the conscience. If one wears the salve thickly and conspicuously enough, who shall dare question whether there is really a wound under it? Just what the fact of having always had a minority in its bosom has done to the national conscience and self-consciousness of English Canadians is worth study. I offer this very controversial point, like others in this paper, as bait to those who would explore the full depth and subtlety of the effects upon each other, of two ethnic groups who are parts of a larger whole. Note, too, that in pushing the conception of the relations between two groups so far, we have gone beyond the effort to be merely impartial and just. Impartial judgment implies a standard of justice, legal and moral. This is precisely what two groups are least likely to agree upon, especially in a crisis.

I plead, however, not for less justice of word and action between ethnic groups, races and peoples, but for a more drastically objective, a broader and more penetrating, analysis with which to work.

8

Queries Concerning Industry and Society Growing Out of Study of Ethnic Relations in Industry

A number of sociologists about two decades ago focused their studies of race relations on ethnic divisions of labor found in the colonial regions of the world which capitalistic industry had but recently penetrated.[1] More recently American sociologists have joined in study of race relations in industry in their own country with the aim of learning how we may make fuller use of the American labor force regardless of racial or ethnic distinction. I think it now profitable to draw these two perspectives together; and in so doing, to raise some general questions, not merely about the role of industry in mixing peoples, but concerning the relations between industry and society in various situations. For whenever one scratches a problem of racial and ethnic relations, one uncovers problems concerning society itself; and in this case, concerning industry and society.

First, let me make three sweeping statements which are germane to the whole problem of ethnic relations in industrial economics.

The first is that industry is always and everywhere a grand mixer of peoples. War and trade mix them, too, but chiefly as precursors to the deeper revolutions of work and production in which the more fateful mixing occurs. In no considerable industrial region of the world has an indigenous population supplied the whole working force. Some of it comes from such a distance as to be noticeably different from the local people. The resulting ethnic differences within the industrial population may be small, as between the various parts of Great Britain, or as between Yankees and Southerners in this country; or great, as between Poles, eastern Germans, and western Ger-

Paper read at the annual meeting of the American Sociological Society held in Chicago, December 28–30, 1948. Reprinted by permission of the publisher from the *American Sociological Review*, Vol. 14, April, 1949. Copyright 1949, American Sociological Association.

mans in the Ruhr and Rhineland, or as between English and French-Canadians in Quebec. They may be extreme, as between South African natives and Europeans, or between North Americans and native Indians of Peru. In short, the differences may range in magnitude from those between regions of the same country, through those between different European nationalities, to those between European and non-European, the latter being most extreme when some of the people are of tribal cultures whose institutions of property and work are entirely different from those known in Europe.

Industrial regions vary also as to the positions of local people relative to those of immigrants. At one pole are those regions in which the working force is built around a nucleus of native controlling and technical personnel and skilled workers, and where successive waves of immigrants enter the working force at the bottom of the skill hierarchy. At the other extreme are those regions in which the controlling and highly skilled nucleus goes out to establish industry in a remote, unindustrialized part of the world; the labor is recruited either from a native population, or—and this is common—is imported from still other ethnic areas. It thus may happen that practically the whole industrial personnel is alien to the region, while the various ranks are alien to each other, as in the mines and plantations of the Malay peninsula.

Finally, the industrial regions vary as to the kinds of industrial and social structures which develop and in the degrees of upward mobility possible for various racial and ethnic elements of the working force. Again, at one pole are the somewhat open structures in which there is a theoretical, although practically limited, possibility for a person of any ethnic kind to fill any position; at the other, rigid systems of stratification in which the people of each ethnic group are limited to a narrow range of jobs or ranks. Each of these kinds of variation has its accompaniments in the industrial community, and eventually in the political and social conflicts, alignments, and movements which follow the development of industry.

My second sweeping statement is that modern industry, by virtue of being the great mixer, has inevitably been a colossal agent of racial, ethnic, and religious segregation. For segregation, if it means something more than that isolation in which the peculiarities of race and culture develop, refers to some degree of functional separation of different kinds of people within a common system. Industry brings people together and sorts them out for various kinds of work; the sorting will, where the mixture is new, of necessity follow racial and ethnic lines. For cultures (and when races first meet they are always unlike in culture) differ in nothing more than in the skills, work habits, and goals which they instill into the individual. These differences may tend to disappear in the course of industrial experience, although segregation may tend to keep them alive in some modified form for a long time. At any rate, there is not yet—even among the older industrial regions, where ethnic differences have been reduced by common experience and intermarriage—one in which one may not discern some deviation from chance expectation in the distribution of ethnic and religious groups among the various kinds of work and the several ranks of industrial organizations.[2]

The third of the sweeping statements is that industry is almost universally an agent of racial and ethnic discrimination. There is no question about it if we take the word discrimination in its basic sense of the action of making distinctions. For those who hire industrial help must nearly always choose from among people who are not all alike ethnically, and very often from among ethnic groups whose industrial experience and training are far from equal. Furthermore, when industry actively seeks labor from new sources, it generally has to make an ethnic choice.

In sociological language, discrimination has taken another meaning: that those who pick people for jobs consider, intentionally or unwittingly, traits not directly relevant to work. If we accept this meaning, industry is still almost universally an agent of ethnic discrimination. In all industrial regions, again including the oldest, there is current among managers, foremen, and industrial workers a body of opinion and lore concerning the work capacities and habits of various ethnic groups. Insofar as such belief and lore do not correspond to verifiable fact, they point to discrimination. Certainly they hinder clear perception of the differences between individuals of a given ethnic or racial group. In some industrial regions, discrimination is openly defended; in a few, enforced by law.

We have defined industrial segregation as deviation from chance in the distribution of people of various ethnic groups among the positions in industry. Discrimination we have defined as consideration of racial, ethnic, or religious traits in selection of workers even when the traits are not known to be relevant to work behavior. But segregation is not of itself evidence of discrimination. For there are undoubtedly cases in which even the most objective and sharp selection of workers by known or probable work performance would result in racial and ethnic segregation. On the other hand, we do not know how long it would take, under an aggressively objective policy, for all racial and ethnic disparities in job distribution to disappear. The truth is that no one has worked out a statistical device for establishing the existence or degree of ethnic discrimination. It would be very difficult to do so. For a given organization may have a great variety of jobs and positions, each of which has its own complex of activities and skills, and consequently of required training and experience. The positions have each their own rate of turnover, so that they vary in their sensitivity to ethnic change in the labor supply. Past discrimination leaves its mark in varying degree and for varying length of time. But the lack of such an index need not worry students of the problem unduly. For discrimination is generally admitted, although it may be called by other names when discrimination becomes a bad word. In fact, the evidence of recent studies indicates that at least an unconscious discrimination tends to permeate industrial organizations even in the rare moments when conscious effort is made to avoid it.

It is an interesting and apparently paradoxical observation that modern capitalistic industry, which has developed a strong, sometimes ruthless, ideology of indifference to persons, of choice of the best article for the purpose, and of the best man for the job, and which has shown a great drive, almost a mission, to sweep away beliefs, customs, and institutions which stand in the way of industrial development, should also have become not merely—as one might have expected—an aggressive and grandiose mixer of peoples, but also a great and sometimes stubborn agent of racial and ethnic discrimination and a breeder of racial doctrines and stereotypes. This raises the general question whether and under what circumstances modern industry is really guided by the impersonal concepts of the market and efficiency in choosing and assigning its labor force.

Another tenet of the ideology of modern industrial management has been that all barriers to free movement of labor should be removed in the interest of its economic use. This appeared in the movement to remove restrictions against internal migration in the early days of the industrial revolution in Europe, and in the insistence on treating each worker as an individual whose employment could be terminated at will by either party without interference of any third party. With reference to this tenet we may ask: To what extent and under what circumstances *does* industry rely on purely economic means and incentives applied to freely moving individuals to get and keep a labor supply, and under what circumstances does it use or encourage essentially political means, such as restriction of movement, fixed terms of employment, or differential rules governing the movement and activities of certain categories of people? There are other questions like these concerning the behavior of industrial management in various social settings. I believe it one of the major tasks of people interested in a sociological view of industry to seek the answers to these questions, and that the way to do it is to compare the ways of industry in a variety of settings, including a variety of interracial and interethnic settings.

A first and evident comparison is that between the mother countries of modern technology and industrial institutions, including their closer satellites, and the outlying, newer industrial regions which we may call colonial, whether they are so in a political sense or not.

In the mother countries (England, Belgium, Holland, Germany, parts of other western European countries, and North America), those who manage industry and perform its higher technical functions are native, as are also the central core of skilled workers. At least, they are native to this general area and feel themselves at home in it. Even within these areas, however, managers and technicians may be ethnically somewhat strange to the particular smaller regions in which they work. Many of the founders, engineers, and skilled workers of the early industries in the German Ruhr came from Britain and Belgium, where coal mining and the iron industry had first developed machinery. It was not long, however, before Germany could supply such people in number sufficient for her own industry and for export.

There has been a constant flow of managers, accountants, engineers, and skilled workers from these mother countries to the outlying newly industrialized regions of the Western world itself, as well as to the colonial regions. This movement takes them, and the industries they operate, into regions where they are ethnically strange enough for it to be remarked by themselves and by the native population. Examples are the central and eastern countries of Europe, the French parts of Canada, and even our Southern states. As the prime movers of industry get out into the less industrially minded parts of the Western world, one begins to hear from them those impatient complaints about the perversity of local institutions and people which they utter more or less openly in colonial regions.

In the older industrial regions of the mother country the rank and file working force was generally built around a nucleus of people native to the region and of the same ethnic kind as management. But as industry grew, large and long-continued internal migration and immigration from other countries were necessary to keep up and expand the working force. The consequent ethnic differences are of the order of national differences within the European world. Of the mother countries, only the United States has recruited a sizable part of its labor from outside the European cultures and races. Such people,

Negroes, Orientals, and Latin American mestizos, were generally brought here as labor, not for manufacturing but for industrial agriculture and construction work, just as in the colonial areas. It has been only after a long experience in the Euro-American culture and economy, and usually after turnover of generations that people of other than European ancestry have found their way into the labor force of American manufacturing industry. In spite of these facts, the ethnic differences show up in the strata of power, skill, and prestige in industrial organizations in all Western countries. To the extent that they do not, it seems to be because the ethnic differences have, in effect, ceased to exist.

Now these mother countries of modern industry all have open social-class systems and social ladders of a similar kind. Social mobility is part of their philosophy. The Western communities in which industry is established generally have landed, commercial, and professional middle classes who, being accustomed to prestige and power, may be jealous of the new leaders of industry. This jealousy is perhaps more apparent when the new leaders of industry differ ethnically from the local middle class. On the other hand, the latter often encourage the coming of industry, and seek to take advantage of it by speculating in land for industrial sites, and by building new houses or businesses which, they hope, will be patronized by the incoming industrial population. In any case, some combination of cooperation and antagonism of local middle-class people with the leaders of industry develops; this becomes a major theme of politics. To it is added the politics of labor, as the industrial working force takes form and becomes defined in its own eyes and those of management and the local nonindustrial middle class. Some of the workers, whether native or immigrant, will try to rise in the industrial structure; their success or failure will almost certainly become symbolically important to the workers at large. If it be failure, the flames of ethnic consciousness will be fanned thereby, and local politics will reflect the fire. There may develop a labor movement which defines its enemy, management, in racial or ethnic terms, and which may, at the same time, endeavor to keep out workers of other ethnic or racial kinds. Since these are areas in which all, or nearly all, classes of people are accustomed to take some part in politics, and therefore may be quickly mobilized against industry, management cannot ignore local politics. The various political alignments which develop in such industrial communities, and the circumstances which change them have been talked of, and have, in a few cases, been described and analyzed.[3] There is need of systematic comparison of them in a variety of situations.

Although it must reckon with unfavorable alignments and opposition, industry can count on finding in the Western world the basic matrix of law, institutions, and ideologies in which the special institutions of capitalistic industry grew up. I think it a fair generalization that in the mother countries, industry prefers as little interference of government as possible, excepting only use of the police power to protect their "property" and "right to operate," and of legislation to protect markets. In such countries, industry is, as a rule, against attempts to restrict the flow of labor into and out of the region. An exception appears in marginal areas which share some of the characteristics of the colonial world; such as in the southern United States, where an industrial agriculture had developed slavery and when that was abolished, other devices for holding people to their jobs—a pattern taken over to some extent by early manufacturing industries in the region.

At the opposite pole from the Western mother countries of modern industry stand the colonial areas of the world,[4] whither men of European extraction have gone or sent their agents to gather and fetch to world markets vegetable and mineral products wanted for consumption or manufacture in the industrial mother countries. The first capitalistic industrial enterprises in such regions are usually plantations or mines, which marshal large numbers of people to labor under what is to them an alien system.

Often not enough native people can be immediately recruited to meet the newcomers' demand; in this case, laborers may be imported under indenture or contract from some other nonindustrial, non-European country; generally, the imported labor has come from among the nontribal peoples of Asia where large masses of landless people accustomed to wage-work are willing to hire themselves out for a period of years without hope of advancement. When their terms of work are up, they often go into small trading or commercial farming. They thus become a middle caste of small entrepreneurs, as have the Chinese in the East Indies and the East Indians in South Africa.

The natives themselves are often not accustomed to individual wage-work, at least as a continued and sole means of getting a living. They may have worked only as members of communities, their tasks and their rewards determined by their places in a social system. Hence they are not always willing to work for long periods, if at all, in the new enterprises. In such case the political force of the colonial power is used to recruit and hold workers. A head-tax payable in money of the new system may be used to compel families, tribes, and communities to send out members to work for a time. Penal sanctions may be applied to those who leave jobs. Restrictions on movement in and out of the district and earlier, colonial chattel slavery served the same end.[5] In short, the usual economic incentives do not bring in a labor supply. Industry departs from its mother country practice of encouraging free movement of labor, and uses the police power instead. The problem of early industry in England was to make the people free to move from parish to parish so that they might be available to industry; one could assume that the poor would use the freedom in a way profitable to industry. In colonial regions, that assumption proves not true, and there is a complete reversal of tactic.

This raises the whole question of the relation of industry to the law, institutions, and mores of the communities and regions where it establishes enterprises. In the Western world the representatives of industry claim to believe in as little government as possible, and generally claim to respect the mores, religion, and social beliefs of the communities in which they operate. Indeed, local custom and belief are often pled by industrial management as their reason for racial and ethnic discrimination and segregation. On the other hand, industry has eaten away at many customs and beliefs by its very insistence on continuous operation. But, in the main, the law, sentiments, and symbols of the community are essentially those of the leaders of industry themselves. In the purely colonial regions, they are not. Local institutions and law may not allow for the kind of organization that industry regards essential to its operation; and the policing power may be neither strong enough nor properly minded to support industry. The evidence from colonial situations makes it appear that where the local legal and institutional framework stands in the way, industry is prepared to modify it as much as need be. This it does by support of imperial interference with local authority. An additional means is the establishment of separate industrial communities in which industry and its representatives exercise political and police functions over their employees: thus the familiar colonial institutions of the labor compound, the plantation, and that institution of areas marginal to the colonial world, the company town. One of our tasks should be the close analysis of the behavior of industrial management toward local law, institutions, and beliefs in a whole series of situations, from those in which local society is apparently most favorable to industry to those in which it is least favorable. At the colonial pole we get evidence of a belief in the divine right of industry to modify any society as much as need be to allow it to exploit local markets, resources, and labor; perhaps it is undertaken with the least pang when the local people and culture are of some kind with whom industrial managers feel little human identification. This is one meaning of the "white man's burden."

On the other hand, it may turn out that industry will lose its sense of identification with the law, institutions, and people of an older industrial community if they develop in a way unfavorable to industry beyond some point of tolerance. It is possible that law, institutions, and sentiments are most favorable to industry in Western communities with well-developed concepts of the law relating to property, organization of voluntary corporations, free individual contract, and the like, but not yet highly nor long industrialized—communities still virgin, but ripe for willing embrace.

To resume our comparison, as a result of the importation of labor from other regions, the industrial hierarchy in colonial areas often consists of several ethnic groups, each of which performs some rather distinct function.[6] The new recruits of each group come into the structure at a given level and tend to remain there. There is no ladder of promotion by small rungs from the bottom to the top of the structure. Mobility tends to occur mainly by leaving the industrial organization for some new commercial or service function brought into being by the social revolution accompanying the growth of the new economic system. There is almost complete absence of the kind of industrial mobility which is so strong in the ideology of industry in the Western countries.

A related feature of the colonial regions, well described by J. H. Boeke in his works on the Dutch East Indies, is that the native labor is for a long time only halfway in the new system. When not working in it for wages, they are absorbed again and kept by the familial, tribal, or village societies to which they still belong. In course of time, the power of the native society and economy to reabsorb the industrial workers declines, through loss of land to the new system of things or through pressure of population. At the same time, some of the natives become so weaned from their mother culture as to have no wish to return to it. Their goals are already turned toward the new life. Thus there grows up a group of people who are completely dependent upon the new industrial system, people who—when not working for wages—must now be considered the unemployed of the new system. Such people are inclined to become discontent, to demand a new and higher scale of wages so that they can buy the consumer's goods of the new system, and even to demand that they be allowed to climb higher in the industrial hierarchy.[7]

A similar cycle occurs even in the mother countries of industry when people of "backward" rural regional or ethnic elements are drawn into the less-skilled jobs of industry in times of acute labor shortage. We have seen it in the United States in the case of the rural Southern people, both Negro and white; and in Canada, in the case of "backwoods" people from Quebec and the Maritime provinces. It is a process which contains the problem of hidden social subsidies to industry, and the question whether industry can maintain the level of profit which it has come to expect when all such hidden subsidy has wasted away and the population must be kept from industrial income even when not working for industry.

In the colonial regions, there is either no middle class of natives in the European sense (South Africa), or the middle class (as in India or China) is far removed from any place in industry of control over it. The middle classes may pick up some crumbs of prosperity or power from the presence of the new economic order, or they may be threatened and destroyed by it. In either case, they may be without political power. The masses are at first politically inactive, but may begin showing signs of forming new groups, of a feeling of nationality where once there had been only tribal or village solidarity. A new nationalism may arise, and economic and ethnic unrest may be joined in it. Hence that confusion of racial and class conflict so common in the colonial areas of the world.

Within industry itself, one finds in these colonial areas almost no admission of the native population to the inner and higher positions of prestige and control. The tendency to exclusion of ethnically alien elements is here seen in its extreme; or perhaps it is only more visible because of race and the sharp cultural distinctions between the working many and the managing few. Where this line of effective exclusion is drawn depends upon circumstances and upon the nature of the industry. In South African mining, white men came from England to do the skilled work at first; now that a native labor force which could do the work has been developed, the politically active white men use the full power of the state and racial solidarity to preserve their own monopoly. The line is held at the gate to skilled work; industry puts up with it at great cost. In other cases the line is drawn at supervision and authority. In others, the main concern is to keep merely the higher control of policy and money in the hands of representatives of the dominant, European group.

Here we meet that peculiar phenomenon, the straw boss, and can see his essential function. A native is given supervision over native workers; or a person of some ethnic group alien both to management and the mass of the workers is given this function. The notion is that such a person will know the peculiar ways of the workers, and will deal with them accordingly. He is a liaison man, a go-between. And wherever there are workers of some kind extremely alien to industry and to the managers of industry, someone is given this function. He documents, in effect, the gap between the higher positions and the lower; and symbolizes the fact that there is no easy ladder of mobility from the lower position to the higher. He may be literally bilingual, transmitting the orders given in the European tongue into some vernacular; he is also bilingual in a broader figurative sense. He understands the language—the symbols and meanings—of the industrial world, and translates it into symbols which have meaning to people from another culture, who live in a different set of life-chances. And here we can begin to push harder toward comparison of the mother countries of industry and the colonial industrial regions. In the latter, the straw boss symbolizes limited mobility. He is himself mobile, and ambitious. But the nature of his job rests on the lack of mobility of the masses. In the mother countries, the straw boss turns up, too. He is found wherever some new and strange element is introduced into the labor force in number. The Negro personnel man is one of the latest straw bosses; he acts as a liaison man between management and Negro help. He cannot himself be considered a candidate for any higher position or for any line position in industry; his is a staff position which exists only so long as Negroes are hired in fairly large numbers, and so long as Negro help is considered sufficiently different from other help to require special liaison. If the race line disappeared, or tended to disappear in industry, there would be no need of the Negro personnel man. There might be personnel men who are Negroes. Thus, the Negro personnel man is performing a racial function; he is not part of the regular line of authority, and does not represent a rung in the ladder of regular advancement to higher positions. Industrial organizations in the colonial regions abound in such liaison positions. Just what such positions are, the features of social and industrial organization which they reflect, and the kinds of persons who fill them are all matters whose further analysis would throw light on the nature and internal functioning of industrial organization. It is but one of the several features which appear in clear form in colonial industry, but which may also exist, although commonly overlooked, in the industry of the mother countries.

Now these considerations of structure and mobility again raise questions concerning the fundamental ideology of industry. For industry in the Western world promoted an ideology of mobility, that is, of ambition. In the colonial world, ambition is often regarded as unjustified and dangerous. Even in the Western world, managers speak with nostalgia of the unambitious first generation of Poles, French Canadians, or peasant workers of other ethnic groups; people who were content with their jobs, willing to work hard without hope of advancement. Of course, such people often had objectives outside industry to keep them at work and content; notably, the desire to save money for buying property. In spirit, they were not completely industrialized. A second or later generation which insists on advancement within industry is compared unfavorably with their fathers. The hostile reaction of many managers to ambitious Negroes is too well known to require documenting.

Here is apparently a contradiction: Industry encourages ambition, and complains a good deal about lack of it. On the other hand, it praises some people for not having it, and complains of others who do. This raises another general question: Just how much ambition does an industrial organization want and in how many people and in what kinds of people does it want it? In the colonial world, there is generally a limit on the possibilities of promotion for persons of each ethnic category, although this may change through time. For certain kinds of work, it may actually be to the advantage of industry to hire only people whose ambitions are directed to goals completely outside the industrial system. For others, they may want ambitious people. There may, however, be some balance between the proportion of ambitious and unambitious people which works best even in the oldest of the industrial regions. A clue appears in a phrase current in a large concern in this country. They have a breed known as the "Thank God for" people; the unambitious people who can be counted on to stay where they are, and who keep things running while others are busy climbing the mobility ladder from one job to another. Analysis might show that in the mother countries of industry some adjustment between symbol and reality has occurred, so that a large proportion of workers may give lip service to the mobility ideal, but not too many take it seriously.

Just what proportion of ambitious workers industrial organizations of various kinds can tolerate is a question which merits comparative analysis, although it may be difficult to make the necessary observations in a society where people generally claim to believe in ambition and to be ashamed of lack of it. In colonial regions, the talk on the subject is often franker.

I have already noted that ethnic exclusiveness tends to develop at all levels of colonial industrial hierarchies. The dominant managerial and technical functions remain pretty much in the hands of the founding ethnic group. Sometimes a European group of skilled workers, as in South African mines, holds to its level of jobs and succeeds in excluding the natives. In the less-skilled jobs, some group of natives may manage to keep out others. Even in American industry, such a tendency shows clearly. A number of forces play upon hiring and selection to reinforce or to break up this tendency. If I were to venture a hypothesis it would be something like this: the tendency to exclusiveness is present in all organizations, and in the segments thereof, but the power to maintain it varies. In industry, the necessity of keeping a full labor force operates against exclusiveness in those categories where large numbers are required; generally, the lower levels of skill. The people at these levels have little or no formal power of hiring. They have, in varying degree, informal power of selection and rejection.

The people in the higher levels of the hierarchy have the power to keep their own ranks ethnically exclusive. In the colonial or semicolonial industrial regions, management often quite frankly talks of the necessity of keeping management in loyal h–nds; that is, in the hands of people closely identified with one another by national sentiment as well as by general cultural background. In the mother countries of industry, one does not hear such talk, but it is possible that the mechanism operates without people being aware of it. It may operate through the mechanism of sponsoring, by which promising young people are picked and encouraged in their mobility efforts by their superiors. In the course of their rise, they are not merely given a technical training, but also are initiated into the ways and sentiments of the managerial group and are judged by their internal acceptance of them. Ethnic, national, and class loyalty are undoubtedly factors in the original choice of people to be sponsored and in their later rise. In the Western world individuals ethnically different from those at the top of management may be drawn into the sponsorship circle, but in the course of it effectively lose all symbols of identification with the ethnic group from which they have come and take on those of the receiving group. Where skin color and other racial features are involved, this is not so easy to do. Thus, while modern industry is opposed to nepotism, as contrary to the best choice of people in an open market, as an operating organization it tends to hold power in the hands of a group whose new members are picked from among people thought to be loyal not merely to the particular organization but to the management class and its culture. In the selection and sponsoring process ethnic background plays a large part.

The sponsoring power of lower ranks may be less, but is by no means completely lacking in many situations. Coal miners and railroad workers notoriously have great sponsoring power. And even in the colonial regions the members of an ethnic group or clan, or the inhabitants of a village, may have, in effect, the power to recruit new workers. In a sense, when industry brings in some new ethnic group it has to do it in opposition to the present workers. The actual ethnic composition and changes therein seem then to be a resultant of the operation of demand for new help against the exclusive tendencies of the various segments of the existing working organization. The search of modern industry for new help that can be used with profit has certainly been active and persistent. On the other hand, for a given kind or level of job, the field in which the search is made may be limited by management's own state of knowledge and sentiments. Certainly the evidence is clear that in the colonial regions, and to some extent in the mother countries, there grows up a body of belief about the special working qualities of various ethnic groups. These stereotypes, which may or may not correspond to the facts, act to limit the vision of those who select help and who initiate sponsorship. In a sense, this is like any marketing situation, in that the bargaining of the marketer is limited by his own knowledge and sentiments. The role of sentiments is, however, made somewhat stronger in the hiring and utilization of human labor than in the buying and selling of inanimate commodities by the fact that the human labor is, so to speak, consumed by industry. Industry is not a labor broker, for it uses the labor to build a continuing organization for work; it must live with its laboring people. And in the course of working together the social and political processes get under way as they do in any organization. Industry thus considers its people not merely as technical help, but as actual or potential participants in a struggle for power within industry and society, and as potential close colleagues (or as unfit to be such). When one takes these points into account, many of the contradictions and paradoxes in the behavior of industrial management and workers begin to move toward possible solution. A complete resolution of them might be approached by systematic comparison of the various situations in which industry has operated. I suspect that in such comparison racial and ethnic differences will act as a sort of litmus paper to bring out characteristics and processes which might otherwise be overlooked.

Notes

1. See E. B. Reuter (editor), *Race and Culture Contacts* (New York: McGraw-Hill Co., 1934), in which papers of the 1933 meeting of the American Sociological Society

appear; especially R. D. McKenzie, "Industrial Expansion and the Interrelations of Peoples," and R. E. Park, "Race Relations and Certain Frontiers." See also McKenzie, "Cultural and Racial Differences as Bases for Human Symbiosis," in Kimball Young, *Social Attitudes* (New York: Henry Holt, 1931). For still earlier work on the problem see Sidney Olivier, *White Capital and Coloured Labour* (London, 1906) and *The Anatomy of African Misery* (London, 1927); James Bryce, *The Relations between the Advanced and the Backward Races of Mankind* (London, 1902).

2. This is so obviously true in North America as to need no proof. For evidence concerning western Germany see: Wilhelm Brepohl, *Der Aufbau des Ruhrvolkes in Zuge der Ost-West-Wanderung* (Recklinghausen, Bitter & Co., 1948), Everett C. Hughes, "The Industrial Revolution and the Catholic Movement in Germany," *Social Forces*, XIV (Dec., 1935). There are marked differences between the positions of Flemings and Walloons in Belgium; Protestant and Catholic in Holland; Flemings, Italians, etc., and French in France. It is commonly said that such differences of distribution still exist as between Welsh, Scotch, Irish, and English of various regions of the British Isles.

3. E.g., W. L. Warner and J. O. Low, *The Social System of the Modern Factory* (New Haven: Yale University Press, 1947).

4. For a general definition of colonial status see Raymond Kennedy, "The Colonial Crisis and the Future," in R. Linton, *The Science of Man in the World Crisis* (New York: Columbia University Press, 1945). He notes that Japan is (or was) the one non-European nation to have developed modern political and economic colonies, and that these colonies showed the essential features of colonies of European countries.

5. For material on this subject see: J. H. Boeke, *The Structure of the Netherlands Indian Economy*, New York: Institute of Pacific Relations, 1942; John A. Noon, *Labor Problems of Africa*, Philadelphia: University of Pennsylvania Press, 1944; Sheila van der Horst, *Native Labor in South Africa*, London: Oxford University Press, 1942; Sydney Olivier, *White Capital and Coloured Labour* (London: The Hogarth Press, 1929), and *The Anatomy of African Misery* (London: L. & V. Woolf, 1927).

6. R. D. McKenzie, "Cultural and Racial Difference as Bases of Human Symbiosis," Amos H. Hawley (ed.) *Roderick D. McKenzie on Human Ecology,* Chicago: University of Chicago Press, 1968: pp. 170–201.

7. For one of the best analyses of this process see A. W. Lind, *Economic Succession and Racial Invasion in Hawaii,* University of Chicago Libraries, 1936. In this work (p. 404) is the following passage: "The process by which Hawaii imports large numbers of unskilled laborers from various sections of the globe, exploits their labor power for a few years on the sugar and pineapple plantations, and at the same time initiates them into the great American scramble for a place at the top of the economic ladder, is apparently irreversible and is cumulative in its exactions upon the existing economy and culture. Each new generation of plantation workers occasions an addition to the surplus of competitors for the preferred positions within the system, not alone by graduation of the majority of its number to the ranks of nonplantation pursuits, but even more by the creation of a second generation even more thoroughly inoculated with the American success virus." See also his *An Island Community: Ecological Succession in Hawaii,* Chicago: University of Chicago Press, 1938.

9

Race Relations in Industry

One of the many dramas of modern industry is that of the meeting and of the working together of people unlike each other in race, nationality, and religion. Wherever it has gone—and industry is always moving into new parts of the world—it has put some new combination of the peoples of the earth at work together. The industrial revolution in England mixed the peoples of the South with those of the North and Irishmen with Englishmen. The Protestants of North Germany established industries in the Rhine; Catholic peasants of the region came to work in them. In the cotton mills of India, Hindus of various castes are herded together with their fellow Indians of other religions. Chinese city workers, driven from the urban East to the rural interior of their country by the Japanese invasion, even now find themselves making electrical equipment for war alongside rustics, also Chinese, who speak strange dialects and who until yesterday knew no tools more complicated than the sickle and the hammer.[1]

In our own country, immigrants from the back provinces of all the countries of Europe have met each other in the steel mill, the mine, the packing house, and in the loft where ladies' handkerchiefs are made. Recently, they have been joined by a new wave of rural Americans, some of them as uninitiated to industry as any European peasant who ever landed on Ellis Island, but English of tongue, bred in the most indigenous American traditions of religion, folklore, humor, fighting, and rugged individualism, and physically of the purest Anglo-Saxon stock, or of one of the combinations of African with Indian, Spanish, French, or Anglo-Saxon that we call "Negro" in this country.

Although each of the combinations of peoples thus brought together is unique, there is likeness in their meeting and its consequences. Wherever strange peoples have met to work in industry, some have been more initiated in its ways and have possessed more tools and technical knowledge than others. The new have always had to learn not merely how to use their hands and heads at new tasks

Reprinted by permission of William Foote Whyte from *Industry and Society*, edited by William Foote Whyte, McGraw Hill, New York, 1946.

but also how to live by a new calendar and by the clock, how to deal with new kinds of people in unaccustomed relations to each other, how to use money as their main source of income, and how to order their lives to a new set of contingencies. In nearly all cases, those older and better placed in industry have attributed the newcomers' lack of skill and of the industrial frame of mind to their inherent nature, without being too clear as to whether this nature is a matter of genes or of nurture. The newcomers sooner or later reorganize their ways and their wishes about the new order of things, and become aware of the opinions that their industrial superiors, both workers and employers, have of them. A difference of industrial status that they once accepted as in the nature of things they now question. They speak of discrimination. They act as self-conscious minorities, discontented with their status, always act. To compare these processes, as they have occurred in various places and with various human ingredients, is an intriguing enterprise. We leave it for another day, reminding ourselves only that the races, the nations, and the religions have met again and again in industry, that they will so meet again and again; that they can and do work together, although not always in harmony; and that the groups now oldest in industry learned their industrial lessons from ethnic strangers who considered them poor pupils until they became effective competitors or respected fellow workers. Thus do race relations in industry look in the worldwide, generations-long perspective.

Our special concern, however, is with the relations of Negroes with other persons in American industry at the present time. This requires other perspectives. For, while the Negroes are presently in a phase through which numerous other groups have passed, their situation in American life is unique. It is so in this respect, that the relations of Negro to white Americans have been crystallized into a body of practice enforced upon both races, but more especially upon the Negro, by social pressure, economic sanction, and even by physical force. White Americans have elaborated and then worked deep into their very bones a body of belief about what Negroes are and ought to be like, as well as a complex of fears of what would happen if the practices and beliefs were to change.

Beliefs and fears concerning the Negro as an economic being are interwoven with those concerning him as a citizen, neighbor, and companion. In white American thought, furthermore, strong belief that the Negro is different from other kinds of people is mixed in about equal proportions with fear that he is just like the rest of us. And here lies the essence of the race problem in America; we fear in the Negro those very human qualities that American social philosophy encourages in others. We stubbornly wish that the Negro should be unique. Race relations in American industry must be seen from this perspective also. The danger, however, is not that we should overlook the uniqueness of the relations between Negro and white Americans but that we should magnify it. We cannot avoid the race problem in this country, although many people, especially in the North, would like to. All of us, Negro and white, are a part of the problem. It therefore behooves us to act as intelligently as possible. To do so, we must balance the unique features of the problem against its many likenesses with others. And we must see race relations in all the social matrices in which they occur.

One such matrix is industrial organization, considered as a system of human relations. And if I may present the conclusion of this chapter so near its beginning, that conclusion is not much more than the statement that "in industry" is the important term in the phrase, "race relations in industry." To know about race relations in industry, and to deal with them, one must look upon them as being of the same general order as other relations of people at work, requiring the same kinds of thinking and analysis, demanding the same understanding and skills; and, on the other hand, as little capable of settlement, once and for all, by some sleight-of-hand trick as other human problems in industry, and yet as amenable as others to those tentative, constantly repeated, never perfect, but often successful, decisions and actions by which a working organization is kept going to the moderate satisfaction of most people concerned.

The preceding chapters have presented a way of looking at industrial organization and at human behavior within it. Mr. Gardner gave us the important idea of an informal organization that can be discovered in each case only by close observation made with fundamental concepts in mind. Mr. Warner has shown how industry interacts with the community. Mr. Davis has talked of the life objectives that lead people to work and to have certain attitudes toward their jobs. Analysis of this kind may be applied to race relations in industry. Such analysis, stubbornly continued and applied to a variety of situations, will lead to a better understanding not only of the race problem but also of industrial behavior in general. For what the introduction of a minority into an industry does is to throw into bold silhouette those very features of industrial organization and behavior with which these chapters have been concerned.

Perhaps the best answer to the question, "What is a minority in industry?" is this: if the hiring of persons of a certain kind in an industry, plant, or job is *news*, then that group is a minority. I refer, of course, not to the mild interest created by the coming into the shop of a strange individual or by the promotion of a person long known, but to the much more lively disturbance created by the hiring of workers of a strange category or by the promotion of individuals of a class hitherto limited to certain positions.

By this criterion, women and certain ethnic groups are minorities in industry. Negroes especially are a minority. For their appearance, like a good front-page story in the newspaper, furnishes the talking point for the day and not for the day alone. It causes people to talk, to listen, and to make dramatic gestures of alarm. Everyone recognizes that the decision behind the change is one of policy, very consciously made in the councils of management. The ensuing discussion will treat of the effects of the change on the labor market, postwar unemployment, seniority, and unions. But there will also be talk of things generally thought to be of less import and less related to what are claimed to be the main concerns of labor and management: such as washrooms, lockers, eating facilities, employees' sports and parties, including what to do about the shower to be held for the popular employee who is about to leave to have a baby. The people in the upper regions of management will be heard speculating upon the probable reactions of the humble janitress who will have to clean up washbasins used by the Negro employees. In short, the whole human side of the organization comes to life and to view. Relationships ordinarily unnoticed or even denied are consciously taken into account.

The emphasis upon informal relationships and what are ordinarily considered incidental matters appears not only at the moment when Negroes are introduced into a plant. Later on, managers, personnel men, and union officials attribute their success in integrating Negroes into their organizations to skillful manipulation not of the organization chart but of small groups and cliques and of the sentiments of the workers. A union official tells of setting the stage so that the hiring of Negroes may be defined as a victory for the union, thereby gaining support the members would otherwise have withheld. One company prides itself on having placed its first Negroes in the employment office for all to see, thus forestalling the criticism that the front-office staff was willing to give the shop hands Negro fellow workers but wouldn't have any themselves. Another placed a few on the periphery of a department where trouble was expected and let workers get used to having them around before moving them directly into the department. Others speak of hand-picking their first Negro employees, not so much for their efficiency as to convince fellow workers that Negroes can be intelligent, good looking, and "nice." Other employers, more jealous of their authority, and certainly not very pleased at the idea of hiring Negroes, admit that they did not succeed in getting the white workers to accept them. Indeed, the admission sometimes becomes almost a boast that hell, high water, and the Fair Employment Practices Committee combined couldn't make them do more than make a few defeatist gestures toward employing and promoting Negroes. Even this boastful admission contains the thought that success would require skillful handling of sentiments and the informal organization, rather than merely stronger use of the power to command.

These statements, and the legion of others like them, imply not merely that the informal organization exists as a possible aid or hindrance to the hiring of minority workers, but that this organization is something that can be and sometimes is consciously manipulated. From the fact that such manipulation is possible, people sometimes draw the unwarranted conclusion that the informal organization of workers and the sentiments expressed in their words and action are factors of little account. The facts point to the opposite conclusion, namely, that the manipulation is successful only to the extent that the informal organization and the sentiments of the workers are understood. To understand is not, however, to yield. All in all, it looks as if the greatest success in employing Negro workers has been achieved by a joining of understanding with firm and bold experimental action at the beginning and in the crises that arise later.

But how, in fact, do workers react to the coming of Negroes into their midst, and how does the informal organization operate? Let some examples speak. In a certain plant, Negroes were first hired in a department that, though dirty and smelly and without prestige, has a very stable working force. The men in it, mostly elderly Poles, work in groups of three that produce as units and are so paid as to make treamwork the key to a good income. It was thought that these men would not have much prejudice and that the isolation of the department would allow the hiring of Negroes without much comment. Of several Negro men hired, none stayed more than a few days. The management was disturbed, for it thought that the Negroes were confirming the common opinion that they are unreliable. Interviews with these Negro men brought out a consistent and simple story. The workers in the department had practiced every obvious and subtle art to let the newcomers know that they were not wanted and would never learn (i.e., be taught) the work. Upon hearing all this an aged member of the management, now retired, snorted that no one had ever succeeded in forty years in putting into that department any new man not chosen by the men already there. In this rather extreme case appear two factors: (1) the attitude of the men to the Negro newcomers, and (2) what we may call the molecular structure of their organization. We may leave the first with the remark that all the evidence in the case indicates that those men had no great prejudice toward Negroes as such, but that they had an ingrained suspicion of newcomers. On the second point, it is clear that formal admission of this shop meant nothing without informal admission to one of the work teams.

Now the organization of this particular shop was unusually close grained. The power of each little work team to accept or reject a new worker was much greater than common. Instruction in the job was entirely in their hands. Another shop that we have examined is much more open. Each girl works on her own machine, so that her production does not mechanically depend upon that of another. In this situation it is hard to see how the older girls could prevent the new one from making her quota, and there is no reason to believe that they try. But it is a rare job that is not learned more quickly and satisfactorily if one gets pointers from fellow workers. It is doubtful whether any job, no matter how well organized the formal instruction for it may be, is learned entirely without such aid. The diaries of our fieldworkers are full of this theme. Of course, the instruction given the new worker is not confined to pointers on bettering his production; it includes devices for resisting pressure from management and the workers' own rules for dealing with one another. In fact, what the new worker gets—or does not get—from his fellows is an initiation rather than mere instruction. While he is being initiated, he is also being tried out to see what sort of fellow worker he will be. The place he is to have in the organization is being determined at the same time. What his job will mean to him will depend, in a degree that varies with his personality and objectives, on this place. His performance as well will probably depend upon it. Elton Mayo and his associates have recently found that, in an aircraft plant on the West Coast, absences and turnover are much less frequent among men who are members of a work team with some group solidarity.[2]

Our findings suggest that Negroes are not generally initiated into existing teams and cliques of white workers. Occasionally we learn of such cases as that of a white group leader of southern extraction, who, being anxious to keep a good gang together in an unstable shipyard and finding that a Negro welder was a good and agreeable worker, invites the Negro to eat with the white group in order to be sure of keeping him. Individual Negroes are sometimes accepted as good fellows, although the price may be that they allow themselves to be considered exceptions, different from and superior to the common run of Negroes; a definition intended to be flattering to the individual, but derogatory of Negroes as a group. Sometimes, the initiation of the Negro includes a trying out of horseplay and nicknames on him, putting him in the dilemma of accepting the role of a comic inferior or of resisting and perhaps finding that the price of equality is isolation. Our files contain the statements of many Negro men who prefer to walk and work in lonely dignity; of others who become sensitive and aggressive; and of a few who by a combination of wit and good humor achieve both respect and friendship.

In a few plants that we have been able to analyze in some detail, however, such informal groupings of Negroes as exist are somewhat separate from white groupings. It seems plausible and, from the data, likely that informal organization has not developed so far among Negro workers in plants where they are new as among white workers. In a plant now being observed the Negro women in one department show signs of elaborating a system of cliques, with leaders who are not those whom the supervisors consider to be leaders.

While our data on this point are far short of what they should be, they indicate, as would our other knowledge of industrial behavior, that the formation of cliques, work teams, and leaders has and will have the same effect upon Negro workers as upon workers generally. It may be assumed that if there are to be leaders among Negro workers, they will arise only when there is something for them to lead, namely, cliques, work teams, and the like. It therefore becomes important to know what relations grow up or can be brought about between Negro groups and Negro leaders and their white counterparts. A significant lead on this problem lies in what appears to be true in certain racially mixed unions: that the knitting of the organization of the two races occurs not so much in the washroom and lunchroom gossip groups—the primary level of contact and interaction—but a little higher, at the level of minor leadership, where the enthusiasm for a common cause and the necessities of strategy favor a solidarity that transcends the race line.

An ulterior motive has led me to put off consideration of what is usually the main theme of discussions of race relations—what the races think and feel about each other. I wished first to direct your attention to the setting within which people's thoughts and sentiments are put into gesture and action. What, then, is the Negro in the minds of the white people who make industry's policies and put them into effect, of those lower supervisors whose identification with management has lately become a matter of dispute, of union leaders, and of workers? Again we shall emphasize general points rather than to give a detailed survey.

The American industrial executive prides himself on two things pertinent to our subject. First, on his progressive, scientific attitude toward industrial processes. He wants new things done, but he wants them to be tested; boldness, with enough caution not to go wrong, is his formula. His second point of pride is his ability to choose men. He is proud of the "comers" he has picked out and given their chance. But Herman Feldman, who made a survey of racial factors in American industry about fifteen years ago, found that, while nearly all employers had positive opinions about the characteristics of various nationalities and races as workers, they had little or no systematic evidence on the subject. "Actual analysis," he said, "of the comparative capacity of different racial groups is not part of the practice of industrial concerns."[3] Our own evidence confirms the impression that the view of most industrial managers is clouded by the brand names of race and nationality in about the same measure as that of other people. On a number of occasions I have been asked to discuss race relations in industry with groups of industrial men in managerial posts, from the very modest, but promising, to the highest. Invariably I have been asked to talk about the matter in a practical way; i.e., to stick to the experience that industries have had in adjusting the relations of Negro and white workers. After complying with this request I have always been showered with questions. Of the questions asked by these practical men, the great majority have been questions about the Negro, not race relations in industry; i.e., not about the kinds of situations that arise when Negroes of certain kinds and in certain proportions work with non-Negroes of certain kinds and in certain proportions under different circumstances. The questions, furthermore, have been affirmative in mood, beginning with an "Is it not true that Negroes . . . ?" or "When will Negroes learn . . . ?" The affirmations ill concealed in these questions had not to do so much with the Negro's aptitudes for learning manual and mental skills, as with his social nature. Taken together, they express the American stereotype of the Negro, a creature unfit for any but the marginal positions in industry because of his laziness, primitiveness, and childlikeness, yet full of an unjustified desire to have what he does not have and should not want to have, up to and including marriage with the manager's secretary. Let me hasten to assure you that these questions were usually answered by other members of the same groups, less numerous, but keenly interested in reporting their own

experience and in learning from the experiences of others. The fact
that the bulk of these men of managerial rank think of race relations
in much the same way as other Americans does not prove that they
are incompetent managers, or that many of them have not very successfully hired Negroes to work alongside their white workers. Many
of them have done so.

The fact that many people in managerial positions so think of the
Negro is, however, significant. It means that the decision to hire Negroes at all where they have not been employed before, or to hire
them for new kinds of jobs, is generally regarded as a step into a
dangerous unknown. It indicates that the natural and normal thing is
not to employ Negroes, and that to employ them or to extend their
employment to new fields, to skilled work, or to the office, has the
weight of sentiment and precedent against it.

Another consequence of this kind of thinking is a strong disposition
to regard the employment of Negroes as a very tentative experiment,
something to do only in an emergency. There are two extremes of the
experimental frame of mind. One is that stubborn and determined
attitude that makes the experimenter look closely for the causes of
any apparent failures. His disposition is to retain faith in his experiment and to seek the causes of failure in the manner of application
rather than in the idea itself. The other frame of mind is that of
trying, timorously and tentatively, against one's own conviction, some
unfortunately necessary departure from routine. In this frame of mind,
that of many representatives of management toward the hiring of
Negroes, one is sensitive to the objections of others in his own organization, touchy about the "I told you so" that perhaps accords with
his own feelings. This frame of mind is revealed in the inclination of
many managements to see a racial issue in any difficulty in which
Negroes are involved. This tendency is of course given strength by a
like tendency of employees, both Negro and white. In a typical case
of this kind management frantically called the representative of an
agency that tries to settle such matters to say they were having race
trouble and would have to establish separate locker rooms. The investigator found that the plant had grown tremendously during the war,
without any increase in locker-room facilities. For two years employees had been complaining of crowding in the locker room and of
having to share their lockers with workers on other shifts. When
Negroes were hired, the matter came to a head; the white employees
demanded separate locker rooms. This case was settled by immediately building new but not segregated locker rooms well placed about

the plant. The racial way of thinking in this case gave a ready definition for a chronic problem.

Such a timorous and tentative attitude cannot but influence the already unfavorable views of workers and lower supervisors toward Negro workers and encourage their resistance. One cannot expect people to change a satisfying and socially supported attitude unless there is some countersatisfaction or support. Workers, like other people, look for rewards. They talk and act to the gallery more than they are given credit for. Management, by and large, has not thought much of how to reward and support the employee in a change of attitude toward strange ethnic groups and Negroes. The lower supervisors do not generally do so. Fellow workers certainly are more inclined to reward a person for thinking and acting in the conventional way toward Negroes. Unions act sometimes one way and sometimes another; there is a great difference between them in this regard.

To turn more directly to the attitudes of workers, the diaries of observers in industry indicate a certain rewarding of the dramatic, unqualified, rather than of the moderate, statement of attitudes. A worker may be taken down a peg if he boasts about how he talked back to the boss, not because of the attitude expressed, but because he is suspected of not having done it in the way he said. When a company says it will hire Negroes, if people don't mind, some of their people say they will quit. They are needled afterward, not for the threat, but for the failure to carry it out. We have found no case, except in some of the unions that have set about to alter racial attitudes, in which either fellow workers or supervision give the individual worker any efficacious reward for expressing a favorable attitude toward Negroes.

If we look at the structure of the thinking of workers about Negro fellow workers, we will find in it not merely the conventional American attitude toward Negroes, but also the general inclination of workers to view with disapproval, born of anxiety, the hiring of new kinds of workers for their particular jobs. Their anxiety relates not only to security but to status and prestige as well. Jobs and departments in an industry are rated by everyone concerned. We expect that. Less attention has been given to the fact that the kinds of people hired for a given job determine to some extent the job's prestige. Thus, if women are hired for a job that only men have done, the men may take the hiring of women, not as proof that women are rising in status, but as proof that the job's status is threatened. We have heard of one industry in which Italians, who had been limited to poorer jobs, were annoyed when Negroes were hired to work alongside them; not because they disliked Negroes particularly, but on the ground that—since they knew what people thought of Negroes—the hiring of them was additional evidence that management had a low opinion of the Italians. Like most other actions of management, the hiring of new kinds of workers is regarded as a social gesture, as an expression of management's opinion of the job and of the people already on the job. It also changes the situation of the workers, in that they have to size up and judge how the new, unknown people will act toward the work group, the union, and management. Much talk is required among the workers to arrive at new common understandings about how to behave. The disposition of the workers is, at the beginning, to resist changes in the composition of their work group, and to give the rewards to those who crystallize the unfavorable opinion rather than to those who explore the situation for favorable aspects and interpretations.

On the other hand, while workers do not like the prospect of new kinds of fellow workers, they have a disposition to "go along" with most people hired. An American girl of Polish descent spoke for thousands of workers in northern cities when she said of Negroes, "I'd rather not work with them myself, but I wouldn't quit because of them. I guess they have to work somewhere, but I wish it didn't have to be here." A good many white workers report that, in their place of work, there is an "exceptional" Negro, who is a good worker, doesn't try to "mix too much," and who himself is the first to assert that most Negroes aren't much good. Others speak of a Negro who is an effective shop steward or member of a grievance committee. Still others report that the Negro girls in their shop are clean, agreeable, or of a good class. These reactions indicate that racial stereotypes, even though believed in, are to some extent seen for what they are and are not always applied to individuals whom one knows well enough to define in terms of the qualities considered desirable in fellow workers.

We have said but little about the protagonist of race relations in American industry, the Negro industrial worker. As a matter of fact, in our research we have learned more from him than from any other source and more about him—and her—than about anyone else. Being a self-conscious member of a minority, he knows more and will tell more about the problem than white workers. What is to others a passing incident is to him his fate. He is clearly of one of the most rapidly changing groups in the country; his skills and experience are being transformed. His hopes and demands, no less so. And if one reads through the hundreds of interviews in which Negro workers tell us the story of their experiences in industry, he will see laid before him all that variety of life objectives by which Americans gauge the worth and meaning of their jobs. The main difference is the preoccupation of all Negroes—each in a way that reflects his backgrounds, his conception of himself, and his views of the realities of the American world in which he has to live—with the race problem.

These observations concerning American workers who are Negroes give an easy excuse for ending this chapter, like a good sermon, where it began. The differences among Negroes in the qualities pertinent to their behavior as workers and fellow workers are significant only to those people—employers, union leaders, and workers—who are in that stubbornly experimental frame of mind of which we spoke; the frame of mind in which one applies to the problem of race relations all that we know and can learn about human relations in industry.

Notes

1. Shih Kuo-Heng, *China Enters the Machine Age*, Harvard University Press, Cambridge, 1944.

2. Mayo, Elton, and George F. F. Lombard, *Teamwork and Turnover in the Aircraft Industry of Southern California*, Harvard University Graduate School of Business Administration, Boston, 1944.

3. Feldman, Herman, *Racial Factors in American Industry*, p. 192, Harper & Brothers, New York, 1931.

10

The Knitting of Racial Groups in Industry

Elton Mayo has recently given the name "rabble hypothesis"[1] to the assumptions which, he claims, still guide not merely many managements in dealing with workers, but also many of those who investigate industrial behavior. He refers to the belief that an industrial organization is an aggregation of individuals each seeking his own gain without reference to other persons, and consequently each capable of being induced to greater effort by devices focused upon this desire for advantage. To this assumption Mayo opposes the view that a working force normally consists of social groups, whose members are highly responsive to each other's social gestures and identify their fates with those of their fellows; social groups which, further, are related to others in the larger system of social relations in and about industry. Mayo argues that a state of good cooperation is dependent upon the existence of such groups, even though one of their functions may be some restriction of individual production. He believes, finally, that the "solitary," the person who does not feel himself part of any such group, is actually somewhat disorganized, and not likely to function well in the long run.

The theme of my remarks is that a fruitful way of analyzing race relations in industry is to look at them against whatever grid of informal social groupings and of relations within and between such groups exists in the industries, departments, and jobs in which Negroes or other new kinds of employees are put to work. Recent experience suggests that this grid of relationships, and the manner in which Negroes are introduced into it, are more significant in the success of a policy of hiring Negroes than are the generalized racial attitudes of the white workers concerned.

Polling of white workers to find whether they favor the hiring of Negroes as their equal and close fellow workers would almost anywhere result in an emphatic "No." Workers generally prefer not to have any new kinds of workers introduced among and equal to them-

Paper read before American Sociological Society at 40th Annual Meeting, 1946. *American Sociological Review*, Vol. XI (Oct., 1946). Reprinted by permission.

selves. But Negroes have been successfully employed among white workers; and many other new kinds of workers have been introduced among older kinds of workers who were not enthusiastic about them. Polling of attitudes, on this simple basis, gives little clue to the probable behavior of the old workers to the new. The simple "No" of the workers to many proposals of management is not to be taken at face value; for industry has not been run by majority vote of the workers, and a "No" is often no more than a demonstration of protest. In fact, workers more or less expect each other to object to changes proposed by management.

It does not follow that racial preferences and dislikes have no bearing on the question whether the races will work well together. Racial attitudes themselves take on new dimensions when looked at in the framework of the human relations prevailing in industry. It is characteristic of industry that groups of workers who have knit themselves into some kind of organization in and about their work develop some set of expectations, considered little short of rights, that their jobs and their work fellowship should be limited to persons of some certain kind—as to age, sex, race, ethnic qualities, education, and social class. Mr. Orvis Collins, in a recent paper,[2] shows how the management of a New England factory got itself into an impasse by violating the expectation that certain kinds of jobs should belong to Irishmen. We could do with a good deal more investigation of what workers in various jobs and industries consider the proper kind of fellow worker, what they think are their own rights in the matter, and of the devices which they use to expel newcomers not of the kind they want and of those which management and unions have used to get the newcomers accepted. Such expectations are not likely to be stated formally; they may not even be admitted informally. Defense of the breach of them is likely, as in the case reported by Mr. Collins, to be hidden by indirection of various kinds. It is also probable that some of the so-called noneconomic behavior attributed to people new to industry—erratic changing of jobs, failure to respond to wage incentives, quitting industrial work entirely and returning home to farms—may be due not merely to unfamiliarity with the ways of industry. It may be a reaction to rejection by those among whom they have been put to work.

I used the expression "grid of informal relations." By this I mean simply the pattern of groupings which prevails in a place of work. The factory cafeteria, shown in Figure 1, exhibits such a grid; this is the pattern which renews itself every day at noon, when there are the most and the greatest variety of people there. The employees sort

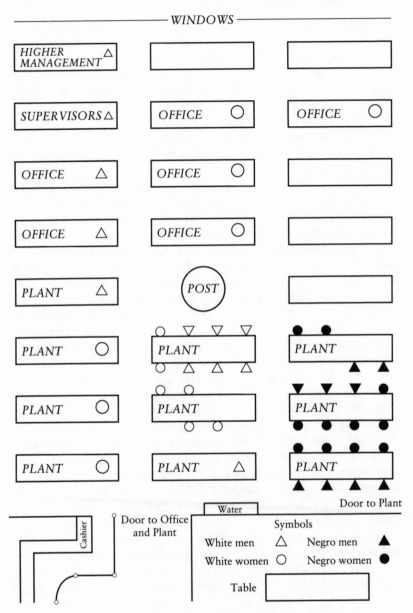

Figure 1. Seating by Rank, Sex, and Race in a Factory Cafeteria.

themselves according to their rank, sex, and race, and to their places in the office or out in the plant. The observers found also, that while it was seldom possible for all of the workers who belonged to a given close circle to come to the cafeteria and find places at the same table, they did—so far as possible—eat together.

The individual thus finds his table in a grid of rank, sex, race, and personal relations. At a union picnic the unit of the pattern was the table, each serving as headquarters for one or two family parties. The management families were in one corner of the grounds; the mass of the Negro families were concentrated toward the opposite corner. In the middle zone were some tables at which a Negro family party and a white family party sat, but so grouped that Negro faced Negro and white faced white. Near the platform used for announcements, dancing, and contests, were the only tables with racially mixed parties. These were the union leaders in charge of the picnic. Thus, in this grid, the family—which is by American definition not racially mixed—and rank within the factory worked together to form a pattern, which the union slightly disturbed by drawing a few people away from the family and away from factory rank to form a small nucleus based on special function.

I mention these examples first, not because of the inherent significance of seating arrangements in cafeterias and at picnics, but because they illustrate so vividly what I mean by a grid of relationships. Incidentally, in both cases the Negroes—with the exception of the few union committeemen at the picnic—fitted into that space in the pattern whose occupants were most numerous and of the lowest rank. None of them had characteristics which would set up any expectation that they might fit anywhere else.

On the job itself, the patterns of relationship are subject in varying measure to the physical layout of the shop, the distribution of workers of different races among the various kinds of jobs, by the degree of dependence of one worker upon others for successful performance of his work, as well as by the social atmosphere created by management, supervision, the union, and the workers themselves. Furthermore, the informal relations among workers are not always so immediately visible as in the cafeteria and at the picnic. But generally such relations are there, although not all workers are part of any network of groups of people who cooperate in some special way to control what goes on with reference to work or other matters.

The Fixing Room

A department called the Fixing Room in a certain plant illustrates one kind of grid or grouping at work and its consequences for race relations. The work is done by teams of three men. The members of a team meet and exchange tools and materials without a word and without even a direct look at each other. In fact, there is something of a cult of silence among them. The bonus, which is a large part of their income, is based upon the product of a team. The skills are learned on the job from the other members of the team to which one is assigned. The men are nearly all Poles, past middle age, bound together by kinship and neighborhood. The teams and the whole group together are notoriously and successfully impervious to management's attempts to control their relations, and even the choice of new employees. They pick their own fellows. The labor shortage of the war dried up the sources of new men of their kind and management tried to get new help—Negroes. Several Negro men were hired, but all left after a few days. Interviews with these Negro men revealed that they were subjected to a not-very-subtle, but very effective, torture by the other members of the teams to which they were assigned. Later, the management tried the device of hiring a whole Negro team, which complicated the matter of learning the job; they stayed for some time, achieved a very creditable rate of production, and recently quit in a group. We have not yet found out what happened, but I venture to say that it was fundamentally a case of rejection by the older workers. In this shop there is no place for the solitary individual. One must be integrated into a team-clique to work at all. The homogeneity and traditional solidarity and autonomy of the whole department conspired to make the men unwilling to accept new kinds of workers and make management impotent to bring about change against their will.

The power of resistance was probably increased by connivance of the foremen. Many of the foremen in this plant are old-timers, who

Figure 2. Fixing Room. (Each circle is a closed work team of three men.)

worked for the father of the present manager. They have a sort of proprietary interest in the departments they supervise; their idiosyncrasies are rather affectionately tolerated. The foremen can thus be, in effect, leaders of departmental cliques. A change of policy thus meets a very dense and intricate resisting structure. In their efforts to hire Negroes in the Fixing Room, management did not succeed in penetrating it.

The Polishing Room

The Polishing Room in another plant shows another type of both formal and informal organization operating in relation to race. In this room, each girl works independently on a machine like all the others. At intervals, all workers are moved along to the next machine. No one has a vested interest in a machine. By dint of good production and long service workers hope to get on the day shift. Many of the white girls of longer service have gravitated to this shift; it is about two-thirds white, in fact. The swing shift has a larger proportion of Negroes; the night shift, a strong majority of them. The few white girls on the night shift appear to prefer it because of some family reason. A girl cannot by especially high production increase her income; seniority alone brings small fixed increases of hourly wage; long service also brings certain benefits and an annual bonus. Something is made of the principle that only those who have good production records will be kept on when and if layoffs become necessary. There is thus very little in the situation and in the policies of management to induce either a strong individualism or a close grouping of the employees. One would expect it to be a situation into which Negro help could be fairly easily introduced, and so it has been. But there is, nevertheless, an informal organization of workers. To quote from the report of the observers:

> An analysis of clique formation and membership provides some clearer insights into such acceptance as the Negro has achieved and into the attitudes and expectation of Negro workers in the plant. There are several recognizable cliques in the Polishing Room; their functions are well defined by their members. The clique is concerned with production and procedure, and with the status and behavior of the individual workers.
> The cliques in this room are not mutually exclusive and sharply defined. There is a central group, the "Old Girls," made up of young women of from twenty-two to thirty-three years of age and of an average length of service of about five years. The "Old Girls" eat in the cafeteria; each

usually manages to eat with at least one or two of her clique fellows. Another group, also of long service, bring their lunches and eat in the lounge. But there is little association between them and the "Old Girls" clique. There are a number of smaller satellite cliques, each attached by at least one common member to the "Old Girls." It appears likely that a new girl may be sponsored into the organization through the satellite cliques. We observed one girl who was, when first interviewed, unfriendly toward other workers, a "lone wolf." Two months later she had been accepted, had ceased to be a rate-busting "horse" and had even become much more tolerant to the Negro girls.

The clique organization of the Polishing Room may be shown as in Figure 3.

The girls in the central clique, and those oriented towards them,

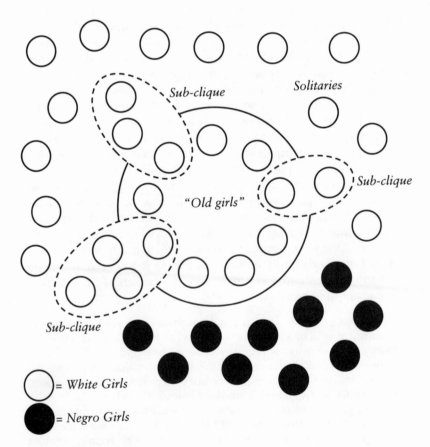

Figure 3. Polishing Room.

seem to be of such skill that they are without anxiety about being able to keep up to or even to surpass the usual rate; they maintain good levels of production, but make statements which make it clear that one of the functions of the group is control of the average rate of production.

White workers have defined a "good day's work" as falling within the limits of one hundred and one hundred and six. Many say that it would be easy to produce more. The girls who say this claim to be fast workers; they explain their failure to produce more by a well-developed rationale: to do more would be to ruin the job for the diligent, but slower workers. But "ratebreaking" is condoned for a day or so for a worker who has fallen behind and wants to bring her average up to par. Apparently a girl who is socially well established in the group can consistently break the rate a little with only mild teasing as punishment. But outsiders who break the rate are severely punished by ridicule and scorn; if they persist, they remain outsiders and, if associations are important to them, they may be forced off the job. Here is an apparent paradox: Admittance to the group may be secured only by adherence to the established definitions of the group, while unquestioned membership carries the privilege of some deviant behavior.

This is, of course, not a paradox at all; for it is characteristic of social groups to demand of the newcomer a strict conformity which will show that he accepts the authority of the group; then, as the individual approaches the center of the group and becomes an established member, they allow him a little more leeway.

Outside the organization are some white women and all the Negro women. The white women outsiders are a varied lot. Some are older women who must, or think they must, struggle to produce enough to keep their jobs. Some of them say that they are no longer young enough to be able to play. Others show in one way or another that some outside concern is so important as to make them defy or ignore the opinions of their fellow workers. Some are probably not acceptable for one reason or another—perhaps dress, personal hygiene, or general queerness.

But no Negro girl, no matter what her length of service, her production rate, or her personality, has found a place in the system of cliques of the white girls. The observers report that among the girls in the cliques, "It is generally understood that Negro workers are to be accorded tolerance and a measure of friendliness. There is ample evidence that there was opposition at first to the hiring of Negroes. In the two years that have elapsed, a studied, but tentative, acceptance has occurred. Negro and white workers meet each other with good will and friendliness on the job. They carry on conversations at their machines. But this friendliness does not extend beyond the work situation, and it varies in degree within the lesser cliques. White and Negro workers do not eat together except occasionally by accident. Not in any case is a Negro a member of a clique of white girls, and apparently conversation between the races seldom touches problems that are mutually important."

This means, in effect, that the Negro girls do not take part in the conversation of social gestures by which the rules and sentiments of the group are communicated to the newcomer, and by which she is offered membership in the clique as a reward for accepting its discipline. Insofar as white girls complain of the conduct of their Negro fellow workers, it is in precisely the terms they use about white girls who are not in the cliques. The Negro girls, they say, "are all for themselves; they don't try to help each other." One white girl summed up the matter thus:

> Some colored girls . . . don't care what the next person does. They're that way about everything. If one of them makes a hundred and ten (a very high production), the rest of them don't care. Now when a white girl makes that much, we make her slow down because we know how hard it is for some of 'em to make the average.
> *Interviewer:* Why do you think the Negro girls don't try to pull their rates down?
> Well, they're just like that about everything. They don't even try to help each other.
> *Interviewer:* What do you mean?
> They don't get into a group. They just mingle with everybody. I don't think the colored girls have any little groups like we have. . . .
> *Interviewer:* How do you account for that?
> It's 'cause they're all for themselves. Now you take the white girls; the younger ones will mix with the older girls and they find out what they are supposed to do.

The same worker said of a new white girl, "She won't keep no high average. She's mingling more with the other girls, now." Thus she implicitly recognized mingling with other girls and sensitivity to their opinions as a desirable, steadying experience. She apparently did not see that the very reason for the Negro girl's undesirable production habits is probably that she is excluded from the rewards of group membership. In effect, she is complaining that the Negro girls do not form their own cliques.

That the Negro girls have not developed an organization in this case is borne out by the observers. We do not know why this is so. But certain considerations concerning the probable reasons bear directly on the points thus far made and on the final one which I have to make.

Some of the white girls are, to use Mayo's expression, "solitaries." Most of the Negro girls are so. The records of production seem to indicate this, as well as their other actions and talk. A few Negro girls have very high rates, and indulge in racing with other workers. Some are erratic in production. Others anxiously struggle to get their rates up to the point where they can feel secure against being the first to be laid off. There is evidence that they think that they are on trial. This is highly individualistic behavior; it is also typically anxious behavior.

We may ask, although we cannot answer with much assurance, why the Negro girls in this room are so unorganized. First, they are not in the white clique organization because they are not given the chance to be in it. Then, why do they not form an organization of their own? Perhaps because they are new, relatively speaking. Perhaps because on the day shift, where the main white clique developed, they—the Negro girls—are in the minority and would hesitate to form what would be considered a rival group. Perhaps it is that there are no Negro girls who feel secure enough in their positions to form a disciplining group which would, as part of its discipline, control production. In this particular plant the management has undoubtedly made a strong attempt to reduce discrimination. Now the way they have done it is to emphasize that the Negro girl will be hired, kept, and promoted strictly according to her individual merits.

This is a point on which we may make some tentative generalizations. This very emphasis on treating the individual on his merits can become a source of overindividualistic anxiety. For the statement "You will be judged on your own merits," repeated too often, becomes a dinning into one's ear of the thought, "You are on trial. I doubt whether you can make it, but if you do I will give you credit. Most people of your kind can't make it. I shall be astonished if you do. If you do, you will certainly be an exception. You've got to show me." This bit of imagined talk is, in fact, not far from what foremen do say to Negro workers in many plants. It contains an invitation, almost a threatening command, to the Negro worker to be a "solitary."

Now this might not work with Negroes of the least ambitious class or those working at traditional Negro jobs. But in the Polishing Room the Negro girls show potential or actual middle-class behavior and sentiments, as do also most of the white girls; nor are they employed at "Negro jobs." And this brings us to our general point. The individualistic or "rabble" hypothesis of industrial management—that each worker is an individual who may be induced, and who ought to be able to be induced, to work for his own ends without regard to his fellows—is almost unconsciously applied with redoubled force to the Negro worker. The behavior it encourages is, in its essence, the behavior of the ambitious person. The ambitious white worker may dissociate himself from his fellows to some extent, and in spite of being somewhat disliked he may get promotions for it. The Negro worker apparently feels and is made to feel in some situations that he has to dissociate himself from others and be a "solitary" in order merely to keep his job. I do not think the Polishing Room is a situation in which this is unusually so. But the combination of individually separate work, with the particular pattern of white informal organization from which Negroes are excluded, and a management policy which gives the Negro girls definite hope that they can gain security by individual effort—and in no other way—might be expected to keep them a somewhat anxious series of solitaries rather than a stable organized group.

The Fixing Room illustrates the problem which arises in a shop where the informal organization consists of a series of closely related tight teams into which the individual worker—white or Negro—must fit in order to work at all. The Polishing Room has an open formal structure, easy for the individual to enter; and a moderately open, but nevertheless, powerful, informal structure of cliques. But it is not quite open to Negroes, and the results are as have been reported.

These two cases are, however, alike in that no attempt has been made to modify the informal organization so as to relate Negroes to it. In the Fixing Room, after a first attempt to put Negroes into existing teams failed, management attempted to set up Negro teams, but without trying to define their relations to existing teams. In the Polishing Room, management tried to create general tolerance. In other cases, a union or management has made a more definite effort in this regard. It seems fairly common for a vigorous union administration successfully to encourage biracial groups of shop leaders. We have observed a few cases in which foremen, who are the centers of informal groups of their own workers, have developed something of an interracial organization. More often the opposite occurs where the foreman occupies such a position. I cite these additional cases, without the description necessary for you to judge of them, to indicate the variety of situations which may occur, and also to introduce a final point; namely that the situation may often be changed by some active force, either union or management, which takes the pattern of informal relations into account.

Notes

1. Elton Mayo, *The Social Problems of an Industrial Civilization.* Boston Graduate School of Business Administration, Harvard University 1945. Chapter II et passim.

2. Orvis Collins, "Ethnic Behavior in Industry." *American Journal of Sociology.* LI (January, 1946), 293–98.

11

Institutional Office and the Person

The conscious fulfilling of formally defined offices distinguishes social institutions from more elementary collective phenomena. This paper will discuss the nature of institutional offices and their relations to the peculiar roles and careers of persons.[1]

Office and Role

Sumner insisted that the mores differentiate, as well as standardize, behavior, for status lies in them.[2] Status assigns individuals to various accepted social categories; each category has its own rights and duties. No individual becomes a moral person until he has a sense of his own station and the ways proper to it. Status, in its active and conscious aspect, is an elementary form of office. An office is a standardized group of duties and privileges devolving upon a person in certain defined situations.

In current writing on the development of personality, a great deal is made of social role. What is generally meant is that the individual gets some consistent conception of himself in relation to other people. This conception, although identified with one's self as a unique being, is a social product; Cooley would have said, a product of primary group life. But role, however individual and unique, does not remain free of status. Indeed, Linton says "a role is the dynamic aspect of a status."[3] Role *is* dynamic, but it is also something more than status. Status refers only to that part of one's role which has a standard definition in the mores or in law. A status is never peculiar to the individual; it is historic. The person, in status and in institutional office, is identified with a *historic role*. The peculiar role of a prophet or a political leader may be transformed into the historic role or office of priesthood or kingship. Every office has had a history, in which the informal and unique have become formal and somewhat imper-

Reprinted by permission of the publisher from *The American Journal of Sociology*, Vol. XLIII, November, 1937. Copyright 1937, University of Chicago Press.

sonal. The story of an institution might well be told in terms of the growth of its offices, with which have been identified the personal roles of series of individuals.

Entrance into a status is not always a matter of choice. That does not prevent persons from being aware that they are entering it, from focusing their wills upon it, or from fulfilling the attendant obligations with consciously varying degrees of skill and scruple. Status gives self-consciousness and the conscience something to bite on.[4]

Every social order is, viewed in one way, a round of life. Anthropologists almost invariably describe it so, and show how persons of different status fit their activities into this round. But beyond routine, even in simple and stable societies, occur great ceremonial occasions and crucial enterprises. On such occasions some person or persons become the center of enhanced attention. Collective expression and effort are coordinated about them. Status may determine the selection of these persons, but they must perform special offices appropriate to the occasion. They become, within the limits of their offices, especially responsible for the fate of their fellows and for the integrity of their communities.[5]

The person who fills such a great office is judged not as the common run of mankind but with reference to his predecessors in office and to the popular conception of what the office should be. He is exposed to special demands. He is also protected, insofar as the office sets the limits of his responsibility, from both the bludgeons of critics and the sharp thrusts of his own conscience.

Objective differentiation of duty reaches its ultimate rigidity in ritual office. The subjective aspect of such rigidity is punctiliousness.[6] The responsibilities of ritual office are so clear-cut as to allow the incumbent a feeling of assurance that he is doing his whole duty. The anxiety lest he fall short is but the greater.[7] Anxiety and responsibility are alike focused upon the office, as something transcending the individual. The incumbent tends to be impatient of the criticisms of others. He wards them off by declaring that whoever criticizes him attacks the sacred office.

In the performance of ritual one may realize profoundly that he, even he, is playing a historic role; he may be transfigured in an ecstasy in which his personal attributes are merged with those of the office. Each meticulous gesture bursts with symbolic meaning. E. Boyd Barrett writes thus of his feeling while celebrating his first mass.

On the snow-white altar cloth before me lay a chalice of wine and on a paten a wafer of unleavened bread. Presently *at my words,* at my repetition of the eternal formula of consecration, the wine would become the blood of Christ, and the bread the body of Christ. My hands, soiled and sinful though they were, would be privileged to raise aloft in adoration the Son of God, the Saviour of the world. . . . . Surely the words "Sanctus! Sanctus! Sanctus!" were none too sacred to pronounce in presence of this mystery of mysteries. . . . . My first mass was an ecstasy of joy. . . . . I gave myself confidently and wholeheartedly to God and I felt that He gave himself to me.[8]

While devotion and sense of office may be at their maximum in such moments, judgment is in abeyance. It is in the nature of ritual that it should be, since each action is part of a sacred whole. Furthermore, rituals are performed under compulsion often backed by a vow. A vow allows no turning back, no changing of the mind, no further exercise of judgment.[9]

An office may eventually become so ritualistic that the successive incumbents are but symbols rather than responsible agents. A rigid etiquette is observed in approaching them, and sentiments of reverence become so intense that the office is worshipped. This final point of impersonal institution of an office is reached at the cost of the more active functions of leadership. In ongoing collective life, contingencies arise to require decisions. Even a ritual may not go on without a stage manager. Furthermore, every ritual is proper to an occasion. The occasion must be recognized and met. An office may become purely symbolic only if the meeting of contingencies is allocated to some other office.[10]

Coming down to earth, the person cannot, apart from ritual, escape judgments. His peculiar social role asserts itself and may come into conflict with the office which he fills. The fusion of personal role and office is perhaps never complete save in ritual.

One of the extreme forms in which one's personal role appears is that of a call or peculiar mission. The person's conception of his mission may carry him beyond the conception which others have of his office. As an office becomes defined, there arise devices by which one's fellows decide whether one is the person fit to fill it. The first leader of a sect may be "called" to his task; his successors, too, are "called," but the validity of the call is decided by other men, as well as by himself.[11] Thus the "call," a subjective assurance and compulsion, is brought under the control of one's fellows. But the sense of mission may be so strong that it makes the person impatient of the discipline exercised by his colleagues.[12]

There are other ways in which personal role and office may conflict. It is sufficient for our present purposes to suggest that the very sense of personal role which leads one into an institutional office may make him chafe under its bonds. The economy of energy and will, devotion and judgment, peculiar to the individual does not completely disappear when he is clothed with an established, even a holy, office. The more secular offices make fewer formal demands upon the individual; they require less suppression of the individuality. They are less symbolic and more subject to the test of effectiveness in action. A free, secular society, from this point of view, is one in which the individual may direct his energies toward new objects; one in which he may even succeed in creating a new office, as well as in changing the nature and functions of existing ones.

Career and Office

In any society there is an appropriate behavior of the child at each age. Normal development of personality involves passing in due time from one status to another. Some stages in this development are of long duration; others are brief. While some are thought of as essentially preparatory, and their length justified by some notion that the preparation for the next stage requires a set time, they are, nevertheless, conventional.

In a relatively stable state of society, the passage from one status to another is smooth and the experience of each generation is very like that of its predecessor. In such a state the expected rate of passage from one status to another and an accompanying scheme of training and selection of those who are to succeed to instituted offices determine the ambitions, efforts, and accomplishments of the individual. In a society where major changes are taking place, the sequence of generations in an office and that of offices in the life of the person are disturbed. A generation may be lost by disorder lasting only for the few years of passage through one phase.

However one's ambitions and accomplishments turn, they involve some sequence of relations to organized life. In a highly and rigidly structured society, a career consists, objectively, of a series of status and clearly defined offices. In a freer one, the individual has more latitude for creating his own position or choosing from a number of existing ones; he has also less certainty of achieving any given position. There are more adventurers and more failures; but unless complete disorder reigns, there will be typical sequences of position, achievement, responsibility, and even of adventure. The social order will set limits upon the individual's orientation of his life, both as to direction of effort and as to interpretation of its meaning.

Subjectively, a career is the moving perspective in which the person sees his life as a whole and interprets the meaning of his various attributes, actions, and the things which happen to him. This perspective is not absolutely fixed either as to points of view, direction, or destination. In a rigid society the child may, indeed, get a fixed notion of his destined station. Even in our society he may adopt a line of achievement as his own to the point of becoming impervious to conflicting ambitions. Consistent lines of interest and tough conceptions of one's destined role may appear early in life.[13]

Whatever the importance of early signs of budding careers, they rarely remain unchanged by experience. The child's conception of the social order in which adults live and move is perhaps more naïve than are his conceptions of his own abilities and peculiar destiny. Both are revised in keeping with experience. In the interplay of his maturing personality and an enlarging world the individual must keep his orientation.

Careers in our society are thought of very much in terms of jobs, for these are the characteristic and crucial connections of the individual with the institutional structure. Jobs are not only the accepted evidence that one can "put himself over"; they also furnish the means whereby other things that are significant in life may be procured. But the career is by no means exhausted in a series of business and professional achievements. There are other points at which one's life touches the social order, other lines of social accomplishments— influence, responsibility, and recognition.

A woman may have a career in holding together a family or in raising it to a new position. Some people of quite modest occupational achievements have careers in patriotic, religious, and civic organizations. They may, indeed, budget their efforts toward some cherished office of this kind rather than toward advancement in their occupations. It is possible to have a career in an avocation as well as in a vocation.

Places of influence in our greater noncommercial organizations are, however, open mainly to those who have acquired prestige in some other field. The governors of universities are selected partly on the basis of their business successes. A recent analysis of the governing boards of settlement houses in New York City shows that they are made up of people with prestige in business and professional life, as well as some leisure and the ability to contribute something to the budget.[14]

It would be interesting to know just how significant these offices appear to the people who fill them; and further, to whom they regard themselves responsible for the discharge of their functions. Apart from that question, it is of importance that these offices are by-products of achievements of another kind. They are prerogatives and responsibilities acquired incidentally; it might even be said that they are exercised ex officio or *ex statu.*

The interlocking of the directorates of educational, charitable, and other philanthropic agencies is due perhaps not so much to a cabal as to the very fact that they are philanthropic. Philanthropy, as we know it, implies economic success; it comes late in a career. It may come only in the second generation of success. But when it does come, it is quite as much a matter of assuming certain prerogatives and responsibilities in the control of philanthropic institutions as of giving money. These prerogatives and responsibilities form part of the successful man's conception of himself and part of the world's expectation of him.[15]

Another line of career characteristic of our society and its institutional organization is that which leads to the position of "executive." It is a feature of our society that a great many of its functions are carried out by corporate bodies. These bodies must seek the approval and support of the public, either through advertising or propaganda. Few institutions enjoy such prestige and endowments that they can forgo continued reinterpretation of their meaning and value to the community. This brings with it the necessity of having some set of functionaries who will act as promoters and propagandists as well as administrators. Even such a traditional profession as medicine and such an established organization as the Roman Catholic church must have people of this sort. By whatever names they be called, their function is there and may be identified.

Sometimes, as in the case of executive secretaries of medical associations, these people are drawn from the ranks of the profession. In other cases they are drawn from outside. University presidents have often been drawn from the clergy. In the Y.M.C.A. the chief executive officer is quite often not drawn from the ranks of the "secretaries." But whether or not that be the case, the functions of these executive officers are such that they do not remain full colleagues of their professional associates. They are rather liaison officers between the technical staff, governing boards, and the contributing and clientele publics. Their technique is essentially a political one; it is much the same whether they act for a trade association, the Y.M.C.A., a hospital, a social agency, or a university. There is, indeed, a good deal of competi-

tion among institutions for men who have this technique, and some
movement of them from one institution to another. They are also
men of enthusiasm and imagination. The institution becomes to them
something in which dreams may be realized.[16]

These enthusiastic men, skilled in a kind of politics necessary in a
philanthropic, democratic society, often come to blows with the older
hierarchical organization of the institutions with which they are connected. Therein lies their importance to the present theme. They
change the balance of power between the various functioning parts
of institutions. They change not only their own offices but those of
others.

Studies of certain other types of careers would likewise throw light
on the nature of our institutions—as, for instance, the road to political
office by way of fraternal orders, labor unions, and patriotic societies.
Such careers are enterprises and require a kind of mobility, perhaps
even a certain opportunism, if the person is to achieve his ambitions.
These ambitions themselves seem fluid, rather than fixed upon solid
and neatly defined, objectives. They are the opposites of bureaucratic
careers, in which the steps to be taken for advancement are clearly
and rigidly defined, as are the prerogatives of each office and its place
in the official hierarchy.[17] It may be that there is a tendency for our
social structure to become rigid, and thus for the roads to various
positions to be more clearly defined. Such a trend would make more
fateful each turning point in a personal career. It might also require
individuals to cut their conceptions of themselves to neater, more
conventional, and perhaps smaller patterns.

However that may be, a study of careers—of the moving perspective in which persons orient themselves with reference to the social
order, and of the typical sequences and concatenations of office—may
be expected to reveal the nature and "working constitution" of a
society. Institutions are but the forms in which the collective behavior
and collective action of people go on. In the course of a career the
person finds his place within these forms, carries on his active life
with reference to other people, and interprets the meaning of the one
life he has to live.

Notes

1. W. G. Sumner, *The Folkways*, New York, Ginn & Co, 1956, pars. 40, 41, 56,
61, 63, 67, *et passim*; C. H. Cooley, *Social Organization*, New York, Scribners, 1929,

chaps. iii, xxviii; E. Faris, "The Primary Group: Essence and Accident," *American Journal of Sociology*, XXXVIII (July, 1932), 41–50.

2. *Op. cit.*, par. 73.

3. Ralph Linton, *The Study of Man*, New York, Appleton, 1936, chap. viii, "Status and Role."

4. B. Malinowski, in *Crime and Custom in Savage Society*, London, Routledge, 1926, chap. v *et passim*, attacks the notion, so prominent in evolutionary social theory, that the member of a primitive society adheres to custom unconsciously and automatically. He maintains that among the Trobriand Islanders there is considerable margin between the maximum and minimum fulfilling of obligations and that, within these limits, persons are impelled by motives very like those recognized among us. Some men show an excess of zeal and generosity, banking upon a return in goods and prestige. He points also to a conflict of offices embodied in one person; a man is at once affectionate parent of his own children and guardian of the property and interests of his sister's children. Malinowski suggests that the man is often aware of this conflict.

5. See R. Redfield, *Chan Kom, a Maya Village*, Washington, Carnegie Institution, 1934. Chicago, Univ. of Chicago Press, 1962, pp. 153–59, for description of the *fiesta* and the office of *cargador*; B. Malinowski, *Argonauts of the Western Pacific*, New York: E. P. Dutton, 1922, 1961, for the office of the chieftain in canoe building and expeditions, and that of the magician in gardening.

6. Sumner, *op. cit.*, par. 67.

7. The psychoanalysts trace ritual to anxieties arising from unconscious guilt. In compulsion neurosis the individual ceaselessly performs rituals of *Buss* and *Nichtgeschehenmachen* (see A. Fenichel, *Hysterien und Zwangsneurosen*, Wien, Internationaler Psychionalytischer Verlag, 1931, chap. iv). J. Piaget, in *The Moral Judgment of the Child*, London, Kegan, Paul, 1932, finds that young children play marbles as ritual before they play it as a game. In this early stage they observe punctiliously such rules as they know, attributing their origin to their fathers, the city alderman, and God. They are quick to accuse and facile at self-excuse, but show little regard for their fellow-players.

8. *Ex-Jesuit*, London, Geoffrey Bles, 1931, p. 124. Many Catholics expect special blessings from a priest's first mass.

9. See W. G. Sumner, *War and Other Essays*, New Haven, Yale University Press, 1911, "Mores of the Present and Future," p. 157, in which he says: "One of the most noteworthy and far-reaching features in modern mores is the unwillingness to recognize a vow or to enforce a vow by any civil or ecclesiastical process . . . In modern mores it is allowed that a man may change his mind as long as he lives." The belief that a man may change his mind is an essentially secular attitude. Catholic doctrine recognizes this, by distinguishing resolutions, promises, and vows. Vows are the most sacred, since they are promises to God. "A subsequent change in one's purpose is a want of respect to God; it is like taking away something that has been dedicated to Him, and committing sacrilege in the widest sense of the word." Resolutions are mere present intentions, without a commitment; promises between man and man or to the saints should be kept, but the breach is not so serious as that of a vow (*The Catholic Encyclopedia*, Vol. XV, "Vows"). It is perhaps the residue of the compulsion of a vow that gives ex-priests the sense of being marked men. See E. Boyd Barrett, *op. cit.* Ordinary life may be something of an anticlimax for these men once dedicated to holy office. Such men are also suspect. A French Canadian recently dismissed all that a certain psychologist might say by remarking, "C'est un homme qui a porté la soutane."

There are many instances in sociological literature of the profound changes in an institution that accompany the decline of compulsion in its offices. Redfield, *op. cit.,* tells how in towns and cities the *fiesta* becomes something of a secular enterprise. No longer is it a sacred festival, led by a *cargador* who accepted "the holy burden" from his predecessor. The Webbs, in *English Local Government: the Parish and the County,* London, Longmans, 1906, describe a similar decline of the sense of obligation to serve as parish officers in growing industrial towns.

10. Max Weber, in his "Politik als Beruf" (*Gesammelte politische Schriften,* München, Drei Masken Verlag, 1921, pp. 396–450), essays a natural history of various types of political office. He shows how certain offices, as that of sultan, became purely symbolic, while the wielding of political power and the risk of making mistakes were assumed by others. The position of the emperor of Japan is similar; the emperor is divine, but he speaks only through the voices of men. It is not suggested that these two features do not sometimes appear in the same office. They do, as in the papacy. Offices vary in their proportions of symbol and action.

11. See the *Catholic Encyclopedia,* Vol. XV, "Vocation." While the Catholic church admits the possibility that divine light may be shed so abundantly upon a soul as to render deliberation about the validity of a vocation unnecessary in some cases, it does not regard such inner assurance necessary to vocation. The spiritual director is to discover and develop the germ of vocation by forming the character and encouraging "generosity of the will." The church insists that two wills should concur before one can enter the clergy: the will of the individual and the will of the church. The latter is "external vocation," which is "the admission of the candidate in due form by competent authority."

12. The ardor of a person with a peculiar mission may become an insufferable reproach to his colleagues and contain a trace of insubordination to his superiors. The neophyte who is too *exalté* can be borne, but a certain relaxation of ardor is demanded in course of time. In a well-established institution, ardor must be kept within the limits demanded by authority and decorum; it may not necessarily reach the state in which "men, fearing to outdo their duty, leave it half done," as Goldsmith said of the English clergy.

13. Psychoanalysts trace to very lowly motives the lines of consistency in the individual's conception of his life and the way in which he disciplines and marshals his efforts. Their more important point is that these phenomena rise out of intimate family relationships. They also use the term "mobility of the libido" (cf. Klein, "The Role of the School in the Libidinal Development of the Child," *International Journal of Psychoanalysis,* V [1924], 312–31) to indicate the child's capacity to transfer his affections and energies to objects in a larger world as he grows and extends his circle of activity. A great deal, however, remains to be done in the way of understanding the bearing of early experiences on the subsequent careers of persons. It is evident that the age, as well as the frequency, of appearance of a sense of career varies greatly from family and from class to class. The pressure on children to discipline themselves for careers likewise varies; the psychological by-products of these pressures want studying, for they seem sometimes to thwart the ends they seek.

See H. D. Lasswell, *World Politics and Personal Insecurity,* New York: McGraw-Hill, 1935, pp. 210–12, for a discussion of "career lines."

14. Albert J. Kennedy, Kathryn Farra, and Associates, *Social Settlements in New York,* New York: Columbia University Press, 1935, chap. xiv: T. Veblen, *The Higher Learning in America,* New York: Sagamore, 1918, p. 72 *et passim.*

15. The Junior League frankly undertakes to train young women of leisure for their expected offices in philanthropic agencies.

16. The reports made by the American Association of University Professors on conflicts between professors and college presidents sometimes reveal in an interesting way the characteristics of both and of the offices they fill. See *Bulletin of the American Association of University Professors,* XXI (March 1935), 224–66, "The University of Pittsburgh"; XIX (November, 1933), 416–38, "Rollins College."

17. Mannheim would limit the term "career" to this type of thing. Career success, he says, can be conceived only as *Amtskarriere.* At each step in it one receives a neat package of prestige and power whose size is known in advance. Its keynote is security; the unforeseen is reduced to the vanishing point ("Über das Wesen und die Bedeutung des wirtschaftlichen Erfolgstrebens," *Archiv für Sozialwissenschaft und Sozialpolitik,* LXIII [1930], 458 ff.).

12

Dilemmas and Contradictions of Status

It is doubtful whether any society ever had so great a variety of statuses or recognized such a large number of status-determining characteristics as does ours. The combinations of the latter are, of course, times over more numerous than the characteristics themselves. In societies where statuses[1] are well defined and are entered chiefly by birth or a few well-established sequences of training or achievement, the particular personal attributes proper to each status are woven into a whole. They are not thought of as separate entities. Even in our society, certain statuses have developed characteristic patterns of expected personal attributes and a way of life. To such, in the German language, is applied the term *Stand.*

Few of the positions in our society, however, have remained fixed long enough for such an elaboration to occur. We put emphasis on change in the system of positions which make up our social organization and upon mobility of the individual by achievement. In the struggle for achievement, individual traits of the person stand out as separate entities. And they occur in peculiar combinations which make for confusion, contradictions, and dilemmas of status.

I shall, in this paper, elaborate the notion of contradictions and dilemmas of status. Illustrations will be taken from professional and other occupational positions. The idea was put into a suggestive phrase by Robert E. Park when he wrote of the "marginal man." He applied the term to a special kind of case—the racial hybrid—who, as a consequence of the fact that races have become defined as status groups, finds himself in a status dilemma.

Now there may be, for a given status or social position, one or more specifically determining characteristics of the person. Some of them are formal, or even legal. No one, for example, has the status of physician unless he be duly licensed. A foreman is not such until appointed by proper authority. The heavy soprano is not a prima donna in more than temperament until formally cast for the part by the director of the opera. For each of these particular positions there is also an expected technical competence. Neither the formal nor the technical qualifications are, in all cases, so clear. Many statuses, such as membership in a social class, are not determined in a formal way. Other statuses are ill defined both as to the characteristics which determine identification with them and as to their duties and rights.

There tends to grow up about a status, in addition to its specifically determining traits, a complex of auxiliary characteristics which come to be expected of its incumbents. It seems entirely natural to Roman Catholics that all priests should be men, although piety seems more common among women. In this case the expectation is supported by formal rule. Most doctors, engineers, lawyers, professors, managers, and supervisors in industrial plants are men, although no law requires that they be so. If one takes a series of characteristics, other than medical skill and license to practice it, which individuals in our society may have, and then thinks of physicians possessing them in various combinations, it becomes apparent that some of the combinations seem more natural and are more acceptable than others to the great body of potential patients. Thus a white, male, Protestant physician of old American stock and of a family of at least moderate social standing would be acceptable to patients of almost any social category in this country. To be sure, a Catholic might prefer a physician of his own faith for reasons of spiritual comfort. A few ardent feminists, a few race-conscious Negroes, a few militant sectarians, might follow their principles to the extent of seeking a physician of their own category. On the other hand, patients who identify themselves with the "old stock" may, in an emergency, take the first physician who turns up.[2]

If the case is serious, patients may seek a specialist of some strange or disliked social category, letting the reputation for special skill override other traits. The line may be crossed also when some physician acquires such renown that his office becomes something of a shrine, a place of wonderful, last-resort cures. Even the color line is not a complete bar to such a reputation. On the contrary, it may add piquancy to the treatment of a particularly enjoyed malady or lend hope to the quest for a cure of an "incurable" ailment. Allowing for such exceptions, it remains probably true that the white, male, Protestant physician of old American stock, although he may easily fail to get a clientele at all, is categorically acceptable to a greater variety of patients than is he who departs, in one or more particulars, from this type.

It is more exact to say that, if one were to imagine patients of the various possible combinations of these same characteristics (race, sex, religion, ethnic background, family standing), such a physician could treat patients of any of the resulting categories without a feeling by the physician, patient, or the surrounding social circle that the situation was unusual or shocking. One has only to make a sixteen-box table showing physicians of the possible combinations of race (white and Negro) and sex with patients of the possible combinations to see that the white male is the only resulting kind of physician to whom patients of all the kinds are completely accessible in our society (see table 1).

One might apply a similar analysis to situations involving other positions, such as the foreman and the worker, the teacher and the pupil. Each case may be complicated by adding other categories of persons with whom the person of the given position has to deal. The teacher, in practice, has dealings not only with pupils but with parents, school boards, other public functionaries, and, finally, his own colleagues. Immediately after one tries to make this analysis, it becomes clear that a characteristic which might not interfere with some of the situations of a given position may interfere with others.

I do not maintain that any considerable proportion of people do consciously put together in a systematic way their expectations of persons of given positions. I suggest, rather, that people carry in their minds a set of expectations concerning the auxiliary traits properly associated with many of the specific positions available in our society. These expectations appear as advantages or disadvantages to persons who, in keeping with American social belief and practice, aspire to positions new to persons of their kind.

The expected or "natural" combinations of auxiliary characteristics become embodied in the stereotypes of ordinary talk, cartoons,

TABLE 1* RATIO OF NEGRO AND WHITE PHYSICIANS

	Physician			
Patient	White Male	White Female	Negro Male	Negro Female
White male	....	....	....	....
White female	....	....	....	....
Negro male	....	....	....	....
Negro female	....	....	....	....

*I have not used this table in any study of preferences but should be glad if anyone interested were to do so with selected groups of people.

fiction, the radio, and the motion picture. Thus, the American Catholic priest, according to a popular stereotype, is Irish, athletic, and a good sort who with difficulty refrains from profanity in the presence of evil and who may punch someone in the nose if the work of the Lord demands it. Nothing could be farther from the French or French-Canadian stereotype of the good priest. The surgeon, as he appears in advertisements for insurance and pharmaceutical products, is handsome, socially poised, and young of face but gray about the temples. These public, or publicity, stereotypes—while they do not necessarily correspond to the facts or determine people's expectations—are at least significant in that they rarely let the person in the given position have any strikes against him. Positively, they represent someone's ideal conception; negatively, they take care not to shock, astonish, or put doubts into the mind of a public whose confidence is sought.

If we think especially of occupational status, it is in the colleague-group or fellow-worker group that the expectations concerning appropriate auxiliary characteristics are worked most intricately into sentiment and conduct. They become, in fact, the basis of the colleague-group's definition of its common interests, of its informal code, and of selection of those who become the inner fraternity—three aspects of occupational life so closely related that few people separate them in thought or talk.

The epithets "hen doctor," "boy wonder," "bright young men," and "brain trust" express the hostility of colleagues to persons who deviate from the expected type. The members of a colleague-group have a common interest in the whole configuration of things which control the number of potential candidates for their occupation. Colleagues, be it remembered, are also competitors. A rational demonstration that an individual's chances for continued success are not jeopardized by an extension of the recruiting field for the position he has or hopes to attain, or by some short-cutting of usual lines of promotion, does not, as a rule, liquidate the fear and hostility aroused by such a case. Oswald Hall found that physicians do not like one of their number to become a consultant too soon.[3] Consulting is something for the crowning, easing-off years of a career; something to intervene briefly between high power and high blood-pressure. He who pushes for such practice too early shows an "aggressiveness" which is almost certain to be punished. It is a threat to an order of things which physicians—at least, those of the fraternity of successful men—count upon. Many of the specific rules of the game of an occupation become comprehensible only when viewed as the almost instinctive attempts of a group of people to cushion themselves against the hazards of their careers. The advent of colleague-competitors of some new and peculiar type, or by some new route, is likely to arouse anxieties. For one thing, one cannot be quite sure how "new people"—new in kind—will act in the various contingencies which arise to test the solidarity of the group.[4]

How the expectations of which we are thinking become embodied in codes may be illustrated by the dilemma of a young woman who became a member of that virile profession, engineering. The designer of an airplane is expected to go up on the maiden flight of the first plane built according to the design. He (sic) then gives a dinner to the engineers and workmen who worked on the new plane. The dinner is naturally a stag party. The young woman in question designed a plane. Her coworkers urged her not to take the risk—for which, presumably, men only are fit—of the maiden voyage. They were, in effect, asking her to be a lady rather than an engineer. She chose to be an engineer. She then gave the party and paid for it like a man. After food and the first round of toasts, she left like a lady.

Part of the working code of a position is discretion; it allows the colleagues to exchange confidences concerning their relations to other people. Among these confidences one finds expressions of cynicism concerning their mission, their competence, and the foibles of their superiors, themselves, their clients, their subordinates, and the public at large. Such expressions take the burden from one's shoulders and serve as a defense as well. The unspoken mutual confidence necessary to them rests on two assumptions concerning one's fellows. The first is that the colleague will not misunderstand; the second is that he will not repeat to uninitiated ears. To be sure that a new fellow will not misunderstand requires a sparring match of social gestures. The zealot who turns the sparring match into a real battle, who takes a friendly initiation too seriously, is not likely to be trusted with the lighter sort of comment on one's work or with doubts and misgivings; nor can he learn those parts of the working code which are communicated only by hint and gesture. He is not to be trusted, for, though he is not fit for stratagems, he is suspected of being prone to treason. In order that men may communicate freely and confidentially, they must be able to take a good deal of each other's sentiments for granted. They must feel easy about their silences as well as about their utterances. These factors conspire to make colleagues, with a large body of unspoken understandings, uncomfortable in the presence of what they consider odd kinds of fellows. The person who is the first of his kind to attain a certain status is often not drawn into the informal brotherhood in which experiences are exchanged, competence built up, and the formal code elaborated and enforced. He thus remains forever a marginal man.

Now it is a necessary consequence of the high degree of individual mobility in America that there should be large numbers of people of new kinds turning up in various positions. In spite of this and in spite of American heterogeneity, this remains a white, Anglo-Saxon, male, Protestant culture in many respects. These are the expected character-istics for many favored statuses and positions. When we speak of racial, religious, sex, and ethnic prejudices, we generally assume that people with these favored qualities are not the objects thereof. In the stereotyped prejudices concerning others, there is usually contained the assumption that these other people are peculiarly adapted to the particular places which they have held up to the present time; it is a corollary implication that they are not quite fit for new positions to which they may aspire. In general, advance of a new group—women, Negroes, some ethnic groups, etc.—to a new level of positions is not accompanied by complete disappearance of such stereotypes but only by some modification of them. Thus, in Quebec the idea that French-Canadians were good only for unskilled industrial work was followed by the notion that they were especially good at certain kinds of skilled work but were not fit to repair machines or to supervise the work of others. In this series of modifications the structure of qualities ex-pected for the most-favored positions remains intact. But the forces which make for mobility continue to create marginal people on new frontiers.

Technical changes also break up configurations of expected status characteristics by altering the occupations about which they grow up. A new machine or a new managerial device—such as the assembly line—may create new positions or break old ones up into numbers of new ones. The length of training may be changed thereby and, with it, the whole traditional method of forming the person to the social demands of a colleague-group. Thus, a snip of a girl is trained in a few weeks to be a "machinist" on a practically foolproof lathe; thereby the old foolproof machinist, who was initiated slowly into the skills and attitudes of the trade, is himself made a fool of in his own eyes or—worse—in the eyes of his wife, who hears that a neighbor's daughter is a machinist who makes nearly as much money as he. The new positions created by technical changes may, for a time, lack definition as a status. Both the technical and the auxiliary qualifications may be slow in taking form. The personnel man offers a good example. His title is perhaps twenty years old, but the expectations concerning his qualities and functions are still in flux.[5]

Suppose we leave aside the problems which arise from technical changes, as such, and devote the rest of this discussion to the consequences of the appearance of new kinds of people in established positions. Every such occurrence produces, in some measure, a status contradiction. It may also create a status dilemma for the individual concerned and for other people who have to deal with him.

The most striking illustration in our society is offered by the Negro who qualifies for one of the traditional professions. Membership in the Negro race, as defined in American mores or law, may be called a master status-determining trait. It tends to overpower, in most crucial situations, any other characteristics which might run counter to it. But professional standing is also a powerful characteristic—most so in the specific relationships of professional practice, less so in the general intercourse of people. In the person of the professionally qualified Negro these two powerful characteristics clash. The dilemma, for those whites who meet such a person, is that of having to choose whether to treat him as a Negro or as a member of his profession.

The white person in need of professional services, especially medical, might allow him to act as a doctor in an emergency. Or it may be allowed that a Negro physician is endowed with some uncanny skill. In either case, the white client of ordinary American social views would probably avoid any nonprofessional contacts with the Negro physician.[6] In fact, one way of reducing status conflict is to keep the relationship formal and specific. This is best done by walking through a door into a place designed for the specific relationship, a door which can be firmly closed when one leaves. A common scene in fiction depicts a lady of degree seeking, veiled and alone, the address of the fortuneteller or the midwife of doubtful practice in an obscure corner of the city. The anonymity of certain sections of cities allows people to seek specialized services, legitimate but embarrassing as well as illegitimate, from persons with whom they would not want to be seen by members of their own social circle.

Some professional situations lend themselves more than others to such quarantine. The family physician and the pediatrician cannot be so easily isolated as some other specialists. Certain legal services can be sought indirectly by being delegated to some queer and unacceptable person by the family lawyer. At the other extreme is school teaching, which is done in full view of the community and is generally expected to be accompanied by an active role in community activities. The teacher, unlike the lawyer, is expected to be an example to her charges.

For the white colleagues of the Negro professional man the dilemma is even more severe. The colleague-group is ideally a brother-hood; to have within it people who cannot, given one's other atti-tudes, be accepted as brothers is very uncomfortable. Furthermore, professional men are much more sensitive than they like to admit about the company in which nonprofessionals see them. The dilemma arises from the fact that, while it is bad for the profession to let laymen see rifts in their ranks, it may be bad for the individual to be associated in the eyes of his actual or potential patients with persons, even colleagues, of so despised a group as the Negro. The favored way of avoiding the dilemma is to shun contacts with the Negro professional. The white physician or surgeon of assured reputation may solve the problem by acting as consultant to Negro colleagues in Negro clinics and hospitals.

For the Negro professional man there is also a dilemma. If he accepts the role of Negro to the extent of appearing content with less than full equality and intimacy with his white colleagues, for the sake of such security and advantage as can be so got, he himself and others may accuse him of sacrificing his race. Given the tendency of whites to say that any Negro who rises to a special position is an exception, there is a strong temptation for such a Negro to seek advantage by fostering the idea that he is unlike others of his race. The devil who specializes in this temptation is a very insinuating fellow; he keeps a mailing list of "marginal men" of all kinds and origins. Incidentally, one of the by-products of American mores is the heavy moral burden which this temptation puts upon the host of Americans who have by great effort risen from (*sic*) groups which are the objects of prejudice.

There may be cases in which the appearance in a position of one or a few individuals of a kind not expected there immediately dissolves the auxiliary expectations which make him appear odd. This is not, however, the usual consequence. The expectations usually continue to exist, with modification and with exceptions allowed.

A common solution is some elaboration of social segregation. The woman lawyer may become a lawyer to women clients, or she may specialize in some kind of legal service in keeping with woman's role as guardian of the home and morals. Women physicians may find a place in those specialties of which only women and children have need. A female electrical engineer was urged by the dean of the school from which she had just graduated to accept a job whose function was to give the "woman's angle" to design of household electrical appliances. The Negro professional man finds his clients among Ne-groes. The Negro sociologist generally studies race relations and teaches in a Negro college. A new figure on the American scene is the

Negro personnel man in industries which have started employing Negro workers. His functions are to adjust difficulties of Negro workers, settle minor clashes between the races, and to interpret management's policies to the Negro as well as to present and explain the Negro's point of view to management. It is a difficult job. Our interest for the moment, however, is in the fact that the Negro, promoted to this position, acts only with reference to Negro employees. Many industries have had women personnel officials to act with reference to women. In one sense, this is an extension of the earlier and still existing practice of hiring from among a new ethnic group in industry a "straw boss" to look after them. The "straw boss" is the liaison officer reduced to lowest terms.

Another solution, which also results in a kind of isolation if not in segregation, is that of putting the new people in the library or laboratory, where they get the prestige of research people but are out of the way of patients and the public. Recently, industries have hired a good many Negro chemists to work in their testing and research laboratories. The chemist has few contacts with the production organization. Promotion within the laboratory will put the Negro in charge of relatively few people, and those few will be of his own profession. Such positions do not ordinarily lead to the positions of corresponding importance in the production organization. They offer a career line apart from the main streams of promotion to power and prestige.

These solutions reduce the force of status contradiction by keeping the new person apart from the most troublesome situations. One of the consequences is that it adds new stories to the superstructure of segregation. The Negro hospital and the medical school are the formal side of this. The Negro personnel man and foreman show it within the structure of existing institutions. There are evidences that physicians of various ethnic groups are being drawn into a separate medical system of hospitals, clinics, and schools, partly because of the interest of the Roman Catholic church in developing separate institutions but also partly because of the factors here discussed. It is doubtful whether women will develop corresponding separate systems to any great extent. In all of these cases, it looks as if the highest point which a member of these odd groups may attain is determined largely by the number of people of his own group who are in a position to seek his services or in a position such that he may be assigned by other authority to act professionally with reference to them. On the other hand, the kind of segregation involved may lead professional people, or others advanced to special positions, to seek—as compensation— monopoly over such functions with reference to their own group.

Many questions are raised by the order of things here discussed. One is that of the place of these common solutions of status conflict in the evolution of the relations between the sexes, the races, and the ethnic groups of our society. In what circumstances can the person who is accepted formally into a new status, and then informally kept within the limits of the kind mentioned, step out of these limits and become simply a lawyer, foreman, or whatever? Under what circumstances, if ever, is the "hen doctor" simply a doctor? And who are the first to accept her as such—her colleagues or her patients? Will the growth of a separate superstructure over each of the segregated bottom groups of our society tend to perpetuate indefinitely the racial and ethnic division already existing, or will these superstructures lose their identity in the general organization of society? These are the larger questions.

The purpose of the paper, however, is not to answer these large questions. It is rather to call attention to this characteristic phenomenon of our heterogeneous and changing society and to suggest that it become part of the frame of reference of those who are observing special parts of the American social structure.

Notes

1. "Status" is here taken in its strict sense as a defined social position for whose incumbents there are defined rights, limitations of rights, and duties. See the *Oxford Dictionary* and any standard Latin lexicon. Since statuses tend to form a hierarchy, the term itself has—since Roman times—had the additional meaning of rank.

2. A Negro physician, driving through northern Indiana, came upon a crowd standing around a man just badly injured in a road accident. The physician tended the man and followed the ambulance which took him to the hospital. The hospital authorities tried to prevent the physician from entering the hospital for even long enough to report to staff physicians what he had done for the patient. The same physician, in answer to a Sunday phone call asking him to visit a supposedly very sick woman, went to a house. When the person who answered the door saw that the physician was a Negro, she insisted that they had not called for a doctor and that no one in the house was sick. When he insisted on being paid, the people in the house did so, thereby revealing their lie. In the first instance, an apparently hostile crowd accepted the Negro as a physician because of urgency. In the second, he was refused presumably because the emergency was not great enough.

3. Oswald Hall, "The Informal Organization of Medical Practice" (unpublished Ph.D. dissertation, University of Chicago, 1944).

4. It may be that those whose positions are insecure and whose hopes for the higher goals are already fading express more violent hostility to "new people." Even if so, it must be remembered that those who are secure and successful have the power to exclude or check the careers of such people by merely failing to notice them.

5. The personnel man also illustrates another problem which I do not propose to

discuss in this paper. It is that of an essential contradiction between the various functions which are united in one position. The personnel man is expected to communicate the mind of the workers to management and then to interpret management to the workers. This is a difficult assignment. The problem is well stated by William F. Whyte, in "Pity the Personnel Man," *Advanced Management,* October–December, 1944, pp. 154–58. The Webbs analyzed the similar dilemma of the official of a successful trade union in their *History of Trade-Unionism* (rev. ed.; London: Longmans, Green, 1920).

    6. The Negro artist can be treated as a celebrity. It is within the code of social tufthunting that one may entertain, with a kind of affected Bohemian intimacy, celebrities who, on all counts other than their artistic accomplishments, would be beyond the pale.

III

THE SOCIOLOGICAL
IMAGINATION

13

The Improper Study of Man

The proper study of mankind is man. But what men shall we study to learn most about mankind, or simply about people? Those long dead, those now living, those unborn? The learned or the unlettered? The lowly, or those of high degree? Those nearby and of color and deportment like the student's own, or men of strange mien and demeanour? The men of the kraal, or those of the city? Faithful or infidel, the virtuous or the vicious? Are all equally human, or are some a little more so than others, so that what one learns about them is of wider application? Where should one start? At the earliest possible beginning, working toward the present by way of the peoples who were in some sense more directly our ancestors? Shall we produce the future from the lines of the past? Or should we, exploiting our experience of living men, apply to both past and future the lessons of the present?

And by what means shall we learn of those whom we choose to study? Suppose we elect to study living people. Shall we put our trust in studying great numbers, or at least such numbers as, properly selected, will represent all sorts and conditions of men in true proportion? Or shall we pick a few whose doings we observe as under a microscope and whose minds we probe for thoughts, desires, and memories, even for such as they themselves know not of? By what ideas, schemes, and formulae shall we reduce what we find to order? And, not least, how much of what we learn shall we tell those whom we have studied, the larger public, or our colleagues? What principles shall guide us in the discovery of men's secrets; what, in the telling of them?

Shall we wait for those crucial things to happen which offer most increase to our knowledge of this or that aspect of human life, and travel fast and far to catch events on the wing? Or shall we set up experiments, bringing people together under circumstances so controlled as to get precisely the answers we want next? Shall we study

Reprinted from White, Lynn, Jr. (ed), *Frontiers of Knowledge,* New York, Harper & Row, 1956 pp. 79–93. Copyright © 1956 by Harper & Row Publishers, Inc.

people in small groups and communities, and hope to find ways of
expanding our findings without distortion to the big world? Shall we
look at people where nothing happens save the turn of seasons and
generations, and where men are of one breed and of one mind, taking
that as man's normal state? Or shall we study men in the seething
flux of cities, migrations, crusades, and wars, wherever breeds mingle
and minds clash?

To what of people's doings shall we more closely attend: their
politics, their religion, their work, their play, their poems, their philos-
ophies, their sciences, their crafts? What, finally, should be the form
of our questions: "What were people like and what did they do?"
"What are they doing?" "What will they do?" or "What would they
do if—?"

The academic departments which study people are distinguished
from each other by their choices from among these and similar possibilities. Some aspects of academic man insist on a single answer,
explicitly stated. Most of us combine explicit answers with less-
conscious predilection for some kinds of human material rather than
others. Some like to think of themselves as scientists; others as artists,
critics, or moral judges. Some love the adventure of digging up manu-
scripts long buried in dust. Some like to crack a script, or to put
together the fragments of ancient pots or temples. Others like to express behavior in mathematical formulae. Still others like to study
living men, to discover new things about their own kind still warm,
or to detect commonplace motives under the apparently strange ways
of exotic people. But preference for one kind of study does not prevent
scholars from having a try at other kinds of methods of study now and
again. Again and again some academic people, or even rank outsiders,
discontent with the set ways of academic study, go off on some new
path of discovery, or simply take as their major preoccupation what
others have considered a side issue.

So it was, in the century of evolution, that a number of naturalists,
philosophers, historians, and students of the law assembled, classified,
and sought to put into "evolutionary" order the varied customs reported as practiced throughout the world, and especially by those
peoples most removed from nineteenth-century Europe in time, distance, civilization, and race. Some of these men called their work
sociology. Toward the end of the century English and American phi-
lanthropists and reformers visited the slums of the great and growing
cities, described the ways of the people who lived there, counted and
tabulated the things that appeared the best indicators of their misery.
Their surveys were called *sociology*. Some French legal scholars

sought explanations for the alleged penchant of modern people to follow the crowd rather than their ancestors in both virtues and vices. A sharp-tongued Yale professor, Sumner, and, a decade later, an Italian engineer and economist, Pareto, got concerned about those aspects of human social behavior—usages and sentiments—which did not yield good price curves. They wrote treatises on *sociology*.

In addition to a name, these varied pursuits had in common a concern with the classifying of human doings, with the relations of events rather than with the events themselves. They also cut across that organization of the academic studies of man by which the state, the church, economic life, literature, and the like, as well as the various periods of history and the various regions and countries of the world, were each the special domain of some organized group of scholars, and of one department of a university. As historians of human learning have been quick to say, others had gone off on these tangents before. What was new was that these *sociologists,* and people influenced by them, gained a footing in the universities, especially so in the newer American ones. The older scholarly guilds cried, "Trespass," and those of classical bent slew the sociologists with the true but irrelevant accusation that their name, although of noble lineage, was a bastard, being half Latin, half Greek. As do the members of any budding profession or academic specialty seeking access to the scared precincts, the sociologists sought and found ancient and honored ancestors, founded a society and journals, and have since been arguing about what academic ways to get set in. In the debate and in their deeds they are moving toward a certain combination of answers to the questions raised about the proper study of mankind.

By predilection rather than by logic, most sociologists work on the here and now. Although vast apparatuses have been set up to catch and spread knowledge of current doings, not all is recorded; and of what is recorded, not all is spread abroad. There is an economy of observing, recording, and disseminating the news. There is also a politics of it, a balance between revealing and concealing, in which all people and all organized institutions are in some measure involved. It has become part of the mission of sociologists to catch the goings-on of people and institutions at the time; or at least to catch those parts of them which tend to be overlooked by students of politics and economics, and by those who report on and criticize what are considered the serious works of art and of the mind. The lives of the families across the tracks; the reactions of housewives to the morning soap opera; how the men down in the garage unconsciously weave their own inarticulate anxieties and yearnings into their talk of what happened to L'il Abner this morning; the slow moving changes in the level of schooling of those Americans who are called Negro. These things don't make the news, but they make the story comprehensible when it breaks into the headlines. One might say that part of the calling of sociologists is to push back the frontiers of the news so as to get at the news in the back of, or below, the news, not in the sense of getting at the lowdown, but in that of giving the reported events another dimension, that of the perspective of culture and of social processes.

One part of this job is undertaken by the surveyors of opinion. They have invented all sorts of devices for getting at what people think and do about a great variety of matters, large and small. No one of the particular opinions or actions they report would make the news columns, as does the fiftieth home run of a big league player or the visit of a monarch to a country fair. Neither the actors nor the actions, taken singly, are thought worthy of note. Put together, they are the groundswell on which prominent figures and great projects rise and fall, run their courses, or founder. Mr. Unnamed Millions is, as many have noted lately, more and more a gentleman of leisure, a grand consumer of goods and of the popular arts and of the innumerable "services" of our civilization. His choices make or break the great institutions and enterprises. Keeping abreast of him is a job which, like woman's work, is never done. Predicting what he will do, even in the short run, has some of the features of predicting the weather. Many sociologists specialize in these very jobs; they are the quantitative historians of their own times. One of the risks of their trade is that their errors of prediction are more quickly discovered than those of people in some other lines of human study.

Working on this frontier is not a matter merely of setting up machinery to watch people and to inquire of them what they do and think. For one immediately strikes that other frontier, that of conscious and unconscious secrecy. Even a willing informant seldom can or will tell all that he thinks, knows, or does about a matter; nor is he able to show or explain the many connections between his different thoughts and actions. He will tell more about some things than about others; more in some situations than in others; more to some people than to others. It is common knowledge that a human group—a family, school, business concern, a clique—keeps together and keeps going only by maintaining a delicate balance between discretion and frankness. Students of group behavior have achieved great skill in inserting themselves as participant observers into the interstices of groups so as to observe things which can be perceived only by an insider, but whose significance can be conceived only by an outsider free enough of emotional involvement to observe and report accurately and armed with concepts with which to relate what he sees to other groups. Learning the role of participant observer, including the subtle practice of its ethic, is a basic part of training people for social discovery. Each observer, himself a member of society, marked by sex, age, race, and the other characteristics by which people place one another in various roles or relations, must find out not merely what the significant kinds of people are in the groups and situations he wants to study; he must also learn to perceive quickly and surely what role he has been cast in by the people he is studying. He must then decide whether he can effectively and on honest terms get them to see him in such light that they will trust him.

The role of participant observer can be difficult and trying. A young sociologist spent a considerable time as observer in a public mental hospital. The patients would not believe he was not a physician; they pestered him to help them get out. The other doctors were somehow, they insisted, in a plot with relatives to keep them wrongly locked up. The attendants, accustomed to being spied upon, thought him another and more ingenious kind of detective sent to catch them breaking regulations or stealing public property. The physicians, although used to the idea of research and although briefed about his project, were a bit inclined to consider him a spy, too. Only by skillful and strict adherence to his role of seeing much and to his bargain of telling nothing that would harmfully identify any person, did he succeed in staying and in finding out the inward structure of the social groups which even the mentally ill and their keepers and therapists form.

The author of a well-known book on corner gangs "hung on the corner" with a group of young men in a New England city for three years, always torn between whether to get as involved as they wished, which would have bound him to secrecy; or whether to stay just on the edge, where there was a bit of a question whether they could trust him. Except for one essay into helping them get a man elected to public office by voting several times, he stayed on the edge. As it turned out, that was the way the gang wanted it. He wrote the book and is still friends with several members of the group.

It is conceivable that there are social groups so closed and so suspicious that they cannot be studied by participant observers. They may be so tight that they have no place for people of neutral role. Fanatical religious or political sects, criminal gangs, groups planning some secret strategy for either good or ill, bodies charged with knowledge which must be kept close for the common good, people living in great and vulnerable intimacy with each other, these do not welcome even the most trusted outside observers. However, a great deal can be learnt by projecting on these groups what is known of others which approximate them in some degree, and by setting up experiments which simulate them. A group of social scientists has indeed set up an organization to assemble, evaluate, and draw conclusions from the small amounts of information which can be got about people in the Iron Curtain regions. Some of them have written an intriguing book on how to study cultures from a distance. The problems are in part those of the historian, who is limited to the documents left around, since he cannot ask the dead to write documents to his order; but they are also in part the problems of evaluating the testimony of renegades and converts, people who have left some secret group and from various motives tell, or purport to tell, about what they have left. All of these are the problems of the social rhetoric common to all human intercourse.

The fears which lead people to make it difficult for investigators are often enough well founded; more than that, they lie in the nature of social life. A family has secrets, or it is no family. It is not the public's business, ordinarily, what goes on in the bosom of a family; but it is a matter of basic human and scientific interest to know what kinds of families there are, what makes some hold together and others break up, and what happens to children brought up in one kind of family rather than another. The sociological investigator cracks the secrecy, but buries the secrets, one by one, in a tomb of silence—as do all the professions which deal with the problems of people. This means, of course, that the student of human groups must remain willingly and firmly a *marginal* man in relation to those he studies; one who will keep, cost what it will, the delicate balance between loyalty to those who have admitted him to the role of confidant and to his colleagues who expect him to contribute freely to the accumulating knowledge about human society and methods of studying it.

While some prefer to study people *in situ*, others take them aside and learn from them in long interviews, reassuring their subjects, showing sympathy for the problems of each, and refraining the while from even the gesture of censorship. One of the most powerful of modern social inventions is the psychoanalytic interview, in which the patient is led painfully through a maze of hindrances of conscience, shame, and fear to a fuller expression, hence to fuller knowledge, of his own mind. It is based on the assumption that the injunction to know one's self is one that few of us can follow without help. The prolonged sympathetic interview of the social investigator is less dramatic, but is an effective instrument of social discovery. But every device must be valued by its results. Some students have found that there are situations in which contradiction, calling the subject's bluff, facing him with his own contradictions, and even questioning his sincerity bring out depths and ambivalences which might otherwise remain hidden. Some have undertaken experiments to discover how differences of tactical rhetoric on the part of the interviewer affect the rhetoric of the subjects.

Some investigators prefer to go even further than experimenting with methods of interviewing and observing; they set up their own situations and create their own groups. The social research of the University of Frankfort on the Main used such a method in study of political attitudes in 1951. They got up a letter in which an American soldier who had spent some years in Germany tells the people back home in the United States what he thinks are the German attitudes toward the Nazis, Jews, Americans, and democracy. Germans of various backgrounds were called together in small groups to discuss social and political issues; the letter was read to them from a tape made by a speaker with an English accent. In the conversation following the reading, attitudes such as have not been caught by any political questionnaire in postwar Germany came to light.

Similar methods have been used in study of various matters in the U.S.A. A team of social scientists engaged to find out how juries arrive at their unanimous decisions has had the record of a damage suit read onto tape, using different voices for the various persons in the court: the record is played to groups of twelve who are then left alone to decide the case as if they were a jury. A silent observer with a recorder sits unobtrusively in a corner. The subjects play the role of jurymen with great seriousness. The doings of real juries are properly kept a secret; the experimental device provides an approximation with much better observation than one would in any case be likely to get by asking people what had happened in juries on which they had sat. For the observer keeps a record of those who talk the most, those who change their minds, and what alliances are made in the course of the wearing on of the argument. Combined with surveys of the ways in which people of various incomes, education, and other traits say they would judge various cases submitted to juries, these experiments are teaching us a great deal about the operation of one of our cherished institutions.

Some investigators would eventually replace all study of "natural groups" by experimental devices. Only so, they contend, can the many variable factors in social behavior be kept to such number that one can keep track of them and measure their influence. Some would go further than the Frankfort institute or the jury team. For in these projects, the experimenters were interested in the substance of their findings—the political attitudes of the Germans, and the operation of juries in the United States, respectively. The pure experimenters make the substance suit the experiment. They assemble a group of people, and give them a problem to solve to which the experimenter and the subjects are alike utterly indifferent. It is the interaction between people, the influence they have on each other, the way and the mood in which they communicate with one another that is the object of the study. For instance, what difference does it make in the interplay among a number of people whether one of them is so placed that the others can talk to each other only through him, or whether they can all talk to each other at once? One may study the forms of social interaction—social choreography—as a student of poetry may study meters and periods without attending to thought, or as the philologist may analyze grammatical forms and phonetic modulations free of concern for meaning and mood. It is but a narrow step from such study of form in human conduct to the study of form and style in art; one is on the fluttering edge between the abstractions of science and those of art. It is perhaps no accident that Simmel, the German philosopher who first proposed the study of pure interaction, attention to form rather than to content, as the basic concept of sociology, should also have written about money and about art in the same spirit. The more abstract one's way of conceiving things, the more likely one is to make generic discoveries which apply to many concrete fields of natural and human phenomena. As the experimenters penetrate further into the mathematical symmetries of human converse, they may well add to knowledge of other systems of things as well.

If men were gods, big gods with solar systems at beck and call, they might set up control planets, plant people on them, and reproduce millions of years of history, intervening now and then to see what would happen. But students of human society are mortal; our subjects live as long as we do, and usually have as much power over us as we over them. One experimenter has seriously played god by pretending that, in his laboratory as in heaven, a minute is as a hundred years. His naïveté only highlights the problem of translating the findings of small, limited experiments to larger organizations and to the time scale of history; it does not prove that the transfer cannot, with care and in limited degree, be made.

Social experimenting has also raised the problem, both ethical and practical, of manipulating other people. There has been quite a hue and cry about this lately. A psychologist "running rats" is playing a game; the rats play for keeps without even knowing that it is a game. I believe it is suspected that now and again a sly one makes a game of the experiments and laughs up his metaphoric sleeve at the serious psychologist. No one has objected to playing with the rat, but many believe that to manipulate people is an improper way of studying man. But, of course, all politics and much of social life consist of the more or less successful attempts of people to influence one another. Every profession that deals with people is suspected of looking with an experimental and manipulative eye at its clients; indeed, no one would think of going to a lawyer, physician, or even a clergyman who did not look upon his case as one among many from which they had learned their trades. The real problem of manipulating (hence of experimenting upon) humans is not that of manipulation or no manipulation, but that of the proper conditions, limits, means, and ends thereof.

Some sociologists combine the mood of the experimenter with the roving eye of the reporter. They frequent the places where events of the kinds they are interested in are bound to happen, or they get a wide knowledge of some order of human occurrences or problems, and chase down the crucial cases which will give them the combinations of circumstances of which a more general and abstract, yet more refined and useful, knowledge can be built.

Not long ago some social psychologists were studying what happens to a group of people when a great promised event does not occur as predicted by their leaders. When they were in the midst of their project, a small sect gathered about a man who was predicting an early end of the world. Now this has happened many times before, and there are some records of the cases. For instance, when the world didn't come to end on the due date in 1843, the Millerites decided their arithmetic was wrong. A century later their successors, the Seventh Day Adventists (some of them at least) are beginning to say that while Jesus is indeed coming again in the flesh to establish his Kingdom on earth, it is sinfully presumptuous of men to think they can calculate the day and the hour. For did he not say, "Ye know not the day nor the hour?" But the team of psychologists mentioned above quite properly were eager to see a group of living people go through the experience of waiting for the world to end, and they did. Seldom do scholars have such luck.

We are in a time when we have more than common reason to want to know how people will react when disaster strikes. Flying squadrons have been sent in the wake of floods, tornadoes, explosions, and fires to find out tactfully, before memories are clouded and distorted, how people meet such adversity; who rises to the occasion to help others, and who must, on the contrary, be helped. Immediately after a great fire that destroyed half their town, the citizens told a fieldworker what a hero a certain obscure sister superior of a small convent-hospital had been. The nun, they said, had simply taken over and run the rescue services and the whole town. Sometime later the proper order of things had been restored; people appeared to believe that the mayor and an ecclesiastical dignitary had saved the day. In another disaster, the minister of one rather popular church went completely to pieces while the representative of a minority church and a schoolteacher saw the town through its tragedy. The minority minister's hair came out in handfuls some days later when reaction set in; it was the price of his courage. In many cases of such "firehouse" social research, two reports are issued. One is a newsy and perhaps immediately useful report, the other more general, and so phrased as to be useful to others who study human behavior.

If one frees his curiosity of the peculiarities of some one time and place by developing a good set of abstract ideas for comparing one case or situation with another, he will see many situations in various parts of the world comparable to those that originally aroused his interest. He will fall into the delicious conflict between wanting to learn more and more detail about the one dear case and the desire to go elsewhere to add both breadth and nuance to his knowledge. A number of students of American race relations have gone off to Africa, the most tumultuous and massive Negro-white frontier of these days. The relative numbers and the historical situations of people of Negro, European, and other ancestries on the racial frontiers of Africa are varied, and are everywhere quite different from the North American racial frontier. Race relations are still vivid in the United States, for we still consider a man's race an important thing about him. Furthermore, these relations are at a crucial point in which much of both practical and theoretical interest is to be learned. Adventure lies at our own door. But there is also much to be learned by going afield. Race relations have occurred in many historical epochs, in great variety of circumstances, accompanied by various degrees of cultural differences; their course has been influenced by intervening events. Sometimes peoples meet who are alike in race, but different in almost all else. The irreducible core of race relations, as distinguished from the relations of peoples different from each other in other regards, might be found by comparing various communities.

To be sure, one's ability and will to learn languages, one's health, the adaptability and sense of adventure of one's wife, one's knack for playing roles such that one can live among various peoples, not to mention the human life span, limit the number of cultural situations one can study. On the whole, social science has suffered from too little rather than too much getting about (except to conventions). Anthropologists are great people to get around, but only lately have they begun to study the larger and more confused settings where races meet and where new nations are being made. The racially mixed locations and cities of Africa are places where the former subjects of the anthropologists are facing the favorite problems of the sociologist. In fact, sociologists and anthropologists are meeting there, too. In those cities, native prophets and evangelists preach half-Christian, half-tribal gospels and predict great events in which God's black people will come into their own while the white malefactors will be destroyed or driven back to their own land. Such prophets enjoin their people to make themselves pure and ready for their glorious future by a return to some idealized form of the ways of the past. One thinks of the Pharisees tithing mint and rue as part of their program of getting rid of Greek and Roman.

In the *Times* of New York or London, one can follow from day to day the crises of a dozen interracial or intercultural conflicts; in most of them Europeans are reluctantly and bit by bit giving up political, economic, and social power over others. The underdog group is in most cases undergoing revolutionary changes in its culture and social structure and is awakening to a new group-consciousness on larger scale than in the past; it is usually rewriting its history, not because of Carbon-14 or new archaeological finds but because people with a new sense of unity and a new vision of the future seem always to need a new past different both from their traditional ones and from that given them by their foreign masters. Every rewriting of history—especially our own—is grist for the sociologist's mill. Racial and cultural frontiers are but one problem which can be understood only by wide ranging about the world of the present, either in the flesh or in the mind's eye, and about the past, through the eyes of historians and through the works of art and literature in which men have expressed their hopes, hates, and aspirations.

A basic assumption of the study of mankind—hence of individual branches of study such as that called sociology—is that it is important and fascinating to find out what things do and what things do not repeat themselves in human history. Sociologists work rather more on those which are repeated. They assume that although the people of any race, culture, time, or place inherently merit study as much as those of any others, still each historic social time and place may show some special feature which may make it an especially fit laboratory for study of some problem or process of human society. Part of the adventure of the study of human society is the seeking out of the most intriguing living laboratory, prepared by the fortunes of history, for study of the problems we are especially interested in, for use of our particular skills, and for catering to our particular tastes, curiosities, and preoccupations. Our choices may spring from a sense of political and moral urgency, from a desire to advance knowledge for man's good, from some ill-defined identification with all that is human, or from some aesthetic sense.

Some of the students of man's doings should be creatures ready to invade the territory of others, both figuratively and literally, and to compare anything with anything else without shock or apology. It is a friction-generating and improper pursuit. Any social situation is in some measure dear to those in it. To compare it with others is to seem to dull the poignancy of the wrongs of the underdogs, and to detract from the merits of those who have the better place in it. Comparison may violate the canons of status and prestige, as when one compares the code of secrecy of the gentleman's gentleman with that of the lord chamberlain. Comparison of religion with religion appears to reduce the claim of each to a monopoly of truth. Such invasion is also dangerous and improper on the academic front, for any series of human events, any social time and place, and most of man's institutions are each thought to be the game preserve of one of the learned professions. Shoving over scholarly line-fences is even more dangerous than shifting boundary stones in Vermont.

Most perilous and improper of all is it to compare the academic disciplines with one another by pointing out that each is a historical entity which had a beginning and which will probably be superseded by others in the future. If we study man and his institutions with broad-sweeping curiosity, with the sharpest tools of observation and analysis which we can devise, if we are deterred from no comparison by the fallacy which assumes that some people and peoples are more human than others, if we do not allow loyalty to truth to take second place to department or academic guild, we will all be proper students of man. And when we become too respectable, too much bound to past methods, whenever our means show signs of becoming ends, may we all—even the sociologists—be succeeded by people to whom *nihil humanum alienum est.*

14

Social Change and Status Protest:
An Essay on the Marginal Man

The phrase "marginal man" and the phenomenon it designates came formally into the study of society with the publication of Robert E. Park's essay, "Human Migration and the Marginal Man" in 1928. I call it an essay, for it has depth, breadth, and richness of hypotheses, neither required nor expected in an ordinary scientific paper. Park planted seed enough to keep a generation of scientific cultivators busy.

While the phrase came with this publication, the essential idea is much older. Park refers to many others who had sensed the problem; notably Simmel, in his passages on the "stranger" in his *Soziologie* and Gilbert Murray, in his *Rise of the Greek Epic*. He takes Heinrich Heine as a living example of the thing about which he is talking. What Park did was to put the "marginal man" into a broader setting; to see him as a function of the breakup and mixing of cultures attendant upon migration and the great cultural revolutions. He turned a literary and poetic insight into a cluster of related scientific hypotheses. In doing so, he brought it down from the glamour of antiquity and the grandly historical to the level of the most modest European immigrant as well as the oft-despised mulatto, and indeed even to all men in his remark that there are "periods of transition and crisis in the lives of most of us that are comparable with those which the immigrant experiences when he leaves home to seek his fortunes in a strange country."

The first part of Park's paper sketches broadly the relation of migration to cultures and social organization, leading up to its part in the breakup of the smaller traditional societies of which anthropologists have become the most expert students. The latter part focuses attention on the subjective aspects of migration and its effect upon human persons.

The first such effect he notes is "emancipation," the freeing of a

From *Phylon*, The Atlanta University Review of Race and Culture, Vol. X (1st quarter, 1949), pp. 58–65. Reprinted with permission of *Phylon*.

man from customary expectations by travel and migration. Sometimes, we gather, the emancipated man is eager for new things; he
explores and invents. In other cases, he may be painfully homesick
for that which he left behind. Perhaps this homesickness is greatest
when, as in the case of the Greek, that warm and sacred world for
which he yearns no longer exists.

From the completely emancipated man, Park moves on to the "cultural hybrid";

> . . . a man living and sharing intimately in the cultural life and traditions
> of two distinct peoples; never quite willing to break, even if he were permit-
> ted to do so, with his past and his traditions, and not quite accepted,
> because of racial prejudice, in the new society in which he now sought to
> find a place.

The prototype of the "cultural hybrid" he found in the Jew emerg-
ing from the Ghetto. However, the person of mixed blood—to use
the most misleading phrase of common talk about the races—is perhaps the most permanently and fatally condemned of all to the condition of marginality. And that fact, insofar as it is one, points to the
true nature of the marginal position; for while the racial hybrid is
ordinarily also a cultural hybrid, by virtue of the fact that both cultures and races develop their distinguishing marks in relative isolation,
we have plenty of evidence in America that the racial hybrid need not
be a cultural hybrid at all. The American Negro—whether of mixed
blood or not—is not conspicuously a cultural hybrid. But he is a man
with a status dilemma, and the more he, as an individual, acquires of
those elements of American culture which bring to others the higher
rewards of success, the greater is his dilemma.

In addition, the American Negro is a living contradiction of the
canons of status in the American culture. The contradiction lies in the
fact that a member of a group assigned a very humble and limited
status bears other characteristics which ordinarily give or allow the
individual to acquire higher status. The contradiction is objective, in
that it appears to the eyes of others. The dilemma lies in the fact that
he cannot accept the status to which Negroes are ordinarily assigned,
but neither can he completely free himself from it. The dilemma, on
the other hand, is essentially subjective. The Negro who passes as
white no longer presents any contradiction to the eyes of others, but
he still has the inner dilemma.

It is from the angle of status that I propose to analyze the phenomenon of marginality. Status is a term of society in that it refers specifically to a system of relations between people. But the definition of

the status lies in a culture. In fact, one of the essential features of a person's status may be his identification with a culture.

Imagine a society in which the statuses are very well established. The rights and duties pertaining to each are well understood and generally beyond doubt and discussion. The ways by which an individual is assigned to and enters a given status are likewise well defined: by descent, sex, social learning, and accomplishments of various kinds, arriving at a certain age, or by certain rites of passage, such as initiation and marriage. In such a case, one would expect—and the evidence on such societies seems to warrant it—that persons of a given status would exhibit a whole complex of social attributes, all of which seem naturally to pertain to that status. These attributes would be unconsciously woven into a seamless garment. Finally, everyone would know exactly who he is. His status identification would be clear and unquestioned by himself or others.

Imagine now the opposite—a society which is a complete free-for-all. Talents, both the virtuous and the nefarious, have full play. Everybody gets exactly what he has coming to him by virtue of his own efforts. It is a society without a hangover from its past. If an enterprising lad of twenty were fittest to be head surgeon of a great hospital, he would be it. Make it more drastic; if a Jewish Negro girl of twenty, born in Russia and converted to the Witnesses of Jehovah were fittest to be head surgeon of Massachusetts General Hospital, she would be it. In such a society one could, in effect, say that status did not exist. Competition, of some purer sort than any we know, would determine without time-lag what each person would do and be. No such society ever existed. The ones we know are somewhere between this and the other pole. Relatively, our society is nearer the free-for-all than have been most others we know of.

Free as is competition in our society, and strong as is the strain toward allowing talent and accomplishment free rein, there are many positions about which there is a halo of technically irrelevant, but socially expected, characteristics. Thus the physician is still rather expected by most people to be a man. He is expected, further, to be of a certain age, and, often, to have certain ethnic and class characteristics. But in our mobile and changing society new kinds of persons continually acquire the technically and formally demanded skills or qualities of a profession, or other position. Whenever it happens, sociological news is made and a new and unexpected combination of social characteristics appears; thus, the woman senator, the Negro judge, a boy president of a university, a professor in the White House, Cinderella in the Rockefeller mansion. For certain positions there is

a long period of training for inculcating the auxiliary characteristics
of a status as well as the technical skills. Thus, a medical course is a
long *rite de passage*. So is the seminary of the priesthood and the
novitiate of a religious order. Essentially, the function of the novitiate
is to guarantee that there shall be no *marginal* priests or monks. The
marks of the world are washed off, so that the newborn priest shall
be fully a priest, acting as such and judged as such by all other priests
and by all the faithful.

Now it is not merely that the new people who come into positions
lack certain expected characteristics, but that they positively belong
to groups which themselves have a status definition which includes a
combination of expected characteristics (such combinations are called
stereotypes). The woman has certain traditional expected characteristics; she plays certain traditional roles. People are accustomed to act
toward women in certain ways. Likewise, the Negro has a traditional
role. The traditional roles of neither woman nor Negro include that
of the physician. Hence, when either of them becomes a physician the
question arises whether to treat her or him as physician or as woman
or Negro. Likewise, on their part, there is the problem whether, in a
given troublesome situation, to act completely as physician or in the
other role. This is their dilemma. It arises from the fact that the culture
has not yet provided a series of accepted definitions of behavior for
the various situations which arise from the existence of this new kind
of person. So long as the dilemma is present in the mind of the person,
and so long as the existence of such a person appears a contradiction
to others, just so long are the persons concerned in a marginal position.

Their marginality might presumably be reduced in several ways.

1. All such persons could give up the struggle, by retiring completely into the status with which they are most stubbornly identified
by society. This people sometimes do. There are records of turning
back to one's own people, culture, or status which read like those of
religious conversions, with conviction of sin, seeking and finding the
light, doing penance, and retiring into an exclusive world as into a
cloistered religious order. Sometimes, however, such people become
leaders of a cultural revival, which may be either religious or militant
in temper.

People of the statuses threatened by marginal people generally favor this first solution—that of putting them back into their traditional
places. Measures of repression and of exclusion are used to this end.

2. One of the statuses could disappear *as a status*. The word
"woman" could cease to have social meaning, and become merely a

biological designation without any status or role connotations. A few women have set this as the goal of the feminist movement. The word Negro would disappear—as it has tended to do in certain times and countries—in favor of a series of terms which would describe complexion and feature. These terms, in a continuum from black to white or white to black, would be of use mainly to people who are careful about the color of their dresses and neckties, and to the police, whose vocabulary for identifying complexions of wanted persons has always been meager. In short, there would be no Negro group to which to belong.

3. Persons of marginal position might individually resign from the status which interferes with their other status aims. A woman who became a physician would simply not be a woman any more, although other people might remain identified with the status of women. A Negro would declare himself no longer a Negro. Such resignation is both subjectively and objectively difficult. The interplay of these two aspects of the difficulty constitutes a fascinating and sometimes tragic theme of human drama. The temptation to resign, and even to repudiate, is put heavily upon marginal people, as many a Negro can testify. If a Negro worker is somewhat accepted by white fellow workers in industry, they generally seem inwardly compelled to extract from him an admission that he is an exception among Negroes. If he is like them in the rest, why should he not be like them in their stereotypes also. It is a kind of betrayal to which we are all subject in some degree. When we yield, the cock crows thrice.

4. One or both of the statuses might, without disappearing, be so broadened and redefined as to reduce both the inner dilemma and the outward contradiction.

5. Another possible solution is elaboration of the social system to include a marginal group as an additional category of persons with their own identity and defined position. A number of people of similar marginal position may seek one another's company, and collectively strive to get a place for themselves. The Cape Coloured of South Africa, and the Eurasians of India are groups of this kind. In this country, the colored creoles of Louisiana, certain rural communities of light-colored people in both South and North, and the free Negroes in certain Southern communities in slavery times all attempted with some success to establish themselves as recognized groups, neither Negro nor white. During their time of success, they were exclusive of other persons who sought admittance to their ranks as every new member was a potential threat to their special status. They became, in fact, groups of kin-connected families; hence, something closer to

Indian castes than anything else in America has been. But the strain toward keeping the American race system a simple dichotomy has worked against them. In recent times, when nearly everyone must have "papers" for relief, the draft, school, and the like, only the most "backwoodsy" of such groups can escape the fatal dichotomy.

The marginal groups just mentioned consist each of people who are marginal in the same way, and who consciously seek to fortify a common marginal position. Sometimes it happens that marginal people establish and live their lives in a marginal group, hardly knowing that they are doing so. There are whole segments of marginal society, with their marginal cultures among various ethnic and religious groups in this country, some of whom even developed a distinguishing speech. Large numbers of unmarried career women in American cities live in essential isolation from other women and with only formal contacts with men. In addition, there are other marginal groups who are not quite aware of their marginality, by virtue of living together a somewhat insulated life, but who are, furthermore, made up of people of the most diverse backgrounds; people who have in common, to start with, nothing but their marginality. These are to be found in cities and especially among young people. They are the American Bohemians.

All of these solutions appear as themes in the process of social and cultural adjustment and conflict. One can see in social movements—cultural, national, racial, feminist, class—all of these tendencies. The woman's movement has had its advocates of complete eradication of sex as a status determinant, its women who individually resigned from their sex and encouraged others to do so, and those who have quietly or fervently gone back to and idealized the old roles. The main trend has been toward redefinition and broadening of the roles consonant with the status of women, and toward seeking also the integration of women into formerly exclusively male roles. One or another solution may be tried and given up. The internal politics of a social movement turns about choice of these solutions. If you will look inside any movement concerned with the status of a group of people and of their culture, you will find these conflicting tendencies. Shall it be a Negro Renaissance with return to Africa, individual passing, a fight for disappearance of Negro as a status identification, or some broadening and easing of the definition of the Negro status? I need not remind you of the many contingencies in such choices. In reality, a given solution is seldom adopted and stuck to the exclusion of all others. There is a sort of dialectic of them as the pursuit of one changes the situation so as to bring another to the fore.

Up to this point, I have kept women and Negroes before you as illustrations of people with a status dilemma. American Negroes, product of migration and of the mixing of races and cultures that they are, are the kind of case to which the term marginal man has been conventionally applied. I have used the case of women to show that the phenomenon is not, in essence, one of racial and cultural mixing. It is one that may occur wherever there is sufficient social change going on to allow the emergence of people who are in a position of confusion of social identity, with its attendant conflicts of loyalty and frustration of personal and group aspirations. Migration and resulting cultural contact simply create the grand fields on which the battle of status is fought out among humans; a confusing and bloodier battle because its essence is that so many people are in doubt about which side they want to be on or may be allowed to be on.

In our own society, the contact of cultures, races, and religions combines with social mobility to produce an extraordinary number of people who are marginal in some degree, who have some conflict of identity in their own minds, who find some parts of the social world which they would like to enter closed to them, or open only at the expense of some treason to things and people they hold dear. American fiction has been full of such people, as it must be if it is to tell the story of America. Even English fiction of the nineteenth century abounds in such characters. Anthony Trollope's heroes and heroines are generally people who have more breeding than money, or more money than breeding. There are young men who can go into politics and stay in high society if they remain single or marry pots of money; but can be true to a half-promise to some poorer, dearer girl only by giving it all up and going to work for a living. Trollope's own story, told in his autobiography, is that of a boy who went to Harrow School so shabby and penniless that he was the butt of cruel jokes from masters and fellow pupils for the twelve years he was there.

In Trollope's England, marginal social position was almost entirely a matter of class mobility. There was little of ethnic difference in it. In America, marginality is thought of as resulting solely from the mixtures of cultures, races, and religions. There may be more of the problem of class mobility in it, however, than Americans have been accustomed to admit.

In mentioning what you may think the trivial case of Trollope's young man who must choose between his career (class position) and his sweetheart, I incidentally introduced a crucial problem of marginality to which there is little allusion in the formal discussion of the subject, that of life or career contingencies in relation to status marginality.

I suppose a person is furthest from a marginal position if he is so placed that he can go clear through his life without status dilemma. Each of us lives part of his life in retrospect, part in the fleeting present, part in prospect. We see ourselves in a running perspective of the human life cycle. Each phase of our lives offers its own status definitions, rewards, and punishments; each phase also has meaning as the preparation for the next. In Jules Romains' *Men of Good Will* there is a conscientious little boy who promises himself the indulgence of leisure after completion of self-appointed tasks of study repeated so and so many times. The tasks get greater and greater and the indulgence gets put off further and further as he grows up. In the end he becomes very like a case reported by the psychoanalyst, Abraham; that of an artist who promises himself a vacation as soon as he shall have produced a really worthy painting. He ends up, a sleepless wreck, in the hands of a psychiatrist. This is, in varying measure, the theme of life of all people who set high goals for themselves. It is the theme of balancing present and future.

Looking at this same problem from the standpoint of social organization, there are phases of life in which society is more open and more tolerant of diversity than others. Student life is traditionally such a phase. People of various races, ethnic groups, class backgrounds, and of the two sexes mix in an adventuresome spirit of Bohemianism. The essence of Bohemianism is disregard of convention. Convention, in its turn, is in large part a set of definitions of status, hence of proper behavior. Student Bohemianism is a conventional relaxation of convention.

Now university life is two things, a *rite de passage* and a preparation for careers. In England, the two things are crystallized in two kinds of degrees. The Pass Degree is a *rite de passage* for sons of aristocrats and plutocrats; the Honors degree, which requires work, is for people who have to make their way in the world, as most American students must do. But university life is here also a *rite of passage*, not merely from the status of adolescent to that of adult, but from one way of life to another and in many cases, from one culture or subculture to another.

The freedom of student life has always been tolerated by older adults on the assumption that it would, for each given individual, soon come to an end. We must then ask, both as social scientists and as persons with a life to lead, what are the hazards of passing from so free a phase of life into those which follow: of the transition from school to work, from irresponsible singleness to more or less responsible marriage, from young childless marriage to parenthood. Each of these has its hazards. Each of them generally brings one face to face with a stiffer set of status definitions, with greater mutual exclusiveness of social roles and, consequently, with the greater possibility of status dilemma. This aspect of the problem of marginality has been very little studied. It is one of the crucial areas of study if we are really to advance our knowledge of modern society.

Before stopping, let us ask, with regard to social mobility and social change, the same question as we did earlier concerning the relation of migration to marginality. Are mobility and change necessary conditions of marginality, or are they, too, merely the favoring gale? Might there not be, in the most settled society, persons who are in protest against the roles assigned them; persons, even, who want to play some role for which there is no precedent or defined place in their culture? Need one have a woman's movement in order to have the individual woman who feels the masculine protest? Are all the inglorious village Miltons of unpoetic cultures so mute as those in Gray's churchyard? I have often thought that the French-Canadian culture is so stable, not because of its isolation, but because there has been a whole continent for its free-thinkers and other rebels to escape into. I do not think we know the answer to these questions. But we have some clues. They suggest that the human individual does not always passively accept society's answer to the question, "Who am I?" with all its implications of present and future conduct. I suppose we might distinguish between that kind of protest which is merely a squirming within the harness, and that which is a questioning of the very terms and dimensions of the prevailing status definitions. At any rate, there is still much work to be done on the genesis of status protest; or, to put it the other way, on the processes by which the human biological individual is integrated—always in the presence and by the agency of other humans—into a status system.

15

Good People and Dirty Work

... une secte est le *noyau* et le *levain* de toute foule. ... Etudier la foule c'est juger un drame d'après ce qu'on voit sur la scène; étudier la secte c'est le juger d'après ce qu'on voit dans les coulisses.

Sighele, S. *Psychologie des sectes.* Paris, 1898. Pp. 62, 63, 65.[1]

The National Socialist Government of Germany, with the arm of its fanatical inner sect, the S.S., commonly known as the Black Shirts or Elite Guard, perpetrated and boasted of the most colossal and dramatic piece of social dirty work the world has ever known. Perhaps there are other claimants to the title, but they could not match this one's combination of mass, speed, and perverse pride in the deed. Nearly all peoples have plenty of cruelty and death to account for. How many Negro Americans have died by the hands of lynching mobs? How many more from unnecessary disease and lack of food or of knowledge of nutrition? How many Russians died to bring about collectivization of land? And who is to blame if there be starving millions in some parts of the world while wheat molds in the fields of other parts?

I do not revive the case of the Nazi *Endlösung* (final solution) of the Jewish problem in order to condemn the Germans, or make them look worse than other peoples, but to recall to our attention dangers which lurk in our midst always. Most of what follows was written after my first postwar visit to Germany in 1948. The impressions were vivid. The facts have not diminished and disappeared with time, as did the stories of alleged German atrocities in Belgium in the first World War. The fuller the record, the worse it gets.[2]

Several millions of people were delivered to the concentration camps, operated under the leadership of Heinrich Himmler with the help of Adolf Eichmann. A few hundred thousand survived in some fashion. Still fewer came out sound of mind and body. A pair of

Reprinted by permission of the publisher from *Social Problems*, Vol. X, Summer, 1962. Copyright 1962, Society for the Study of Social Problems. (Delivered as public lecture at McGill University shortly after a long visit to Western Germany in 1948.)

examples, well attested, will show the extreme of perverse cruelty reached by the S.S. guards in charge of the camps. Prisoners were ordered to climb trees; guards whipped them to make them climb faster. Once they were out of reach, other prisoners, also urged by the whip, were put to shaking the trees. When the victims fell, they were kicked to see whether they could rise to their feet. Those too badly injured to get up were shot to death, as useless for work. A not inconsiderable number of prisoners were drowned in pits full of human excrement. These examples are so horrible that your minds will run away from them. You will not, as when you read a slightly salacious novel, imagine the rest. I therefore thrust these examples upon you and insist that the people who thought them up could, and did, improvise others like them, and even worse, from day to day over several years. Many of the victims of the camps gave up the ghost (this Biblical phrase is the most apt) from a combination of humiliation, starvation, fatigue, and physical abuse. In due time, a policy of mass liquidation in the gas chamber was added to individual virtuosity in cruelty.

This program—for it was a program—of cruelty and murder was carried out in the name of racial superiority and racial purity. It was directed mainly, although by no means exclusively, against Jews, Slavs, and Gypsies. It was thorough. There are few Jews in the territories which were under the control of the Third German Reich—the two Germanies, Holland, Czechoslovakia, Poland, Austria, Hungary. Many Jewish Frenchmen were destroyed. There were concentration camps even in Tunisia and Algiers under the German occupation.

When, during my 1948 visit to Germany, I became more aware of the reactions of ordinary Germans to the horrors of the concentration camps, I found myself asking not the usual question, "How did racial hatred rise to such a high level?" but this one, "How could such dirty work be done among and, in a sense, *by* the millions of ordinary, civilized German people?" Along with this came related questions. How could these millions of ordinary people live in the midst of such cruelty and murder without a general uprising against it and against the people who did it? How, once freed from the regime that did it, could they be apparently so little concerned about it, so toughly silent about it, not only in talking with outsiders—which is easy to understand—but among themselves? How and where could there be found in a modern civilized country the several hundred thousand men and women capable of such work? How were these people so far released from the inhibitions of civilized life as to be able to imagine, let alone perform, the ferocious, obscene, and perverse actions which they did

imagine and perform? How could they be kept at such a height of
fury through years of having to see daily at close range the human
wrecks they made and being often literally spattered with the filth
produced and accumulated by their own actions?

You will see that there are here two orders of questions. One set
concerns the good people who did not themselves do this work. The
other concerns those who did do it. But the two sets are not really
separate; for the crucial question concerning the good people is their
relation to the people who did the dirty work, with a related one
which asks under what circumstances good people let the others get
away with such actions.

An easy answer concerning the Germans is that they were not so
good after all. We can attribute to them some special inborn or ingrained race consciousness, combined with a penchant for sadistic
cruelty and unquestioning acceptance of whatever is done by those
who happen to be in authority. Pushed to its extreme, this answer
simply makes us, rather than the Germans, the superior race. It is the
Nazi tune, put to words of our own.

Now there are deep and stubborn differences between peoples.
Their history and culture may make the Germans especially suscepti-
ble to the doctrine of their own racial superiority and especially acqui-
escent to the actions of whoever is in power over them. These are
matters deserving of the best study that can be given them. But to say
that these things could happen in Germany simply because Germans
are different—from us—buttresses their own excuses and lets us off
too easily from blame for what happened there and from the question
whether it could happen here.

Certainly in their daily practice and expression before the Hitler
regime, the Germans showed no more, if as much, hatred of other
racial or cultural groups than we did and do. Residential segregation
was not marked. Intermarriage was common, and the families of such
marriages had an easier social existence than they generally have in
America. The racially exclusive club, school, and hotel were much
less in evidence than here. And I well remember an evening in 1933
when a Montreal businessman—a very nice man, too—said in our
living room, "Why don't we admit that Hitler is doing to the Jews just
what we ought to be doing?" That was not an uncommon sentiment,
although it may be said in defense of the people who expressed it that
they probably did not know and would not have believed the full truth
about the Nazi program of destroying Jews. The essential underlying
sentiments on racial matters in Germany were not different in kind
from those prevailing throughout the western, and especially the

Anglo-Saxon, countries. But I do not wish to overemphasize this point. I only want to close one easy way out of serious consideration of the problem of good people and dirty work, by demonstrating that the Germans were and are about as good and about as bad as the rest of us on this matter of racial sentiments and, let us add, their notions of decent human behavior.

But what was the reaction of ordinary Germans to the persecution of the Jews and to the concentration camp mass torture and murder? A conversation between a German schoolteacher, a German architect, and myself gives the essentials in a vivid form. It was in the studio of the architect, and the occasion was a rather casual visit, in Frankfurt am Main in 1948.

The architect: "I am ashamed for my people whenever I think of it. But we didn't know about it. We only learned about all that later. You must remember the pressure we were under; we had to join the party. We had to keep our mouths shut and do as we were told. It was a terrible pressure. Still, I am ashamed. But you see, we had lost our colonies, and our national honor was hurt. And these Nazis exploited that feeling. And the Jews, they *were* a problem. They came from the east. You should see them in Poland; the lowest class of people, full of lice, dirty and poor, running about in their Ghettos in filthy caftans. They came here, and got rich by unbelievable methods after the first war. They occupied all the good places. Why, they were in the proportion of ten to one in medicine and law and government post!"

At this point the architect hesitated and looked confused. He continued: "Where was I? It is the poor food. You see what misery we are in here, Herr Professor. It often happens that I forget what I was talking about. Where was I now? I have completely forgotten."

(His confusion was, I believe, not at all feigned. Many Germans said they suffered losses of memory such as this, and laid it to their lack of food.)

I said firmly: "You were talking about loss of national honor and how the Jews had got hold of everything."

The architect: "Oh, yes! That was it! Well, of course that was no way to settle the Jewish problem. But there *was* a problem and it had to be settled some way."

The school teacher: "Of course, they have Palestine now."

I protested that Palestine would hardly hold them.

The architect: "The professor is right. Palestine can't hold all the Jews. And it was a terrible thing to murder people. But we didn't know it at the time. But I am glad I am alive now. It is an interesting time in men's history. You know, when the Americans came it was like a great release. I really want to see a new ideal in Germany. I like the freedom that lets me talk to you like this. But, unfortunately, that is not the general opinion.

Most of my friends really hang on to the old ideas. They can't see any hope, so they hang on to the old ideas."

This scrap of talk gives, I believe, the essential elements as well as the flavor of the German reaction. It checks well with formal studies which have been made, and it varies only in detail from other conversations which I myself recorded in 1948.

One of the most obvious points in it is unwillingness to think about the dirty work done. In this case—perhaps by chance, perhaps not—the good man suffered an actual lapse of memory in the middle of this statement. This seems a simple point. But the psychiatrists have shown that it is less simple than it looks. They have done a good deal of work on the complicated mechanisms by which the individual mind keeps unpleasant or intolerable knowledge from consciousness, and have shown how great may, in some cases, be the consequent loss of effectiveness of the personality. But we have taken collective unwillingness to know unpleasant facts more or less for granted. That people can and do keep a silence about things whose open discussion would threaten the group's conception of itself, and hence its solidarity, is common knowledge. It is a mechanism that operates in every family and in every group which has a sense of group reputation. To break such a silence is considered an attack against the group; a sort of treason, if it be a member of the group who breaks the silence. This common silence allows group fictions to grow up; such as, that grandpa was less a scoundrel and more romantic than he really was. And I think it demonstrable that it operates especially against any expression, except in ritual, of collective guilt. The remarkable thing in present-day Germany is not that there is so little reference to something about which people do feel deeply guilty, but that it is talked about at all.

In order to understand this phenomenon we would have to find out who talks about the concentration camp atrocities, in what situations, in what mood, and with what stimulus. On these points I know only my own limited experiences. One of the most moving of these was my first postwar meeting with an elderly professor whom I had known before the Nazi time; he is an heroic soul who did not bow his head during the Nazi time and who keeps it erect now. His first words, spoken with tears in his eyes, were:

"How hard it is to believe that men will be as bad as they say they will. Hitler and his people said: 'Heads will roll,' but how many of us—even of his bitterest opponents—could really believe that they would do it."

This man could and did speak, in 1948, not only to the likes of me, but to his students, his colleagues, and to the public which read his articles, in the most natural way, about the Nazi atrocities whenever there was occasion to do it in the course of his tireless effort to reorganize and to bring new life into the German universities. He had neither the compulsion to speak, so that he might excuse and defend himself, nor a conscious or unconscious need to keep silent. Such people were rare; how many there were in Germany I do not know.

Occasions of another kind in which the silence was broken were those where, in class, public lecture, or in informal meetings with students, I myself had talked frankly of race relations in other parts of the world, including the lynchings which sometimes occur in my own country and the terrible cruelty visited upon natives in South Africa. This took off the lid of defensiveness, so that a few people would talk quite easily of what happened under the Nazi regime. More common were situations like that with the architect, where I threw in some remark about the atrocities in response to Germans' complaint that the world is abusing them. In such cases, there was usually an expression of shame, accompanied by a variety of excuses (including that of having been kept in ignorance), and followed by a quick turning away from the subject.

Somewhere in consideration of this problem of discussion versus silence we must ask what the good (that is, ordinary) people in Germany did know about these things. It is clear that the S.S. kept the more gory details of the concentration camps a close secret. Even high officials of the government, the army, and the Nazi party itself were in some measure held in ignorance, although of course they kept the camps supplied with victims. The common people of Germany knew that the camps existed; most knew people who had disappeared into them; some saw the victims, walking skeletons in rags, being transported in trucks or trains or being herded on the road from station to camp or to work in fields or factories near the camps. Many knew people who had been released from concentration camps; such released persons kept their counsel on pain of death. But secrecy was cultivated and supported by fear and terror. In the absence of a determined and heroic will to know and publish the truth, and in the absence of all the instruments of opposition, the degree of knowledge was undoubtedly low, in spite of the fact that all knew that something both stupendous and horrible was going on; and in spite of the fact that Hitler's *Mein Kampf* and the utterances of his aides said that no fate was too horrible for the Jews and other wrongheaded or inferior people. This must make us ask under what conditions the will to know and to discuss is strong, determined, and effective; this, like most of the important questions I have raised, I leave unanswered except as answers may be contained in the statement of the case.

But to return to our moderately good man, the architect. He insisted over and over again that he did not know, and we may suppose that he knew as much and as little as most Germans. But he also made it quite clear that he wanted something done to the Jews. I have similar statements from people of whom I knew that they had had close Jewish friends before the Nazi time. This raises the whole problem of the extent to which those pariahs who do the dirty work of society are really acting as agents for the rest of us. To talk of this question one must note that, in building up his case, the architect pushed the Jews firmly into an out-group; they were dirty, lousy, and unscrupulous (an odd statement from a resident of Frankfurt, the home of old Jewish merchants and intellectual families long identified with those aspects of culture of which Germans are most proud). Having dissociated himself clearly from these people, and having declared them a problem, he apparently was willing to let someone else do to them the dirty work which he himself would not do, and for which he expressed shame. The case is perhaps analogous to our attitude toward those convicted of crime. From time to time, we get wind of cruelty practiced upon the prisoners in penitentiaries or jails; or, it may be merely a report that they are ill fed or that hygienic conditions are not good. Perhaps we do not wish that the prisoners should be cruelly treated or badly fed, but our reaction is probably tempered by a notion that they deserve something, because of some dissociation of them from the in-group of good people. If what they get is worse than what we like to think about, it is a little bit too bad. It is a point on which we are ambivalent. Campaigns for reform of prisons are often followed by countercampaigns against a too-high standard of living for prisoners and against having prisons run by softies. Now the people who run prisons are our agents. Just how far they do or could carry out our wishes is hard to say. The minor prison guard, in boastful justification of some of his more questionable practices, says, in effect: "If those reformers and those big shots upstairs had to live with these birds as I do, they would soon change their fool notions about running a prison." He is suggesting that the good people are either naive or hypocritical. Furthermore, he knows quite well that the wishes of his employers, the public, are by no means unmixed. They are quite as likely to put upon him for being too nice as for being too harsh. And if, as sometimes happens, he is a man disposed to cruelty, there may be some justice in his feeling that he is only doing what others would like to do, if they but dared; and what they would do, if they were in his place.

There are plenty of examples in our own world which I might have picked for comparison with the German attitude toward the concentration camps. For instance, a newspaper in Denver made a great scandal out of the allegation that our Japanese compatriots were too well fed in the camps where they were concentrated during the war. I might have mentioned some feature of the sorry history of the people of Japanese background in Canada. Or it might have been lynching, or some aspect of racial discrimination. But I purposely chose prisoners convicted of crime. For convicts are formally set aside for special handling. They constitute an out-group in all countries. This brings the issue clearly before us, since few people cherish the illusion that the problem of treating criminals can be settled by propaganda designed to prove that there aren't any criminals. Almost everyone agrees that something has to be done about them. The question concerns what is done, who does it, and the nature of the mandate given by the rest of us to those who do it. Perhaps we give them an unconscious mandate to go beyond anything we ourselves would care to do or even to acknowledge. I venture to suggest that the higher and more expert functionaries who act in our behalf represent something of a distillation of what we may consider our public wishes, while some of the others show a sort of concentrate of those impulses of which we are, or wish to be, less aware.

Now the choice of convicted prisoners brings up another crucial point in intergroup relations. All societies of any great size have in-groups and out-groups; in fact, one of the best ways of describing a society is to consider it a network of smaller and larger in-groups and out-groups. And an in-group is one only because there are out-groups. When I refer to *my* children I obviously imply that they are closer to me than other people's children and that I will make greater efforts to buy oranges and cod-liver oil for them than for others' children. In fact, it may mean that I will give them cod-liver oil if I have to choke them to get it down. We do our own dirty work on those closest to us. The very injunction that I love my neighbor as myself starts with me; if I don't love myself and my nearest, the phrase has a very sour meaning.

Each of us is a center of a network of in- and out-groups. Now the distinctions between *in* and *out* may be drawn in various ways, and nothing is more important for both the student of society and the educator than to discover how these lines are made and how they may be redrawn in more just and sensible ways. But to believe that we can do away with the distinction between *in* and *out*, *us* and *them* in social life is complete nonsense. On the positive side, we generally feel a greater obligation to in-groups; hence less obligation to out-groups; and in the case of such groups as convicted criminals, the out-group is definitely given over to the hands of our agents for punishment. That is the extreme case. But there are other out-groups toward which we may have aggressive feelings and dislike, although we give no formal mandate to anyone to deal with them on our behalf, and although we profess to believe that they should not suffer restrictions or disadvantages. The greater their social distance from us, the more we leave in the hands of others a sort of mandate by default to deal with them on our behalf. Whatever effort we put on reconstructing the lines which divide in- and out-groups, there remains the eternal problem of our treatment, direct or delegated, of whatever groups are considered somewhat outside. And here it is that the whole matter of our professed and possible deeper unprofessed wishes comes up for consideration; and the related problem of what we know, can know, and want to know about it. In Germany, the agents got out of hand and created such terror that it was best not to know. It is also clear that it was and is easier to the conscience of many Germans not to know. It is, finally, not unjust to say that the agents were at least working in the direction of the wishes of many people, although they may have gone beyond the wishes of most. The same questions can be asked about our own society, and with reference not only to prisoners but also to many other groups upon whom there is no legal or moral stigma. Again I have not the answers. I leave you to search for them.

In considering the question of dirty work we have eventually to think about the people who do it. In Germany, these were the members of the S.S. and of that inner group of the S.S. who operated the concentration camps. Many reports have been made on the social backgrounds and the personalities of these cruel fanatics. Those who have studied them say that a large proportion were *gescheiterte Existenzen*, men or women with a history of failure, of poor adaptation to the demands of work and of the classes of society in which they had been bred. Germany between wars had large numbers of such people. Their adherence to a movement which proclaimed a doctrine of hatred was natural enough. The movement offered something more. It created an inner group which was to be superior to all others, even Germans, in their emancipation from the usual bourgeois morality; people above and beyond the ordinary morality. I dwell on this, not as a doctrine, but as an organizational device. For, as Eugen

Kogon, author of the most penetrating analysis of the S.S. and their camps, has said, the Nazis came to power by creating a state within a state; a body with its own countermorality and its own counterlaw, its courts and its own execution of sentence upon those who did not live up to its orders and standards. Even as a movement it had inner circles within inner circles; each sworn to secrecy as against the next outer one. The struggle between these inner circles continued after Hitler came to power; Himmler eventually won the day. His S.S. became a state within the Nazi state, just as the Nazi movement had become a state within the Weimar state. One is reminded of the oft-quoted but neglected statement of Sighele: "At the center of a crowd look for the sect." He referred, of course, to the political sect; the fanatical inner group of a movement seeking power by revolutionary methods. Once the Nazis were in power, this inner sect, while becoming now the recognized agent of the state and, hence, of the masses of the people, could at the same time dissociate itself more completely from them in action, because of the very fact of having a mandate. It was now beyond all danger of interference and investigation. For it had the instruments of interference and investigation in its own hands. These are also the instruments of secrecy. So the S.S. could and did build up a powerful system in which they had the resources of the state and of the economy of Germany and the conquered countries from which to steal all that was needed to carry out their orgy of cruelty, luxuriously as well as with impunity.

Now let us ask, concerning the dirty workers, questions similar to those concerning the good people. Is there a supply of candidates for such work in other societies? It would be easy to say that only Germany could produce such a crop. The question is answered by being put. The problem of people who have run aground (*gescheiterte Existenzen*) is one of the most serious in our modern societies. Any psychiatrist will, I believe, testify that we have a sufficient pool or fund of personalities warped toward perverse punishment and cruelty to do any amount of dirty work that the good people may be inclined to countenance. It would not take a very great turn of events to increase the number of such people, and to bring their discontents to the surface. This is not to suggest that every movement based on discontent with the present state of things will be led by such people. That is obviously untrue; and I emphasize the point lest my remarks give comfort to those who would damn all who express militant discontent. But I think study of militant social movements does show that these warped people seek a place in them. Specifically, they are likely to become the plotting, secret police of the group. It is one of the problems of militant social movements to keep such people out. It is of course easier to do this if the spirit of the movement is positive, its conception of humanity high and inclusive, and its aims sound. This was not the case of the Nazi movement. As Kogon puts it: "The SS were but the arch-type of the Nazis in general."[3] But such people are sometimes attracted for want of something better, to movements whose aims are contrary to the spirit of cruelty and punishment. I would suggest that all of us look well at the leadership and entourage of movements to which we attach ourselves for signs of a negativistic, punishing attitude. For once such a spirit develops in a movement, punishment of the nearest and easiest victim is likely to become more attractive than striving for the essential goals. And, if the Nazi movement teaches us anything at all, it is that if any shadow of a mandate be given to such people, they will—having compromised us—make it larger and larger. The processes by which they do so are the development of the power and inward discipline of their own group, a progressive dissociation of themselves from the rules of human decency prevalent in their culture, and an ever-growing contempt for the welfare of the masses of people.

The power and inward discipline of the S.S. became such that those who once became members could get out only by death; by suicide, murder, or mental breakdown. Orders from the central offices of the S.S. were couched in equivocal terms as a hedge against a possible day of judgment. When it became clear that such a day of judgment would come, the hedging and intrigue became greater; the urge to murder also became greater, because every prisoner became a potential witness.

Again we are dealing with a phenomenon common in all societies. Almost every group which has a specialized social function to perform is in some measure a secret society, with a body of rules developed and enforced by the members and with some power to save its members from outside punishment. And here is one of the paradoxes of social order. A society without smaller, rule-making, and disciplining powers would be no society at all. There would be nothing but law and police; and this is what the Nazis strove for, at the expense of family, church, professional groups, parties, and other such nuclei of spontaneous control. But apparently the only way to do this, for good as well as for evil ends, is to give power into the hands of some fanatical small group which will have a far greater power of self discipline and a far greater immunity to outside control than the traditional groups. The problem is, then, not of trying to get rid of all the self-disciplining, protecting groups within society, but one of keeping them integrated with one another and as sensitive as can be to a public opinion which transcends them all. It is a matter of checks and balances, of what we might call the social and moral constitution of society.

Those who are especially devoted to efforts to eradicate from good people, as individuals, all those sentiments which seem to bring about the great and small dirty work of the world, may think that my remarks are something of an attack on their methods. They are right to this extent; that I am insisting that we give a share of our effort to the social mechanisms involved as well as to the individual and those of his sentiments which concern people of other kinds.

Notes

1. "... a sect is the nucleus and the yeast of every crowd. ... To study a crowd is to judge by what one sees on the stage; to study the sect is to judge by what one sees backstage." These are among the many passages underlined by Robert E. Park in his copy, now in my possession, of Sighele's classic work on political sects. There are a number of references to this work in Park and Burgess, *Introduction to the Science of Sociology*, Chicago, University of Chicago Press, 1921, 1969. In fact, there is more attention paid to fanatical political and religious behavior in Park and Burgess than in any later sociological work in this country. Sighele's discussion relates chiefly to the anarchist movement of his time. There have been fanatical movements since. The Secret Army Organization in Algeria is but the latest.

2. The best source easily available at that time was Eugen Kogon's *Der SS Staat, Das System der Deutschen Konzentrationslager*, Berlin. Verlag der Frankfurter Heft, 1946. Many of my data are from his book. Some years later H. G. Adler, after several years of research, wrote *Theresienstadt, 1941–1945. Das Antlitz einer Zwangsgemeinschaft* (Tübingen, J. C. B. Mohr, 1955), and still later published *Die Verheimlichte Wahrheit, Theresienstädter Dokumente* (Tübingen, J. C. B. Mohr, 1958), a book of documents concerning that camp in which Czech and other Jews were concentrated, demoralized, and destroyed. Kogon, a Catholic intellectual, and Adler, a Bohemian Jew, both wrote out of personal experience in the concentration camps. Both considered it their duty to present the phenomenon objectively to the public. None of their statements has ever been challenged.

3. *Ibid.*, p. 316.

16

Bastard Institutions

Institutions distribute goods and services; they are the legitimate satisfiers of legitimate human wants. In the course of distributing religion, play, art, education, food, drink, shelter, and other things—they also define in standard ways what it is proper for people to want. The definition of what is to be distributed, although it may be fairly broad and somewhat flexible, seldom if ever completely satisfies all kinds and conditions of men. Institutions also decide, in effect, to serve only a certain range of people, as does a shop that decides not to carry outsizes and queer styles of shirts. The distribution is never complete and perfect.

Some institutions have resulted from collective protest against either the institutionalized definition of the service, function, or goods in question. One kind of protest is sectarian—protest against the brand of religious doctrine and expression distributed by official clergy. It may be protest against the definition of religious practice, against its distribution, or against alleged connections and identification of the church and its functionaries with the vested interests of certain social classes. Another such protest was that against the established definition of education by the classical colleges. Out of that protest came new educational enterprises such as the Land Grant colleges devoted to pursuit of some single, clearly defined purpose. In time such institutions devolved toward the very patterns against which they revolted and from which they departed. Established institutional patterns are hidden traps into which the best of protest enterprises may fall.

But there are other chronic deviations from established institutions, other kinds of escape from the legitimate channels. There are chronic deviations and protests, some lasting through generations and ages. They may gain a certain stability, although they do not have the support of open legitimacy. They operate without benefit of the law, although often with the connivance of the legal establishment. They may lie outside the realm of respectability.

Regular class lecture in Social Institutions, University of Chicago, Nov. 26, 1951.

Let us call them *bastard institutions*. Some are the illegitimate distributors of legitimate goods and services; others satisfy wants not
considered legitimate. Among bastard institutions are gambling, prostitution (the second oldest profession), rackets, black markets
(whether of babies for adoption, food, or foreign exchange), the fence,
professional crime, bootlegging (of alcoholic liquor or of forbidden
drugs or literature). All take on organized forms not unlike those of
other institutions. Homosexuality takes on certain fairly stable forms:
the homosexual ménage, clubs, cabarets, and such.

Kangaroo courts in prison and armies and the tong courts of the
earlier Chinatowns meted out the justice of a particular group that
did not accept or trust established justice. The popular justice of the
frontier and the lynchings that continued in several Southern states
until the 1920s were bastard institutions, not formally legitimate but
highly conventional and supported by popular opinion. The underworld has its hidden courts for offenses against its rules and interests,
and when an enemy is abroad in the land, the underground—the
maquisards—may try and execute traitors.

Something called quackery lies on the margins of legitimate distribution of medical services. On the outskirts of the educational establishment are the cram schools, to prepare students for admission to
universities or to help them pass the examinations for admission to
the bar. Beyond the gates of military centers, just outside the limits
of middle-class suburbs that allow drinking but not the sale of alcohol,
and just off the property of Utopian industrial towns lie the "Bum-
towns" where people can satisfy their all-too-human wants. Hell is
probably the Bumtown of Heaven.

Some of these bastard institutions are directly against the law, or
the declared moral values of society. They are in direct conflict with
accepted definitions and institutional mandates. Others offer a less
than fully respectable alternative, or allow one to satisfy some hidden
weakness or idiosyncratic taste not provided for, and slightly frowned
on, by the established distributors. Still others quite simply offer a
way to get something not readily available to people of one's kind in
the prevailing institutional system. They are corrections of faults in
institutional definition and distribution.

Whatever they be, and whatever they have in common, these bastard enterprises should be studied not merely as pathological depar-
tures from what is good and right, but as part of the total complex
of human activities and enterprises. In addition, they should be looked
at as orders of things in which we can see the social processes going
on, the same social processes, perhaps, that are to be found in the

legitimate institutions. Weber was interested in the way in which the not-legitimate becomes legitimate, but not especially in the manner in which the chronically illegitimate enterprises of men continue to exist and through what course they run in their effort to survive as against the legitimate definitions of behavior. Park was interested in some of these phenomena. In his later years he became especially interested in the underworlds of the great cities of the world. In them, he believed, there were unusual mixtures of people who, to survive, had somehow to establish a social order among themselves with a minimum of recourse to police and law. Because of their doubtful means of living, it was unwise to attract unnecessarily the agents of law. Because of their variety of origins, traditions, and languages, they could not rely on the customary norms of any one element among them as the basis of their rules of conduct.

Institutions may be described as man's self-created modes, or modal points, of behavior in areas in which there might be many ways of behaving other than the modal one. A mode, of course, is a point in a distribution. The institutional tendency is to pile up behavior at a modal point by definition of what is proper, by sanctions applied against deviating behavior, and by offering devices for distributing only the standardized opportunities and services to people. But while institutions cluster behavior, they do not completely destroy the deviations.

Marriage, for example, is the modal way of organizing the relations between male and female as sexual mates and as procreators and rearers of children. But not all males and females enter into marriages, and not all of those who do so confine their mating to their marriage partners. Some of those who do not enter into marriage have sexual partners, nevertheless, or at least some occasional sexual relations. Now marriage is always defined not merely as an enduring relation between a man and a woman, but as between a man of a certain class, religion, ethnic character, age, income, kin relations, and a woman with appropriate, although not always identical, traits. There are people, in short, who are appropriate mates for each other. Further, as Margaret Mead says in *Male and Female*,[1] only human primate males feed, clothe, and shelter their mates. The ability to do so is not equally distributed among the male population. These factors, combined with the tendency of men and women to move about at different tempos and to congregate in relative isolation from one another, bring it about that there are many people for whom no appropriate marriage partners are easily available or who are not in a position to undertake the obligations of marriage without depriving themselves of other things they value. The upper-class women of Yankee city, whose brothers are slightly less particular about whom they marry, are often without mates. The men of the frontier, the waterfront, the sea, and of armies may be far from the gathering places of the women they might expect to marry. A prolonged military occupation always brings some relief, sometimes resulting in new definitions of what is the acceptable marriage partner—as witness the Japanese wives of the G.I.'s. In present-day England, as Rowntree found in his study of *English Life and Leisure*,[2] many middle-class men, being unable to contract marriage without falling to a lower class level in their style of living and in their associations, merely establish more or less secret liaisons with women of similar circumstances who are quite willing to continue to make their own livings and to enter into such relations rather than to live the life of isolated career women among other career women. A few of the men interviewed said they simply went to prostitutes because the prostitute put no claims on one. A mistress might in time come to have the expectations of a wife, and the man might feel these expectations as obligations. One may, from one point of view, quite properly speak of marriage as a device for distributing men among women, and the available women among the men. The terms of the distribution seem not to fit the facts of present-day English middle-class life so well as they once did.

Now the ancient institution of prostitution is one of the organized ways in which the faulty distribution of mate selection has been compensated for. The most obvious concentrations of houses of prostitution are at those points where men congregate away from home: along the main streets and waterfronts of cities, on the skid roads where loggers and workers on great construction enterprises in the mountains or forests come for relief from the isolation and monotony and complete maleness of their camp life; about hotels, from flophouses to expensive convention hotels; and about military establishments. In the western world at least, prostitution is always frowned on, yet is invariably to be found, and is found most where the distribution of men and women sharply deviates from equality in number and from appropriateness of social status. (Miner found, incidentally, in his French-Canadian rural parish where it was considered very improper for young people to marry without an assured place or piece of land, that a certain married woman in the village was more or less tolerated for many years as a prostitute.)

There is another fault in distribution in sexual relations. Because of the very moral code instilled in children or the vagaries and accidents of temperament, childrearing, and personal experience, often people who are otherwise appropriate marriage partners are not mutually satisfactory sexual partners. There have been various ways of adjustment allowed and various illegitimate (as evaluated by society) ones developed and practiced in various times and among various classes of people to compensate for this maladjustment.

Now this leads me to another side of this same problem, which we do not ordinarily consider in connection with such frowned-upon things as prostitution. One has not discussed the problem of the institutional (the legitimate) and the bastard (the illegitimate) in any aspect of life and behavior until he has also drawn into view the deviation from the institutional norm and from the established way of distributing men and women, in the angelic or saintly direction as well as in the devil's direction. Now, on a quite simple level of analysis, the reason prostitution is such a viable device is that it requires so few women for so many men. It is an economic use of a small number of available, in two senses, women. There is no major contrary device by which one man is distributed among a large number of women (although there are women in modern industrial organizations, hospitals, offices, schools, etc.), gathered in large numbers about a man, or a few men, who occupy enhanced positions and who undoubtedly become for these women, in some measure, substitutes for husbands in many aspects of their relationships. From observations of school teachers and civil servants, it seems to be likely that the man who is nominally their superior and performs merely bureaucratic functions does not become the object of womanly protection and affection, but in their eyes is merely that most unsatisfactory of all males, an old woman in trousers. While the organization of business and industry offers a good many women a share in a man in this way (often, perhaps, a better man than they are likely to pick up on the marriage market), it remains true that in our society there are very large numbers of unmarried women who are not by temperament and vocation devoted to the spinster state. (As a dean of a nursing school remarked lately, it doesn't even do any good to get into a university hospital with an exceptionally good lot of interns. The boys come to medical school already taken these days. This is a blow to women who propose to use their professions to meet men.)

The household of several career women living together in which (although all work) there is some domestic division of labor not unlike that between man and wife, is an essentially unstudied—shall I say institution—that has developed as a result of the maldistribution of males and females under our condition of instituted monogamy. It is not a bastard institution in the extreme sense, but it is often suspected of being one. Those who deviate from expectation in the direction of the angels, but through no wish of their own and through no vocation to blessedness; those who are in the position of having to be better than they would like to be, or better than anyone has a right to expect them to be, are a group seldom studied, although for any full understanding of the operation of moral codes as realized institutional definitions and actual distributions, their case is of special interest. (They are said to be prone to arthritis.) It would be especially important to find out at what points there develops some institutionalizing of adjustments to the position of being better than one wishes. In some countries there is a slight institutionalizing of spinsterhood in the traditions of the Day of St. Catherine. On this day children call at the doors of women recognized as old maids and are given a special candy prepared for the occasion. There must be some inward burning over the decision whether one is to make taffy ahead of time for this occasion, thus recognizing one's estate. Perhaps the children of the neighborhood, egged on by their mothers, enforce the status upon the spinster who clings too long to her youth.

Beyond this, in appearance at least, lies the institutionalizing of celibacy in the name of religion, the spiritual marriage of man and woman to the church accompanied by all the symbols and language of human marriage. There are those who point out that a son dedicated to God by his mother is safe from the clutches of any rival woman. But this is not the order of things that I have in mind to discuss now. It is rather that religious celibacy is the realization in institutional form of deviation from marriage in the direction of the angels—a deviation rationalized in the terms of supposedly supreme values, the higher-than-normal ideals of human conduct. For the individual in such an institution the function may be clear; these institutions allow one to live up to some ideal more nearly than is possible out in the world and in marriage. I emphasize the word *allow*, for the world would merely think a person queer to so live without special declaration, without attachment to an ongoing body devoted to this special deviation from the normal way of life. (In passing, one should not neglect to mention the frequency of stories of famous nuns who had run from the ball where their lovers paid too much attention to someone else to the convent, and there threw themselves into the arms of the mother superior. In the legend they stay on to become themselves mothers superior. There are always stories of girls who enter the convent when their fiancés are lost at sea or in battle.)

Leaving that aside, the institutions of celibacy offer a declared, established, and accepted way of not accepting the modal norm of

behavior; perhaps a nobler and more satisfying way of accepting the
fate that a fault of distribution in existing institutions condemns one
to. They may be considered also as institutional provision for those
higher lights of idealism that, although engendered by the established
teaching of the virtues, are not provided for in the modal definitions
to which institutional machinery is generally geared. Let it be noted,
however, more emphatically than I stated it earlier, that society very
often accepts such deviation in an organized institutional form, when
it would scarcely accept it as isolated individual behavior. In recent
decades, the decades of the Great Wars, the western countries have
been more and more inclined to regard military service as an obligation of every man and yet to accept somewhat the pacifism of certain
historic religious sects. They have, however, been hard on the individual who arrived at pacific philosophy and behavior on his own account or who considered himself individually called to set the Christ-
like example of turning the other cheek. The individual deviation
may appear as a threat to the whole accepted system; the organized
deviation, however, may appear as a special adaptation of the system
itself, perhaps as a little special example of what humans are capable
of. The institutional angels may have some vicarious role of pleading
for us all in heaven. Even so, the public nearly always balks when the
saints, not content to be symbolic paragons of virtue, seek to become
active leaders.

There is an important analogy to this in the heresies. One student
of the heresies of the Middle Ages proposes that one kind of heresy
was the doctrine that all men should absolutely live up to some ideal
of virtue commonly proclaimed by the church.[3] Thus, suppose someone says that all sexual relations are sinful and draws the conclusion
that people are in danger of perdition if they marry. Or suppose that
someone turns the virtue of adoration of the sacred Host, enjoined
upon all men, into a mandate that all men should spend most of their
time in such adoration before the altar, to the neglect of their worldly
duties. The church would declare these to be heresies, argues the
author in question, because society, hence the church, would be destroyed by so extreme and absolute practice of any one virtue. The
church could argue further that true virtues must be commuted with
each other if man is to live. Without going further, it is clear that
society idealizes, in statements and symbolic representation, degrees
of virtue that are not in fact realizable by all people or are not realizable in combination with other virtues and in the circumstances of
ongoing real life. It appears that society allows some people to approach these levels of one virtue or another in some institutionalized

form that will at once provide the spiritual lift and satisfaction of seeing the saintly example before one, without the personal threat that would come from mere individual saintliness offered as something that all of us should seriously emulate and the social threat of a contagious example. The saint's saintliness should be contagious, but only slightly, so that only a few should catch it as badly as he, and the rest of us, though we should catch it, should catch it only in its lighter form. In effect, these apparently heroic deviations stand, in a functional sense, in a parasitic relation to the rest of life: they breed in, are the products of, and live upon the larger, less heroic organism.

When I drew up my outline for this discussion, I meant only to mention, but not to discuss at such length, the bastard substitutes for marriage. And I did not propose to explore the deviation from the norm of institutionalized virtue in the better-than-modal direction. In any case, I have not really said much about the many social phenomena to which the term *bastard institution* might be applied, some of which I named at the beginning. The prototype of all bastard institutions is perhaps that kind of thing which has come to be called "the racket." It is likewise, in its true form, a sort of parasite on the shady side of the institutional tree. On second thought, discussion of that problem had better wait. And I am not too unhappy about my departure from the outline planned, for I think we have done something not common in sociological discussion: namely, to take some matter, some aspect of human life, which is highly institutionalized and is the object of much moral sanctioning, and to treat the whole range of behavior with respect to it: the institutionalized norms and the deviations in various directions from the norm. I do not say that we have surveyed all deviations; that was not the aim. But we have seen the norm, the institutionally defined and distributed relations between adult males and females, as a special point in the fuller range of possible and actual behavior, and have at least indicated some possible functional relations between the instituted and the deviation in both the bastard and the angelic directions.

Notes

1. Margaret Mead, *Male and Female,* New York, William Morrow & Co., 1949 Mentor Book, 1955.

2. B. Seebohm Rowntree and G. R. Lavers, *English Life and Leisure,* New York, Longmans, Green & Co., 1951.

3. Emmanuel Aegerter, *Les Hérésies du Moyen Age.* Paris. Ernest Leroux, 1939.

17

The *Gleichschaltung* of the German Statistical Yearbook

"Racial Classification of People Who Married in 1938." In the summer of 1953, my eye fell by chance upon this heading of a table in the Statistical Yearbook of the German Reich for 1941–42, the last published by the Nazi regime. From earlier work with German official statistics, I was practically certain that the pre-Nazi German had had a religion, but not a race. The statistical German was the opposite of the statistical American, who had a race but no religion. The accident of noticing this change of categories in the German census led me to ask a question: What changes did the statistician of the German Reich have to make in his official Yearbook when the Nazis came to power? Behind it lie more general questions for professional statisticians: How politically neutral is their work? To what extent are the very categories in which they report their data subject to political demands?

I do not know the answers to these general questions. But I did go through all of the German statistical yearbooks from the last one of the pre-Nazi Weimar republic, 1932, through the Nazi period, and including the first postwar volume, to see what changes of category and of reporting occurred along with the radical political changes. I don't know how deeply the Nazis dug into the private opinions of the Reich statistician, or whether Party people were put in his office to watch over him. I have only the internal evidence of the Statistical Yearbooks themselves. The last Weimar volume, and all of the Nazi Yearbooks except the last, are signed by one Dr. Reichardt of the Reich Statistical Office. The last Nazi volume, 1941–42, is signed Godlewski. Whether Dr. Reichardt simply reached the age of retirement about the end of 1940 or whether he finally turned out to be not sufficiently *gleichgeschaltet* (coordinated), I don't know. Many a man did try to get on with his work by making little compromises, only to find one day that it was impossible to continue and fatal to

Reprinted from *The American Statistician*, Vol. IX, No. 5, December, 1955.

quit. I must add that I do not know what happened to Godlewski either; he certainly did not sign the first Yearbook of the new Bonn republic.

The Foreword to the last pre-Nazi Yearbook, 1932, is the exact, dull little statement one expects of a faithful public servant who is accustomed to going modestly on with his work while prime ministers and cabinets come and go. It contains no word about parties or government policies. It uses no political symbol. When, in November, 1933, Dr. Reichardt signed the next Yearbook, Hitler had been Reichschancellor for the better part of a year. The Foreword takes no notice of the change. It is the same little businesslike statement about the contents of the book. In the next Foreword, 1934, however, Dr. Reichardt feels called upon to tell the reader that the Yearbook now contains a series of "German economic curves, showing the economic events since the taking over of power by the Nationalsocialist regime." In 1935, the mention becomes a plug, "In the many tables of the Yearbook there come to expression the powerful accomplishments made by the New State in all fields of folk and economic life in the three years since the taking over of power by the Nationalsocialist regime." He especially notes the great success of measures against unemployment. In passing he mentions some new family statistics, and tables on the Special Census of the Occupational and Social Distribution of *Glaubensjuden* (Jews by faith) and Foreigners.

From 1935 on, the Foreword always tells how many years it has been since the Nationalsocialists took power, and reports in more and more glowing terms the accomplishments of the New State. The statement is typically like this: "The Yearbook gives an accounting in sober, but eloquent figures of the measures taken by the New State in all fields of folk and economic life, and the results in population, economics, and in cultural and political affairs." Dr. Reichardt even notes that the Yearbook has to be bigger because of the increased activity of the New State. From 1936 on, curves showing economic progress are put on the inside of the front cover where they are the first thing to be seen when one opens the book. In 1938 the flyleaf shows a map entitled "Folk and Space since the Assumption of Power." It shows how the empire has been expanded by the assimilation of Austria and Sudetenland. In 1939–40, a similar map shows most of Western Europe under German "protection." Under the map is a summary table showing the increase of territory and population accomplished by the New State. Dr. Reichardt tells us in his 1938 Foreword that the Yearbook now reports the Greater German Reich; he regrets that not many of the tables take account of the new territories, since comparable statistics do not yet exist. The last two books, done in wartime, no longer bother to plug for the New State. A brief Foreword says that the Yearbook was produced under difficulties, "because the needs of the State and the Party require it." Readers are enjoined, under penalty, to keep copies in metal safes and to divulge the contents to no one not in government service.

The 1932 Yearbook shows the results of all Reichstag elections from 1919 to 1932, with the number of votes for each party. The most recent election, that of July 31, 1932, was reported in even greater detail. The 1933 book gives the same summary of past elections, and includes the detail of two new elections. One was the election of November, 1932, in which there was a considerable decline of the Nazi vote. In spite of that, Hindenburg had called upon Hitler to form a government. The other was the election of March, 1933, the only free election in the Hitler time; in it the Social-Democrats held their own, the Catholic Centre gained a little, and the Nazis gained tremendously. The Communists apparently contributed most to the Nazi increase, since they lost a million votes from November, before Hitler came in, to March, just after he came to power. But this is an aside. The Yearbook merely reports the figures. In 1934 and after, each Yearbook reports only the new-style Yes and No elections of the current year. I do not know whether Dr. Reichardt was told to stop reporting the elections of the late Weimar republic, or whether he gave it up for purely technical reasons. It would make no sense to try to compare the results of free elections in which a dozen or more parties struggled for slight gains in their popular vote and for more seats in parliament with those of the new style, high-pressure plebiscites in which the choice was to be for or against Hitler. Maybe Dr. Reichardt was not coordinated on this point; it was sufficient that the elections were coordinated.

But this Yearbook did not even bother to compare the Nazi elections with one another. Perhaps the Nazis missed a propaganda chance here; for it is quite an accomplishment to increase a party's vote from 43.9% of the total to 95.3% in the course of a few months, as did the Nazis between March and November, 1933. Of course, the percentage for the Fuehrer dropped back to 89.9% in August, 1934, but they soon got it up again. In 1936, 99.5% of all qualified voters did their duty, and 98.8% did it right by casting ballots "For the List and for the Fuehrer." There were by now so few negative votes that the statistical office simply lumped them together with the invalid ballots. After the great success in getting an expression of the people's will to follow the leader in 1936, there was no new plebiscite until the empire had expanded to take in more of the German folk. In April, 1938, the Austrians were allowed to show how devoted they were to the Fuehrer and how glad to be absorbed by the New State. The Sudeten Germans were given the same privilege in due time. After that there were no plebiscites. The war was on. But in the reporting of 1938 elections in the 1939 Yearbook a slight change was made. What had been called Austria in 1938 was now called "former Austria." One must remember that the German name for Austria means Eastern Empire, obviously not a fit name for a rather insignificant part of the all-inclusive eternal Greater German Empire.

Race, in the pre-Nazi Yearbooks, was a characteristic of stallions. The number of their registered services for the propagation of their respective races was faithfully recorded in the agricultural part of the book. Men, on the other hand, had religion. They were Christians of Protestant or Roman-Catholic confession, or they were Israelites. That took in most Germans; a handful of others were lumped together. The 1932 book showed how many of each of these categories had lived in various parts and in the whole of Germany in 1910 and in 1925. The only other tables of religion are those which show the religion of each partner in all marriages of the previous year. Religion is indirectly shown in the tables of membership in trade unions and professional organizations, for some such organizations were Catholic or Protestant. None was specifically Jewish. In the first Hitler Yearbook, 1933, the references to religion are exactly as before—with one exception. The trade unions had already been dissolved. The book listed the divisions of the new Labor Front, but regretted that membership figures were not yet available. They were not in the next book, or the one after that, or ever. Perhaps, since all workers belonged to the Labor Front by definition, it would have been silly to give figures; they would have been the same as the figures of people employed in each occupation and industry.

The expressions Jew, Jewess, and Jewish do not occur in the pre-Nazi books or in the first Hitler Yearbook, 1933. Some people were of Israelite religion; some men and women of Israelite religion were married to women and men of the same religion or of Protestant, Roman Catholic, or other faiths. That was all. The 1934 Yearbook reports a new religious Census made in 1933, and compares the religious composition of the population of that year with that of 1925. The 1910 comparison was dropped. The same words are still used for the various religions. But in 1935, although the same figures and the same words were used, there is a whole new set of tables which tell us all about some people called "Glaubensjuden," of whom a special census had been taken on the 16th of June, 1933. They must be the same people who were formerly of Israelite religion, because there are exactly as many of them. But the change is more than one of name. The 1935 Yearbook picks these Glaubensjuden out for special attention not given people of other religions. We are shown what percent Jews form of the population in all geographic divisions; how many of them live in cities of more than 100,000, more than 50,000 and so on. The Jewish populations of Berlin, Hamburg, Frankfurt, Breslau, and a few other large cities are shown in a separate table. The places of birth of Jews are tabulated, also the number and percent of them who are of German or foreign birth, and subjects of Germany or of other countries.

By this time, the Nuremberg laws had made a distinction between people who are subjects of Germany and those who are citizens. The Jews were subjects but could not be citizens. No such facts are presented for the population at large, or for Protestants or Catholics. It is clear that statistics on the Jew are of special interest to the government. We may fairly assume that the statistician had been told to prepare special data on Jews—and to change their names. The name Glaubensjuden (Jews by faith) is still one without racial connotation. Only in the tables on marriages and the religion of people who were born or who died in Prussia were there still people of Israelite religion. In fact, Israelites continued to be born, get married, and to die right down until 1939–40, while people called "Jews by faith" had occupations and lived in various places. In the 1939–40 Yearbook this name is dropped, and tables give us some new categories which take account of the finer distinctions of the Nuremberg laws: Jews, Jewish mixtures of the first degree, and Jewish mixtures of the second degree in all parts of Germany, including Austria, for 1939. The same book still gives a table on the religion of the people, including Israelite. But in 1941–42, there is no longer an Israelite religion in German statistics. The religious categories are Protestant, Roman Catholic, Believers in God, and others. The Gleichschaltung of the statistics is complete. Jews are a race, not a religious group. German statistical segregation is also complete. Jews appear nowhere as simply another category of people in tables which include other Germans. There is one little exception: the good old Prussian vital statistics still show that people of Israelite religion are born and die. The Prussian civil servant is a stubborn fellow. He does his duty, come what may. Or maybe no one issued a new form for recording births and deaths in Prussia, and the officials just had to go on using the old ones.

Of all Israelite women married in 1930, one in eight married a

Christian; of Israelite men, one in four married a Christian. From 1933 on, these proportions constantly decreased. In 1936, about one in fifty married out. The people of Germany were being *gleichgeschaltet;* but the statistical Yearbook stuck to its old form of reporting marriages by religion. Only in 1939–40 does racial reporting take the place of religious in marriage tables. There is in the book of that year a table showing the "Racial Classification of People Who Married in 1938." Marriage partners are now of five kinds: German-blooded, Jewish mixtures of the first degree, Jewish mixtures of the second degree, Jews and Jewesses, and persons of other foreign blood. Twenty-five German-blooded men married Jewesses, and thirty-three Jewish men married German-blooded women in that year. But these traitors to German blood were nearly all of foreign nationality; in 1939, no German-blooded subject of the Reich married a Jew or Jewess. Gleichschaltung both of marriage and marriage statistics was complete.

The Reichstatistician was prodded, I suspect, into setting up tables and graphs to show at a glance the progress of the New State's program of prosperity and territorial expansion. He never showed in a summary and graphic way the success of the program to rid the country and the folk of foreign (Jewish) blood. One has to dig the facts out from many tables. In 1910 there were 538,909 people of Israelite religion in the Reich; 564,379 in 1925; 499,682 in 1933. One can also figure it out that in 1939 there were 451,451 of the people called Jews, Jewish mixtures of the first degree, and Jewish mixtures of the second degree in the new Greater Germany. The Nazi regime could have taken credit for most of the decrease of Jewish people between 1925 and 1933, and certainly they could claim as their own the whole decrease of 48,000 between 1933 and 1939. They could have made their success more impressive by reminding the reader that the new Germany of 1939 included new eastern territory in which many Jews had lived. They could have shown in a more prominent place the reduction in percentage of Jewish population. In 1910 and 1925 nearly one German in a hundred had been a Jew; in 1939, only about one in 190. The Yearbook could also have made a better story out of emigration. It reported only those emigrants who went overseas, and failed to tell how many of them were Jews rather than people of true German blood. This was corrected in later books; for the years 1937, 1938, and 1939 Jewish overseas emigrants are shown separately from others. Until then the total number of overseas emigrants per year had remained between 12,000 and 15,000 since before the Nazi time. Emigration overseas was 14,203 in 1937; 22,986 in 1938;

25,818 in 1939. One can see in a separate table that 7,155 of the emigrants in 1937 were Jews; 16,561 in 1938, and 22,706 in 1939. The reader has to figure out for himself that while in 1937 only half of the emigrants were Jews, over 90% of them were Jews in 1939. In still another table, the reader could learn that true Germans were actually coming home from overseas in greater number than they were leaving. In 1939, only 3,112 people not of Jewish blood emigrated overseas, while 10,455 came back to live or die under the New Order. The statistician could have put these things all together so that a person could follow with pride the purifying of his folk. But no; he reported it only bit by bit, grudgingly.

He did a little better for Prussia. Prussia, in its old-fashioned way, kept right on reporting births and deaths by religion, and persisted in considering that there was an Israelite religion—a fallacy that the New State had given up. If this kind of reporting had been done for all of Germany, one could have had an ideal record of the progress of the liquidation of the Jews. As it is, we do know from various tables that there were 370,348 Prussian Israelites in 1910; 404,446 in 1925; 361,826 Prussian Jews by faith in 1933; and 233,727 Jews, Jewish mixtures of the first and second degrees in the larger Prussia in 1939. Some measure of success is seen in the fact that actually one person in a hundred was a Jew in 1925 in Prussia, but only about half a person in a hundred in 1939. But how was the success achieved? Through encouraging emigration and the death rate? Or by discouraging the birth rate? One has to work hard to get some idea of the weights of these various methods. By using a lot of tables and making some assumptions of the kind that statisticians make, one can estimate that about 42,000 Prussian Jews emigrated overseas from 1933 to the end of August, 1939. As to the births, 2,100 children were born to Jewish mothers in Prussia in 1933, and about 100 to other mothers but of Jewish fathers. The births decreased steadily until 1939, when only 478 were born to Jewish mothers and less than fifty to other mothers and Jewish fathers. This was a good solid reduction of 75% in the number of Jews being produced by birth. But that is a slow method of liquidation. It depends too much upon the life span. In the meantime, in spite of the smaller number of Jews left in Prussia, the death figure held up very well. In 1933, when there were 361,826 Jews in Prussia, 5,565 died. The number of deaths remained above 5,000 a year right along. In 1938, for instance, 5,632 died.

In 1939 the number of deaths weakened a little to 5,182. But since there were then only 233,727 Jews and mixtures left in Prussia, the death rate was more than holding its own. Just think of it: the Jewish population was down 128,099 in six years, a good 35%, without making a dent in the number of Jews who died every year! A pretty good record, all in all, when one remembers that the big campaign had not really started yet. But the statistician should have saved the reader all this trouble. He should have coordinated his statistics about this program of the New State, just as for others. I begin to think he wasn't really *gleichgeschaltet* at all. It is too late for him to make it good now. The 1941–42 Yearbook was the eighth and last put out by the 1,000-Year Reich.

To be sure, a new series of Yearbooks has been started. The first is out: Statistical Yearbook of the German Federal Republic, 1952. It looks a lot like the old ones. The Foreword, signed by one Dr. Gerhard Fuerst, is short and businesslike. He tells of the technical difficulties caused by loss of records and by changes in boundaries. A lot of the tables are devoted to the many refugees from the east. The New State of the Nazis, like the new eastern-zone Democratic German Republic, exported refugees. The new western Federal Republic of Germany receives refugees.

The new western statistical German has lost his race and got back his religion. Some of them even belong to "the Jewish religious community." Not many; just 17,116 as compared with 103,293 in the same territory in 1939. I am glad to say that the new statistician doesn't even try to tell us what happened to the others. I wish him well, and hope he will never have to face the problems of his immediate predecessors.

Index

adult socialization, 33
African-Americans. *See* Negro
ambition. *See* ideology of mobility
American Journal of Sociology, 6–7, 10

bastard institutions, examples of, 193–94
Berlin, Isaiah (quoted), 13–14
Bohemianism, 178
Brandeis University, E. Hughes at, 8

career: aspects of, described, 33–35; and office, 139–42
celibacy, institution of, 197–98
Chicago, University of, Hughes at, 3–4, 6–8, 10
class mobility, 177–78
"code of ethics," as value-laden term, 59–60
colleague-group: residence of, to "new people," 149–50, 155n4; and status conflict, 149–51, 152–53
collective guilt, 184–86
collective silence, 184–86; analogies to, in Germany, 186–88
credat emptor, motto of all professions, 39
"cultural contributions," of ethnic groups, 93
cultural hybrid, as effect of migration, 172

deviation, individual, and organized, 198–99
"dirty work," 62–64, 77n1. *See also* *Endlösung* (final solution)
discrimination, 133; industrial, analyzed, 99–100. *See also* segregation
division of labor, 23–25; in academics, 86–89; inside professions, 42–43; in legal profession, 52; in medical profession, 52–55; psychological and moral, 81; and social interaction, 50–51, 55–56. *See also* personal services
doing *for,* or *to,* people, 51

emancipation, as effect of migration, 171–72
emigration, and German statistical yearbooks, 205–6
Endlösung (final solution), 180–81; and *gescheiterte Existenzen,* 188–91; and race relations in Germany, 181–83, 185; reaction of ordinary German to, 183–86; and the S.S., 180, 188–90. *See also* German statistical yearbooks
English Canadians, 92–93. *See also* ethnic groups
English Life and Leisure (Rowntree and Lavers), 195
ethnic groups: "cultural contributions" of, 93; defined, 91–92; as essential research focus, 93–96; and industrial economics, 97–99
exchange, as basic social process, 24–25
exclusiveness, tendency toward, in organizations, 109–10

failure, establishing criteria of. *See* mistakes, defining
"firehouse" social research, 167–68
Fixing Room, the, and grid of informal relationships, 128–29, 134
fox and hedgehog analogy, 14
French Canada in Transition (E. Hughes), 6–7
French Canadians, 92–95. *See also* ethnic groups

German statistical yearbooks: and emigration, 205–6; and *Glaubensjuden* (Jews by faith), 201, 203–5; and Israelites, 203–5; marriage statistics in, 204–5; race in, 203–5; and Reichstag election results, 202–3; religion in, 203–5, 207; and statistical segregation, 203–5, 207
Germany. *See* collective silence; *Endlösung* (final solution); German statistical yearbooks

209